German

phrasebooks
and
Gunter Muehl

German phrasebook
3rd edition – March 2008

Published by
Lonely Planet Publications Pty Ltd ABN 36 005 607 983
90 Maribyrnong St, Footscray, Victoria 3011, Australia

Lonely Planet Offices
Australia Locked Bag 1, Footscray, Victoria 3011
USA 150 Linden St, Oakland CA 94607
UK 2nd fl, 186 City Rd, London, EC1V 2NT

Cover illustration
Cheers! by Mick Ruff

ISBN 978 1 74059 980 1

text © Lonely Planet Publications Pty Ltd 2008
cover illustration © Lonely Planet Publications Pty Ltd 2008

10 9 8 7 6 5 4 3

Printed through Colorcraft Ltd, Hong Kong
Printed in China

acknowledgments

Lonely Planet Language Products and editor Emma Koch would like to get up on the table and thank the whole, noisy *Bierhalle*:

Publishing manager Jim 'Goethe' Jenkin whose great vision saw the new series develop from the ground up and who generously offered his German language expertise.

Editor Francesca 'Dietrich' Coles for her invaluable assistance on the project and in-house native German speaker Birgit 'Bauhaus' Jordan for answering queries.

Language expert Gunter Muehl for the German translations, the pronunciation guides, for proofing and for excellent advice on all things German. Freelance proofer Adrienne 'Baroque' Costanzo for her sharp eyes and language awareness and the Swiss family Robinson for survival castles.

Layout designer Daniel 'Love Parade' New for the great illustrations, freelance layout designer Patrick 'Vee Dub' Marris for contributing his layout prowess to the German project, layout designer Sally 'Wunderkind' Morgan for support in layout and series designer Yukiyoshi 'Kraftwerk' Kamimura for his input into the project.

Specialist projects managing cartographer Paul 'Lagerfeld' Piaia and map editor Wayne 'Bismark' Murphy for the language map.

Commissioning editors Karin 'Hingis' Vidstrup Monk and Karina 'Nina' Coates for getting the ball rolling and helping out with layout checks.

Project manager Fabrice 'Kafka' Rocher and managing editor Annelies 'Blue Danube' Mertens who helped bring the project to completion.

And last but not least, Language Products editors Piers 'Lederhosen' Kelly, Ben 'Wagner' Handicott, Meg 'Oom pah pah' Worby and Quentin 'Einstein' Frayne who all contributed to the German cause in various ways.

Special thanks to Gunter Muehl for the creation of the Sustainable Travel section for this new edition.

make the most of this phrasebook ...

Anyone can speak another language! It's all about confidence. Don't worry if you can't remember your school language lessons or if you've never learnt a language before. Even if you learn the very basics (on the inside covers of this book), your travel experience will be the better for it. You have nothing to lose and everything to gain when the locals hear you making an effort.

finding things in this book

For easy navigation, this book is in sections. The Tools chapters are the ones you'll thumb through time and again. The Practical section covers basic travel situations like catching transport and finding a bed. The Social section gives you conversational phrases, pick-up lines, the ability to express opinions – so you can get to know people. Food has a section all of its own: gourmets and vegetarians are covered and local dishes feature. Safe Travel equips you with health and police phrases, just in case. Remember the colours of each section and you'll find everything easily; or use the comprehensive Index. Otherwise, check the two-way traveller's Dictionary for the word you need.

being understood

Throughout this book you'll see coloured phrases on the right-hand side of each page. They're phonetic guides to help you pronounce the language. You don't even need to look at the language itself, but you'll get used to the way we've represented particular sounds. The pronunciation chapter in Tools will explain more, but you can feel confident that if you read the coloured phrase slowly, you'll be understood.

communication tips

Body language, ways of doing things, sense of humour – all have a role to play in every culture. 'Local talk' boxes show you common ways of saying things, or everyday language to drop into conversation. 'Listen for ...' boxes supply the phrases you may hear. They start with the phonetic guide (because you'll hear it before you know what's being said) and then lead in to the language and the English translation.

contents

5

german

Denmark
Copenhagen ○

Berlin ○
GERMANY

Brussels
○
Belgium

Luxembourg ○ **Luxembourg**

Prague ○
Czech Republic

Liechtenstein

Vienna ○

○ *Bern* ‡ *Vaduz*
Switzerland

Austria

○ *Budapest*
Hungary

0 ——————— 200 km
0 ——————— 100 mi

■ official language

■ widely understood

EUROPE

For more details see the **introduction**.

INTRODUCTION

Romantic, flowing, literary ... not usually how German is described, but maybe it's time to reconsider. After all, this is a language that has played a major role in the history of Europe and remains one of the most widely spoken languages on the continent. Outside of Europe, it's taught throughout the world and chances are you're already familiar with a number of German words that have entered English – kindergarten, kitsch and waltz are all of German origin.

German is spoken by approximately 100 million people, and is the official language of Germany, Austria and Liechtenstein, and one of the official languages of Belgium, Switzerland and Luxembourg. It's also understood in a number of countries in Eastern Europe. German did not spread across the rest of the world with the same force as English, Spanish and French. This is largely due to the fact that Germany only became a unified nation in 1871 and never established itself as a colonial power.

In recent years, however, the reunification of East and West Germany has seen the language become more important in global politics and economics. Its role in science has long been recognised and German literature lays claim to some of the most famous written works ever printed. Just think of the enormous influence of Goethe, Nietzsche, Freud and Einstein.

at a glance ...

language name: German

name in language:
Deutsch doytsh

language family:
West Germanic

key country: Germany

approximate number of speakers: 100 million

close relatives: Afrikaans, Dutch, English, Frisian, Yiddish

donations to English:
numerous contributions including aspirin, chromosome, eiderdown, hamburger, hamster, plunder, poodle and spanner

introduction

German is commonly divided into two forms – Low German (*Plattdeutsch*) and High German (*Hochdeutsch*). Low German is an umbrella term used for the dialects spoken in Northern Germany. High German is considered the standard form and is understood throughout German-speaking communities: it's the form of German used in this book.

Both German and English belong to the West Germanic language family, along with a number of other languages including Dutch and Yiddish. What this means is that as well as having recognisable words, the grammar of German will also make sense to an English speaker. Don't be put off by the fact that words can have 'different endings' or that there are many ways of saying 'the'. Even with a slight grasp of German grammar, you'll still manage to get your point across.

From the Swiss Alps to the cosy cafes of Vienna, this book gives you the words you need to get by, as well as all the fun, spontaneous phrases that will enrich your experience. Need more encouragement? Remember, the contact you make through using German will make your travels unique. Local knowledge, new relationships and a sense of satisfaction are on the tip of your tongue, so don't just stand there, say something!

> abbreviations used in this book

f	feminine
inf	informal
m	masculine
n	neuter
pl	plural
pol	polite
sg	singular

German is not difficult to pronounce because almost all its sounds are also found in English.

vowel sounds

As in English, vowels can be pronounced short or long with different meanings (compare 'ship' and 'sheep'). Vowels are pronounced crisply and cleanly with your mouth tenser than English, so Tee (tea) is pronounced tay not tay·ee.

symbol	english equivalent	german example
a	run	*hat*
ah	rather	*habe*
ai	aisle	*mein*
air	hair	*Bär*
aw	saw	*Boot*
ay	say	*leben*
e	red	*Bett/Männer/kaufen*
ee	bee	*fliegen*
er	teacher	*schön*
i	bit	*mit*
o	pot	*Koffer*
oy	boy	*Leute/Häuser*
oo	moon	*Schuhe*
ow	house	*Haus*
ü	(ee with rounded lips, so half-way between ee and oo)	*zurück*
u	foot	*unter*

pronunciation

consonant sounds

All German consonant sounds exist in English except for the kh and r sounds — you might need to spend some time getting familiar with them.

The kh sound is generally like the 'ch' in 'Bach' or the Scottish 'loch', also pronounced at the back of the throat. After the vowels e and i it's pronounced more forward in your mouth, almost like a sh sound. A kh sound, however, will always get you by. In this book we've used one symbol for both sounds to simplify things.

The r sound is pronounced at the back of the throat, almost like saying a g sound, but with some friction, a bit like gargling.

symbol	english equivalent	german example
b	big	*Bett*
ch	chili	*Tschüss*
d	din	*dein*
f	fun	*vier*
g	go	*gehen*
h	hit	*helfen*
k	kick	*kein*
kh	loch	*Sprache/ich*
l	loud	*laut*
m	man	*Mann*
n	no	*nein*
ng	sing	*singen*
p	pig	*Preis*
r	run	*Reise*
s	so	*heiß*
sh	show	*schön*
t	tin	*Tag*
ts	hits	*Zeit*
v	van	*wohnen*
y	yes	*ja*
z	zoo	*sitzen*
zh	pleasure	*Garage*

word stress

Stress in German is straightforward – almost all native German words are pronounced with stress on the first syllable. There are just a couple of things to watch for.

Some prefixes aren't stressed, like *ver-* in the verb *verstehen* fer·*shtay*·en (understand). Also, words borrowed from other languages keep their original stress, like *Organisation* or·ga·ni·sa·*tsyawn* (organisation) and *Student* shtu·*dent* (student) and may have the stress on a different syllable than in English.

While these are handy rules of thumb, you can always rely on the coloured pronunciation guide which shows the stressed syllable in *italics*.

intonation

German intonation is quite similar to English. If you're asking a question, your voice goes up at the end, just like in English: *Bist du fertig?* bist du *fer*·tikh (Are you ready?) or *Tee?* tay (Tea?). If you start with a question word, however, your voice falls, also like in English: *Woher kommst du?* vo·*hair* komst du (Where are you from?).

Note that, like in English, a rise in intonation can indicate that the speaker hasn't finished. For example, if someone asks you where you're from, you can say *Melbourne ... eine Stadt ... In Australien mel*·bawn ... *ai*·ne shtat ... in ow·*stra*·li·en (Melbourne ... a city ... in Australia), rising on the first two parts, and everyone will wait with bated breath!

reading & writing

The relationship between German sounds and the characters that represent them in writing is a regular one, so once you become familiar with them, you should be able to pronounce a new word without a hitch. Also, German doesn't have silent letters – you pronounce the *k* at the start of *Kneipe knai·*pe (pub) and the *e* on the end of *ich verstehe* ikh fair·*shtay·*e (I understand).

The examples in the tables on the previous pages show the correspondence between the sounds (in the first column) and how they're typically spelt (in the third column). However, there are a few features worth noting:

- the letter *ß* stands for *ss* (but the rules for when you can use *ß* or *ss* are confusing to Germans themselves so you can ignore these!)
- the letters *sp* and *st* at the start of a word are pronounced like shp and sht (eg, *Sport* (sport) is pronounced shport)
- final *d*, *g*, and *b* are 'unvoiced', ie, pronounced more like t, k and p (eg, *Geld* (money) *is pronounced* gelt)

Don't be intimidated by the length of some German words. Unlike English, which often uses a number of separate words to express one single idea or notion, German tends to join words together. After a while you'll start to recognise parts of words and you'll find it easy to also understand longer words. For example, *Haupt-* howpt· means 'main', so *Hauptpost* howpt·post means 'main post-office' or 'GPO', and *Hauptstadt* howpt·shtat (literally 'main city') means 'capital'.

a–z phrasebuilder

This chapter is arranged alphabetically and is designed to help you create your own sentences. If you can't find the exact phrase you need in this book, remember this: there are no rules, only particular ways of saying things. Some grammar, a few gestures, a couple of well-chosen words and you'll generally get the message across.

adjectives see describing things

a/an

Is that a bank or a museum?

Ist das eine Bank oder   ist das *ai*·ne bank *aw*·der
ein Museum?   ain mu·*zay*·um
(lit: is that a bank or a museum)

German has three words for the articles 'a' or 'an'. The gender of the noun (see **gender**) determines which word you use.

a/an					
masculine	*ein*	ain	a guide	*ein Reiseführer*	ain *rai*·ze·fü·rer
neuter	*ein*	ain	a room	*ein Zimmer*	ain *tsi*·mer
feminine	*eine*	*ai*·ne	a ticket	*eine Fahrkarte*	*ai*·ne *fahr*·kar·te

articles see a/an and the

be

The food is great!
> *Das Essen ist fantastisch!*   das e·sen ist fan·*tas*·tish
> (lit: the food is great)

I'm tired.
> *Ich bin müde.*   ikh bin *mü*·de
> (lit: I am tired)

Just as in English, the verb 'be' changes depending on who or what is the subject of the sentence:

to be		sein		
I	am	*ich*	*bin*	ikh bin
you sg	are	*du*	*bist*	doo bist
he/she/it	is	*er/sie/es*	*ist*	er/zee/es ist
we	are	*wir*	*sind*	veer zind
you pl	are	*ihr*	*seid*	eer zait
they	are	*sie*	*sind*	zee zind
you sg&pl pol	are	*Sie*	*sind*	zee zind

case see **me, myself, I**

describing things

My meal is cold.
> *Mein Essen ist kalt.*   main e·sen ist kalt
> (lit: my meal is cold)

Adjectives don't change their endings if they come after 'be', as in the example above. However, if they come before a noun, eg, *das kaltes Essen*, you have to add endings which roughly follow the same pattern as the article 'the' (see **the**). Nevertheless, using the basic form given in the dictionary, you'll still be understood.

future see **planning ahead**

gender

The cathedral, the gallery and the museum are on Möhl Street.

> *Der Dom, die Galerie*   dair dawm die ga·le·*ree*
> *und das Museum sind*   unt das mu·*zay*·um zint
> *in der Möhlstrasse.*   in dair *merl*·shtra·se
> (lit: the cathedral the gallery
> and the museum are
> on the Möhl-street)

All nouns – words that denote a person, place, thing or concept, such as *Claudia*, *Berlin*, *Schlüssel* (key) or *Hunger* (hunger) – in German are assigned a gender. (Nouns are really easy to spot in written German, as they always begin with a capital letter.) They're classified as masculine, feminine or neuter. These distinctions have nothing to do with sex, for example, *Schlüssel* (key) is masculine and *Mädchen* (girl) is neuter even if the girl is obviously female.

Gender affects the appearance of words which accompany the noun, like the articles 'a' and 'the' (as in the example above), 'some', 'none' and adjectives. If you're not sure what gender a word has, don't worry because people will still understand you.

There are no hard and fast rules for predicting the gender of German nouns, but below are some useful generalisations:

- nouns ending in *-er* are generally masculine,
  eg, *der Lehrer* dair *lair*·rer (the male teacher)
- nouns ending in *-in* are feminine,
  eg, *die Lehrerin* dee *lair*·re·rin (the female teacher)
- young people and animals are neuter,
  eg, *das Baby* das *bay*·bi (the baby)

See also **a/an**, **the**, **some**, **none** and **describing things**.

m before f

In this book, masculine forms appear before the feminine forms. If letters have been added to the masculine word to form the feminine word (often *in*), these will appear in parentheses. Where the change involves more than the addition of *in*, two words are given, separated by a slash. The neuter form – where applicable – is mentioned last.

have

I have a flat tyre.
Ich habe eine Reifenpanne.   ikh *hah*·be *ai*·ne *rai*·fen·pa·ne
(lit: I have a flat-tyre)

Do you have a quieter room?
Haben Sie ein   *hah*·ben zee ain
ruhigeres Zimmer?   *roo*·i·ge·res *tsi*·mer
(lit: have you a quieter room)

As with all verbs in German, 'have' changes depending on who or what 'has' something.

have		haben		
I	have	*ich*	*habe*	ikh *hah*·be
you sg	have	*du*	*hast*	doo hast
he/she/it	has	*er/sie/es*	*hat*	er/zee/es hat
we	have	*wir*	*haben*	veer *hah*·ben
you pl	have	*ihr*	*habt*	eer hapt
they	have	*sie*	*haben*	zee *hah*·ben
you sg&pl pol	have	*Sie*	*haben*	zee *hah*·ben

more than one

I'd like two tickets, please.
Ich möchte zwei   ikh *merkh*·te tsvai
Fahrkarten, bitte.   *fahr*·kar·ten *bi*·te
(lit: I would-like two tickets please)

There are a number of ways of forming plurals in German. It can be difficult to predict plural endings, but the most common ones are:

- *-n* for words ending in *-e*, or *-en* for some words ending in a consonant,
  eg, *Fahrkarte* 'ticket' becomes *Fahrkarten* 'tickets' and *Fink* 'finch' becomes *Finken* 'finches'

- *-e* for some words ending in a consonant,
  eg, *Tag* 'day' becomes *Tage* 'days'
- *-e* + umlaut (two dots) over the vowel for some words
  ending in a consonant, eg, *Zug* 'train' becomes *Züge* 'trains'

If in doubt, just put a number in front of a singular noun and
you will be understood. For more on numbers, see **numbers &
amounts**, page 27.

me, myself, I

In English you use the subject, eg, 'I', before a verb, but the
object, eg, 'me', after a verb. You would say, for example, 'She
likes me' and not 'She likes I'. German is similar and uses the
following forms:

subject			object		
I	*ich*	ikh	me	*mich*	mikh
you sg	*du*	du	you sg	*dich*	dikh
he	*er*	air	him	*ihn*	een
she	*sie*	zee	her	*sie*	zee
it	*es*	es	it	*es*	es
we	*wir*	veer	us	*uns*	uns
you pl	*ihr*	eer	you pl	*euch*	oykh
they	*sie*	zee	them	*sie*	zee
you sg&pl pol	*Sie*	zee	you sg&pl pol	*Sie*	zee

German does this with other words too. For example, the
masculine word for the article 'the', *der* dair, changes to *den* dayn
after a verb:

The tour guide is handsome.
Der Reiseführer ist schön.   dair rai·ze·fü·rer ist shern
(lit: the tour-guide is handsome)

I love the tour guide.
Ich liebe den Reiseführer.   ikh lee·be dayn rai·ze·fü·rer
(lit: I love the tour-guide)

There are other forms like this, which are beyond the scope of this book, but if you come across an unfamiliar short word (like *dem* or *des*) it's likely to be a variation on the word for 'the'.

my & your

You room is on the second floor.
> *Ihr Zimmer ist im*   eer *tsi·*mer ist im
> *zweiten Stock.*   *tsvait·*en shtok
> (lit: your room is on-the second floor)

Here is my passport.
> *Hier ist mein Pass.*   heer ist main pas
> (lit: here is my passport)

The possessive pronouns like 'my' and 'your' in English follow the same pattern as the article 'a/an' – they change depending on the gender or number of the nouns they refer to.

	masculine		neuter		feminine	
my	*mein*	main	*mein*	main	*meine*	*mai·*ne
your sg	*dein*	dain	*dein*	dain	*deine*	*dai·*ne
his	*sein*	sain	*sein*	sain	*seine*	*sai·*ne
her	*ihr*	eer	*ihr*	eer	*ihre*	*ee·*re
its	*sein*	sain	*sein*	sain	*seine*	*sai·*ne
our	*unser*	*un·*zer	*unser*	*un·*zer	*unsere*	*un·*ze·re
your pl	*euer*	*oy·*er	*euer*	*oy·*er	*eure*	*oy·*re
their	*ihr*	eer	*ihr*	eer	*ihre*	*ee·*re
your sg&pl pol	*Ihr*	eer	*Ihr*	eer	*Ihre*	*ee·*re

negative see not

not

I don't smoke.
Ich rauche nicht.   ikh *row*·khe nikht
(lit: I smoke not)

Saying you don't do something is much easier in German than in English – just add *nicht* nikht (not) after the verb. You don't need to add 'don't' like you often do in English.

planning ahead

Tomorrow I'm travelling to Berlin.
Ich fahre morgen   ikh *fah*·re *mor*·gen
nach Berlin.   nakh ber·*leen*
(lit: I travel tomorrow to Berlin)

The easiest way to talk about future events or plans is to use a word like 'tomorrow', or a phrase like 'next week', 'at 3 o'clock' and so on. If you want to talk about future plans but don't have a specific time in mind, you can use the constructions below. This equates to the English construction 'going to'.

I'm going to travel to Berlin.
Ich werde nach   ikh *ver*·de nakh
Berlin fahren.   ber·*leen fah*·ren
(lit: I am-going-to to
Berlin travel)

We're going to take a day trip.
Wir werden einen   veer *ver*·den *ai*·nen
Tagesausflug machen.   *tah*·ges·ows·flookh *ma*·khen
(lit: we are-going-to a
day-trip make)

The verb *werden* changes depending on who or what is going to do something. People will understand if you just use *werden* in all cases, but the correct forms of the verb are given on the next page in case you want to give them a try:

going to		*werden*		
I	am going to	*ich*	*werde*	ikh ver·de
you sg	are going to	*du*	*wirst*	doo veerst
he/she/it	is going to	*er/sie/es*	*wird*	er/zee/es veert
we	are going to	*wir*	*werden*	veer ver·den
you pl	are going to	*ihr*	*werdet*	eer ver·det
they	are going to	*sie*	*werden*	zee ver·den
you sg& pl pol	are going to	*Sie*	*werden*	zee ver·den

plural see more than one

pointing something out

That's my bag and those are her suitcases.

Das ist meine Tasche und   das ist *mai*·ne *ta*·she unt
das sind ihre Koffer.   das zint *ee*·re *ko*·fer
(lit: that is my bag and
  those are her suitcases)

It's very easy to point something out in German. Use *das ist* (that is) and *das sind* (that are) no matter what the gender. The only thing you have to think about is whether you're pointing out one or more things.

possession see have and my & your

question words

An easy way to form a question is by using a question word. These are as follows:

question words

who?	*Wer?*	vair
Who is that?	*Wer ist das?* (lit: who is that)	vair ist das
what?	*Was?*	vas
What is that?	*Was ist das?* (lit: what is that)	vas ist das
which?	*Welcher?*	vel·kher
Which station is this?	*Welcher Bahnhof ist das?* (lit: which station is that)	vel·kher bahn·hawf ist das
when?	*Wann?*	van
When does it open?	*Wann öffnet es?* (lit: when opens it)	van erf·net es
where?	*Wo?*	vaw
Where is the station?	*Wo ist der Bahnhof?* (lit: where is the station)	vaw ist dair bahn·hawf
how?	*Wie?*	vee
How do you say it in German?	*Wie sagt man das auf Deutsch?* (lit: how says one that in German)	vee zagt man das owf doytsh
how much?	*Wieviel?*	vee·feel
how many?	*Wie viele?*	vee fee·le
How much is it?	*Wieviel kostet es?* (lit: how much costs it)	vee·feel kos·tet es
why?	*Warum?*	va·rum
Why is it shut?	*Warum ist es geschlossen?* (lit: why is it shut)	va·rum ist es ge·shlo·sen

some

I'd like some ham, please.
Ich möchte etwas   ikh *mer*·khte *et*·vas
Schinken bitte.   *shin*·ken *bi*·te
(lit: I would-like some ham please)

To ask for 'some' is really simple – just use *etwas* (some), in the same way you'd say 'some' in English.

the

The cathedral, the gallery and the museum are on Möhl Street.
Der Dom, die Galerie   dair dawm die ga·le·*ree*
und das Museum sind   unt das mu·zay·um zint
in der Möhlstrasse.   in dair *merl*·shtra·se
(lit: the cathedral the gallery
    and the museum are
    on the Möhl-street)

Unlike English, where there's only one form of the article 'the', German has a number of words which would all be translated in English as 'the'. Which word you use depends on the word it refers to and the way that word fits into the rest of the sentence. It can get a bit complicated, but if you use the simplest forms of 'the', as outlined below, you'll get your message across.

the					
masculine	*der*	der	the guide	*der Reiseführer*	dair *rai*·ze·fü·rer
neuter	*das*	das	the room	*das Zimmer*	das *tsi*·mer
feminine	*die*	dee	a ticket	*die Fahrkarte*	dee *fahr*·kar·te
plural	*die*	dee	the trains	*die Züge*	dee *tsü*·ge

See also **a/an** and **gender**.

this/these

This dish is fantastic!
Dieses Gericht ist fantastisch!   dee·zes ge·*rikht* ist fan·*tas*·tish
(lit: this dish is fantastic)

The word *dieser* (this/these) follows the same pattern as 'the':

this/these					
masculine	*dieser*	*dee*·zer	this guide	*dieser Führer*	*dee*·zer *fü*·rer
neuter	*dieses*	*dee*·zes	this room	*dieses Zimmer*	*dee*·zes *tsi*·mer
feminine	*diese*	*dee*·ze	this ticket	*diese Fahrkarte*	*dee*·ze *fahr*·kar·te
plural	*diese*	*dee*·ze	these trains	*diese Züge*	*dee*·ze *tsü*·ge

yes/no questions

The hotel is on Potsdamer Square?
Das Hotel ist am Potsdamerplatz?   das *haw*·tel ist am *pots*·dah·mer·plats
(lit: the hotel is on-the Potsdamer-square)

There are three main ways of forming yes/no questions. The one which requires least effort is to make a statement, but to say it like a question, rising in intonation towards the end of the sentence, as illustrated above.

The hotel is on Potsdamer Square, isn't it?
Das Hotel ist am   das *haw*·tel ist am
Potsdamerplatz, nicht wahr? *pots*·dah·mer·plats nikht var
(lit: the hotel is on
  Potsdamer-square not true)

The second example shows that you can also add *nicht wahr* (not true) to the end of a statement. This is much easier than in English, where you'd use a variety of question tags, such as 'isn't it?', 'aren't you?' and 'doesn't it?'.

Is the hotel on Potsdamer Square?
Ist das Hotel am   ist das *haw*·tel am
Potsdamerplatz?   *pots*·dah·mer·plats
(lit: is the hotel on-the
  Potsdamer-square)

Finally, the third example shows you can turn a statement into a question by reversing the order of the subject and the verb.

Also see **word order**.

word order

I'm travelling to Berlin.
Ich fahre nach Berlin.   ikh *fah*·re nakh ber·*leen*
(lit: I travel to Berlin)

Tomorrow I'm travelling to Berlin.
Morgen fahre ich   *mor*·gen *fah*·re ikh
nach Berlin.   nakh ber·*leen*
(lit: tomorrow travel I to Berlin)

In a straightforward German statement, the verb is the second element (note that this does not necessarily mean it's the second word as the first element can contain more than one word).

The verb would usually follow the subject, ie, the concept or thing you're talking about. So if you start the sentence with a word like 'tomorrow', you have to reverse the order of the subject and verb to keep the verb in second spot, as illustrated above. To turn a statement into a question, you can reverse the order of the subject and verb: the verb comes first – see the example at the top of this page.

language difficulties
sprachprobleme

There are two forms of the second person singular pronoun 'you'. Use the polite form *Sie* with anyone you don't know well. You should only use the informal form *du* with people you know very well. All the phrases in this chapter use *Sie* – use your intuition to work out when to use formal and informal forms.

Do you speak English?
Sprechen Sie Englisch?   *shpre·khen zee ong·lish*

Does anyone speak English?
Spricht hier jemand   *shprikht heer yay·mant*
Englisch?   *eng·lish*

Do you understand (me)?
Verstehen Sie (mich)?   *fer·shtay·en zee (mikh)*

Yes, I understand (you).
Ja, ich verstehe (Sie).   *yah ikh fer·shtay·e (zee)*

No, I don't understand (you).
Nein, ich verstehe (Sie) nicht.   *nain ikh fer·shtay·e (zee) nikht*

I (don't) understand.
Ich verstehe (nicht).   *ikh fer·shtay·e (nikht)*

I speak a little German.
Ich spreche ein   *ikh shpre·khe ain*
bisschen Deutsch.   *bis·khen doytsh*

How do you ...?	*Wie ...?*	vee ...
pronounce this	*spricht man*	shprikht man
	dieses Wort aus	dee·zes vort ows
say 'ticket' in	*sagt man 'ticket'*	zagt man ti·ket
German	*auf Deutsch*	owf doytsh
write 'Schweiz'	*schreibt man*	shraipt man
	'Schweiz'	shvaits

What does *'Kugel'* mean?
| *Was bedeutet 'Kugel'?* | vas be·*doy*·tet *koo*·gel |

Could you please ...? *Könnten Sie ...?* kern·ten zee ...

repeat that	*das bitte wiederholen*	das *bi*·te vee·der·*haw*·len
speak more slowly	*bitte langsamer sprechen*	*bi*·te *lang*·za·mer *shpre*·khen
write it down	*das bitte aufschreiben*	das *bi*·te *owf*·shrai·ben

false friends

Many German words look like English words but have a completely different meaning, so be careful! Here are a few examples:

blank	blank	shiny
	not 'blank', which is *leer*, leer	
Chef	shef	boss
	not 'chef', which is *Koch*, kokh	
komisch	*kaw*·mish	strange
	not 'comical', which is *lustig*, *lus*·tikh	
Konfektion	kon·fekt·*tsyawn*	ready-made clothes
	not 'confectionary', which is *Konfekt*, kon·*fekt*	
sensibel	zen·*zee*·bel	sensitive
	not 'sensible', which is *vernünftig*, fer·*nünf*·tikh	
Tip	tip	advance information
	not 'tip', which is *Trinkgeld*, *trink*·gelt	

numbers & amounts

cardinal numbers

kardinalzahlen

1	*eins*	ains
2	*zwei*	tsvai
3	*drei*	drai
4	*vier*	fccr
5	*fünf*	fünf
6	*sechs*	zeks
7	*sieben*	zee·ben
8	*acht*	akht
9	*neun*	noyn
10	*zehn*	tsayn
11	*elf*	elf
12	*zwölf*	zverlf
13	*dreizehn*	*drai*·tsayn
14	*vierzehn*	feer·tsayn
15	*fünfzehn*	*fünf*·tsayn
16	*sechzehn*	zeks·tsayn
17	*siebzehn*	zeep·tsayn
18	*achtzehn*	akht·tsayn
19	*neunzehn*	noyn·tsayn
20	*zwanzig*	tsvan·tsikh
21	*einundzwanzig*	ain·unt·tsvan·tsikh
22	*zweiundzwanzig*	tsvai·unt·tsvan·tsikh
30	*dreißig*	drai·tsikh
40	*vierzig*	feer·tsikh
50	*fünfzig*	fünf·tsikh
60	*sechzig*	zekh·tsikh
70	*siebzig*	zeep·tsikh
80	*achtzig*	akht·tsikh
90	*neunzig*	noyn·tsikh
100	*hundert*	hun·dert
1,000	*tausend*	tow·sent
1,000,000	*eine Million*	ai·ne mil·yawn

ordinal numbers

1st	erste	ers·te
2nd	zweite	tsvai·te
3rd	dritte	dri·te
4th	vierte	feer·te
5th	fünfte	fünf·te

fractions

brüche

a quarter	ein Viertel	ain fir·tel
a third	ein Drittel	ain dri·tel
a half	eine Hälfte	ai·ne helf·te
three-quarters	drei Viertel	drai fir·tel
all	alles	a·les
none	nichts	nikhts

amounts

mengen

How much?	Wieviel?	vee·feel
How many?	Wie viele?	vee fee·le
(100) grams	(100) Gramm	(hun·dert) gram
half a dozen	ein halbes Dutzend	ain hal·bes du·tsent
a kilo	ein Kilo	ain kee·lo
a packet	eine Packung	ai·ne pa·kung
a slice	eine Scheibe	ai·ne shai·be
a tin	eine Dose	ai·ne daw·ze
less	weniger	vay·ni·ger
(just) a little	(nur) ein bisschen	(noor) ain bis·khen
much/a lot	viel	feel
many	viele	fee·le
more	mehr	mair
some	einige	ai·ni·ge

telling the time

die uhrzeit

What time is it?	*Wie spät ist es?*	vee shpayt ist es
It's (ten) o'clock.	*Es ist (zehn) Uhr.*	es ist (tsayn) oor
Quarter past one.	*Viertel nach eins.*	fir·tel nahkh ains
Twenty past one.	*Zwanzig nach eins.*	tsvan·tsikh nahkh ains
Half past one.	*Halb zwei.*	halp tsvai
	(lit: half two)	
Twenty to one.	*Zwanzig vor eins.*	tsvan·tsikh fawr ains
Quarter to one.	*Viertel vor eins.*	fir·tel fawr ains
It's 2.12 pm.	*Es ist*	es ist
	14:12.	feer·tsayn oor tsverlf
am	*vormittags*	fawr·mi·tahks
pm	*nachmittags/*	nahkh·mi·tahks/
	abends	ah·bents

---

the time of your life

English uses 'pm' to denote any time between midday and midnight, but German is a bit more specific. Use *nachmittags* for times between midday and six in the evening, and *abends* between six and midnight.

---

days of the week

die wochentage

Monday	*Montag*	mawn·tahk
Tuesday	*Dienstag*	deens·tahk
Wednesday	*Mittwoch*	mit vokh
Thursday	*Donnerstag*	do·ners·tahk
Friday	*Freitag*	frai·tahk
Saturday	*Samstag*	zams·tahk
Sunday	*Sonntag*	zon·tahk

time & dates

months

January	Januar	yan·u·ahr
February	Februar	fay·bru·ahr
March	März	merts
April	April	a·pril
May	Mai	mai
June	Juni	yoo·ni
July	Juli	yoo·li
August	August	ow·gust
September	September	zep·tem·ber
October	Oktober	ok·taw·ber
November	November	no·vem·ber
December	Dezember	de·tsem·ber

seasons

die jahreszeiten

summer	Sommer	zo·mer
autumn	Herbst	herpst
winter	Winter	vin·ter
spring	Frühling	frü·ling

dates

das datum

What date?
Welches Datum? vel·khes dah·tum

What date it is today?
Der Wievielte ist heute? dair vee·feel·te ist hoy·te

It's 18 October.
Heute ist der hoy·te ist dair
18. Oktober. akh·tsayn·te ok·taw·ber

present

die gegenwart

now	*jetzt*	yetst
right now	*jetzt gerade*	yetst ge·*rah*·de

this ...		
afternoon	*heute*	*hoy*·te
	Nachmittag	*nahkh*·mi·tahk
month	*diesen Monat*	dee·zen *maw*·nat
morning	*heute Morgen*	*hoy*·te *mor*·gen
week	*diese Woche*	dee·ze vo·khe
year	*dieses Jahr*	dee·zes yahr

today	*heute*	*hoy*·te
tonight	*heute Abend*	*hoy*·te *ah*·bent

past

die vergangenheit

day before yesterday	*vorgestern*	*fawr*·ges·tern
last month	*letzten Monat*	*lets*·ten *maw*·nat
last night	*vergangene Nacht*	fer·*gang*·e·ne nakht
last week	*letzte Woche*	*lets*·te vo·khe
last year	*letztes Jahr*	*lets*·tes yahr
since (May)	*seit (Mai)*	zait (mai)
a while ago	*vor einer Weile*	fawr *ai*·ner *vai*·le
(three) days ago	*vor (drei) Tagen*	fawr (drai) *tah*·gen
(half an) hour ago	*vor (einer halben) Stunde*	fawr (*ai*·ner *hal*·ben) *shtun*·de
(five) years ago	*vor (fünf) Jahren*	fawr (fünf) *yah*·ren

yesterday ...		
	gestern ...	*ges*·tern ...
afternoon	*Nachmittag*	*nahkh*·mi·tahk
evening	*Abend*	*ah*·bent
morning	*Morgen*	*mor*·gen

future

day after tomorrow	*übermorgen*	*ü*·ber·mor·gen
in (six) days	*in (sechs) Tagen*	in (zeks) *tah*·gen
in (five) minutes	*in (fünf) Minuten*	in (fünf) mi·*noo*·ten
next month	*nächsten Monat*	*naykhs*·ten *maw*·nat
next week	*nächste Woche*	*naykhs*·te *vo*·khe
next year	*nächstes Jahr*	*naykhs*·tes yahr
tomorrow ...	*morgen ...*	*mor*·gen ...
afternoon	*Nachmittag*	*nahkh*·mi·tahk
evening	*Abend*	*ah*·bent
morning	*früh*	frü
until (June)	*bis (Juni)*	bis (*yoo*·ni)
within a month	*in einem Monat*	in *ai*·nem *maw*·nat
within an hour	*in einer Stunde*	in *ai*·ner *shtun*·de

during the day

It's early.	*Es ist früh.*	es ist frü
It's late.	*Es ist spät.*	es ist shpayt
afternoon	*Nachmittag* m	*nahkh*·mi·tahk
dawn	*Dämmerung* f	*de*·me·rung
day	*Tag* m	tahk
evening	*Abend* m	*ah*·bent
midday	*Mittag* m	*mi*·tahk
midnight	*Mitternacht* f	*mi*·ter·nakht
morning	*Morgen* m	*mor*·gen
night	*Nacht* f	nakht
noon	*Mittag* m	*mi*·tahk
sunrise	*Sonnenaufgang* m	zo·nen·owf·gang
sunset	*Sonnenunter-gang* m	zo·nen·un·ter·gang

How much is it?
Wie viel kostet es? vee feel *kos*·tet es

Can you write down the price?
Können Sie den Preis *ker*·nen zee dayn prais
aufschreiben? *owf*·shrai·ben

Do you accept ...?	*Nehmen Sie ...?*	*nay*·men zee ...
credit cards	*Kreditkarten*	kre·*deet*·kar·ten
debit cards	*Debitkarten*	*day*·bit·kar·ten
travellers cheques	*Reiseschecks*	*rai*·ze·sheks
I'd like to ...	*Ich möchte ...*	ikh *merkh*·te ...
cash a cheque	*einen Scheck einlösen*	*ai*·nen shek *ain*·ler·zen
change money	*Geld umtauschen*	gelt *um*·tow·shen
change some travellers cheques	*Reiseschecks einlösen*	*rai*·ze·sheks *ain*·ler·zen
get a cash advance	*eine Barauszahlung*	*ai*·ne *bahr*·ows·tsah·lung
withdraw money	*Geld abheben*	gelt *ap*·hay·ben
Where's the nearest ...?	*Wo ist der/die nächste ...?* m/f	vaw ist dair/dee *naykhs*·te ...
automatic teller machine	*Geldautomat* m	gelt·ow·to·maht
foreign exchange office	*Geldwechsel-stube* f	gelt·vek·sel·shtoo·be

What's the ...?	*Wie ...?*	vee ...
charge for that	*hoch sind die Gebühren dafür*	hawkh zint dee ge·*bü*·ren da·*für*
commission	*hoch ist die Kommission*	hawkh ist dee ko·mi·*syawn*
exchange rate	*ist der Wechselkurs*	ist dair *vek*·sel·kurs

It's free.

Das ist umsonst.   das ist um·*zonst*

It costs (30) euros.

Das kostet (30) Euro.   das *kos*·tet (*drai*·tsikh) *oy*·ro

---

money talks

Talking about prices is really easy in German because you don't need to add a plural ending to the currency. Twenty dollars is simply *zwanzig Dollar*. Below are a few currencies translated into German to get you started:

cent	*Cent*	sent
dollar	*Dollar*	*do*·lahr
euro	*Euro*	*oy*·ro
franc	*Franc*	frank
pence	*Pence*	pens
pound	*Pfund*	pfunt
rouble	*Rubel*	*roo*·bel
yen	*Yen*	yen

getting around

herumreisen

What time does the ... leave?	*Wann fährt ... ab?*	van fairt ... ap
boat	*das Boot*	das bawt
bus	*der Bus*	dair bus
train	*der Zug*	dair tsook

What time does the plane leave?
Wann fliegt das Flugzeug ab? van fleekt das flook·tsoyk ap

What time's the ... bus?	*Wann fährt der ... Bus?*	van fairt dair ... bus
first	*erste*	ers·te
last	*letzte*	lets·te
next	*nächste*	naykhs·te

I'd like a/an ... seat.	*Ich hätte gern einen ...*	ikh he·te gern ai·nen ...
aisle	*Platz am Gang*	plats am gang
non-smoking	*Nichtraucher-platz*	nikht·row·kher·plats
smoking	*Raucherplatz*	row·kher·plats
window	*Fensterplatz*	fens·ter·plats

How long will it be delayed?
Wie viel Verspätung wird es haben? vee feel fer·shpay·tung virt es hah·ben

listen for ...

... ist ge·shtri·khen ... *ist gestrichen.*	The ... is cancelled.
hat fer·shpay·tung ... *hat Verspätung.*	The ... is delayed.

Is this seat free?
Ist dieser Platz frei?   ist *dee*·zer plats frai

That's my seat.
Dieses ist mein Platz.   *dee*·zes ist main plats

Can you tell me when we get to (Kiel)?
Könnten Sie mir bitte   *kern*·ten zee meer *bi*·te
sagen, wann wir in   *zah*·gen van veer in
(Kiel) ankommen?   (keel) *an*·ko·men

I want to get off here.
Ich möchte hier   ikh *merkh*·te heer
aussteigen.   *ows*·shtai·gen

buying tickets

fahrkarten kaufen

Where can I buy a ticket?
Wo kann ich eine   vaw kan ikh *ai*·ne
Fahrkarte kaufen?   *fahr*·kar·te *kow*·fen

Do I need to book?
Muss ich einen Platz   mus ikh *ai*·nen plats
reservieren lassen?   re·zer·*vee*·ren *la*·sen

A ... ticket to (Berlin).	Eine ... nach (Berlin).	*ai*·ne ... nahkh (ber·*leen*)
1st-class	Fahrkarte erster Klasse	*fahr*·kar·te *ers*·ter *kla*·se
2nd-class	Fahrkarte zweiter Klasse	*fahr*·kar·te *tsvai*·ter *kla*·se
child's	Kinderfahrkarte	*kin*·der·fahr·kar·te
one-way	einfache Fahrkarte	*ain*·fa·khe *fahr*·kar·te
return	Rückfahrkarte	*rük*·fahr·kar·te
student's	Studentenfahrkarte	shtu·*den*·ten·fahr·kar·te

Two (return tickets), please.
   Zwei (Rückfahrkarten) bitte.   tsvai (*rük*·fahr·kar·ten) *bi*·te

How much is it?
   Was kostet das?   vas *kos*·tet das

It's full.
   Es ist ausgebucht.   es ist *ows*·ge·bookht

How long does the trip take?
   Wie lange dauert die Fahrt?   vee *lang*·e *dow*·ert dee fahrt

Is it a direct route?
   Ist es eine direkte   ist es *ai*·ne di·*rek*·te
   Verbindung?   fer·*bin*·dung

Can I get a stand-by ticket?
   Kann ich ein Standby-Ticket   kan ikh ain stend·*bai*·ti·ket
   bekommen?   be·*ko*·men

I'd like to	*Ich möchte meine*	ikh *merkh*·te *mai*·ne
my ticket, please.	*Fahrkarte bitte ...*	*fahr*·kar·te *bi*·te ...
cancel	*zurückgeben*	tsu·*rük* gay·ben
change	*ändern lassen*	*en*·dern *la*·sen
confirm	*bestätigen*	be·*shtay*·ti·gen
	lassen	*la*·sen

getting there

German distinguishes between different types of journeys, depending on the transport used:

| *Fahrt* f | fahrt | **journey by road or rail** |
| *Flug* m | flook | **journey by plane** |

This distinction is reflected in the names of the tickets used for these journeys:

| *Fahrkarte* f | *fahr*·kar·te | **train/bus/underground ticket** |
| *Flugticket* n | *flook*·ti·ket | **plane ticket** |

This chapter mostly uses *Fahrkarte*, except in the plane section, so make sure you use the appropriate word when you're buying tickets.

luggage

gepäck

My luggage has been ...	*Mein Gepäck ist ...*	main ge·*pek* ist ...
damaged	*beschädigt*	be·*shay*·dikht
lost	*verloren*	fer·*law*·ren
	gegangen	ge·*gang*·en
stolen	*gestohlen*	ge·*shtaw*·len
	worden	*vor*·den

My luggage hasn't arrived.
Mein Gepäck ist　　　　main ge·*pek* ist
nicht angekommen.　　　nikht *an*·ge·ko·men

I'd like a luggage locker.
Ich hätte gern ein　　　ikh *he*·te gern ain
Gepäckschließfach.　　　ge·*pek*·shlees·fakh

Can I have some coins/tokens?
Können Sie mir　　　　*ker*·nen zee meer
ein paar Münzen/　　　ain pahr *mün*·tsen/
Wertmarken geben?　　　*vert*·mar·ken *gay*·ben

plane

flugzeug

When's the next flight to ...?
Wann ist der nächste　　van ist dair *naykhs*·te
Flug nach ...?　　　　　flook nahkh ...

What time do I have to check in?
Wann muss ich　　　　　van mus ikh
einchecken?　　　　　　*ain*·che·ken

For phrases about getting through customs, see **border crossing**, page 48.

bus

Which bus	Welcher Bus	vel·kher bus
goes to ...?	fährt ...?	fairt ...
Cologne	nach Köln	nakh kerln
the station	zum Bahnhof	tsum *bahn*·hawf
the youth	zur Jugend-	tsur *yoo*·gent·
hostel	herberge	her·ber·ge
the city centre	zum Stadt-	tsum *shtat*·
	zentrum	tsen·trum

This one.	Dieser hier.	*dee*·zer heer
That one.	Der da.	dair dah
Bus number ...	Bus Nummer ...	bus *nu*·mer ...

See numbers & amounts page 27.

where to?

German uses two different words for the English word 'to'. With place names, use *nach*:

to Germany	nach Deutschland	nakh *doytsh*·lant
to Salzburg	nach Salzburg	nakh *zalts*·boorg

For all other destinations, use zum/zur/zum m/f/n:

to the station	zum Bahnhof m	tsum *bahn*·hawf
to the youth	zur Jugend- f	tsur *yoo*·gent·
hostel	herberge	her·ber·ge
to the city	zum Stadt- n	tsum *shtat*·
centre	zentrum	tsen·trum

train

What station is this?
Welcher Bahnhof ist das?   vel·kher *bahn*·hawf ist das

What's the next station?
Welches ist der   vel·khes ist dair
nächste Halt?   *naykhs*·te halt

Does this train stop at (Freiburg)?
Hält dieser Zug in   helt *dee*·zer tsook in
(Freiburg)?   (*frai*·boorg)

Do I need to change trains?
Muss ich umsteigen?   mus ikh *um*·shtai·gen

Which carriage is (for) ...?	*Welcher Wagen ...?*	vel·kher vah·gen ...
dining	*ist der Speisewagen*	ist dair shpai·ze·vah·gen
Munich	*geht nach München*	gayt nahkh mün·khen
1st class	*ist erste Klasse*	ist ers·te kla·se

boot

boot

Are there life jackets?
Gibt es Schwimmwesten?   gipt es *shvim*·ves·ten

What's the sea like today?
Wie ist das Meer heute?   vee ist das mair *hoy*·te

I feel seasick.
Ich bin seekrank.   ikh bin *zay*·krangk

taxi

taxi

I'd like a taxi ...	*Ich hätte gern*	ikh *he*·te gern
	ein Taxi für ...	ain *tak*·si für ...
now	*sofort*	*zo*·fort
tomorrow	*morgen*	*mor*·gen
at (9am)	*(9 Uhr)*	(noyn oor)

Are you free?
Sind Sie frei?   zint zee frai

Please put the meter on.
Schalten Sie bitte den   *shal*·ten zee *bi*·te dayn
Taxameter ein.   tak·sa·*may*·ter ain

How much is it to ...?
Was kostet es bis ...?   vas *kos*·tet es bis ...

Please take me to (this address).
Bitte bringen Sie mich zu   *bi*·te *bring*·en zee mikh tsoo
(dieser Adresse).   (*dee*·zer a·*dre*·se)

I'm really late.
Ich bin wirklich spät dran.   ikh bin *virk*·likh shpayt dran

Please slow down.
Fahren Sie bitte langsamer.   *fah*·ren zee *bi*·te *lang*·za·mer

Please wait here.
Bitte warten Sie hier.   *bi*·te *var*·ten zee heer

Stop ...	*Halten Sie ...*	*hal*·ten zee ...
at the corner	*an der Ecke*	an dair *e*·ke
here	*hier*	heer

car & motorbike

> car & motorbike hire

Where can I	Wo kann ich	vaw kan ikh
hire a/an ...?	... mieten?	... mee·ten
I'd like to	Ich möchte	ikh merkh·te
hire a/an ...	... mieten.	... mee·ten
automatic	ein Fahrzeug	ain fahr·tsoyk
	mit Automatik	mit ow·to·mah·tik
car	ein Auto	ain ow·to
4WD	ein Allradfahr-	ain al·raht·fahr·
	zeug	tsoyk
manual	ein Fahrzeug	ain fahr·tsoyk
	mit Schaltung	mit shal·tung
motorbike	ein Motorrad	ain maw·tor·raht

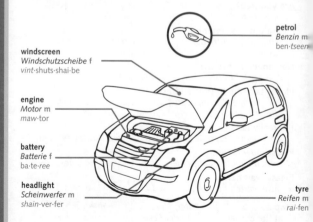

petrol
Benzin m
ben·tseen

windscreen
Windschutzscheibe f
vint·shuts·shai·be

engine
Motor m
maw·tor

battery
Batterie f
ba·te·ree

headlight
Scheinwerfer m
shain·ver·fer

tyre
Reifen m
rai·fen

PRACTICAL

42

How much is it per ...?	Wie viel kostet es pro ...?	vee feel kos·tet es praw ...
day	Tag	tahk
hour	Stunde	shtun·de
week	Woche	vo·khe

> on the road

Does this road go to ...?
Führt diese Straße nach ...?
fürt dee·ze shtrah·se nahkh ...

What's the ... speed limit?	Was ist die Höchst-geschwindigkeit ...?	vas ist dee herkhst-ge·shvin·dikh·kait ...
city	in der Stadt	in dair shtat
country	auf dem Land	owf daym lant
motorway	auf der Autobahn	owf dair ow·to·bahn

road signs

Ausfahrt	ows·fahrt	Exit
Ausfahrt Freihalten	ows·fahrt frai·hal·ten	Keep Clear
Baustelle	bow·shte·le	Roadworks
Einbahnstraße	ain·bahn·shtrah·se	One-way
Einfahrt	ain·fahrt	Entrance
Einfahrt Verboten	ain·fahrt fer·baw·ten	No Entry
Gefahr	ge·fahr	Danger
Halteverbot	hal·te·fer·bawt	No Stopping
Mautstelle	mowt·shte·le	Toll
Parkverbot	park·fer·bawt	No Parking
Radweg	raht·vayk	Cycle Path
Sackgasse	zak·ga·se	No Through Road
Stopp	shtop	Stop
Überholverbot	ü·ber·hawl·fer·bawt	No Overtaking
Umleitung	um·lai·tung	Detour

(How long) Can I park here?
 (Wie lange) Kann ich   (vee *lang*·e) kan ikh
 hier parken?   heer *par*·ken

Where do I pay?
 Wo muss ich bezahlen?   vaw mus ikh be·*tsah*·len

Where's a petrol station?
 Wo ist eine Tankstelle?   vaw ist *ai*·ne *tangk*·shte·le

diesel	*Diesel* m	*dee*·zel
leaded	*verbleites Benzin* n	fer·*blai*·tes ben·*tseen*
LPG	*Autogas* n	*ow*·to·gahs
petrol (gas)	*Benzin* n	ben·*tseen*
regular	*Normalbenzin* n	nor·*mahl*·ben·tseen
unleaded	*bleifreies Benzin* n	*blai*·frai·es ben·*tseen*

> problems

I need a mechanic.
 Ich brauche einen   ikh *brow*·khe *ai*·nen
 Mechaniker.   me·*khah*·ni·ker

My car/motorbike has broken down (at …).
 Ich habe (in …) eine   ikh *hah*·be (in …) *ai*·ne
 Panne mit meinem   *pa*·ne mit *mai*·nem
 Auto/Motorrad.   *ow*·to/*maw*·tor·raht

I had an accident.
 Ich hatte einen Unfall.   ikh *ha*·te *ai*·nen *un*·fal

The car/motorbike won't start.
 Das Auto/Motorrad   das *ow*·to/*maw*·tor·raht
 springt nicht an.   shpringkt nikht an

I have a flat tyre.
 Ich habe eine Reifenpanne.   ikh *hah*·be *ai*·ne *rai*·fen·pa·ne

---

listen for …

vel·khes fa·bri·*kaht*/mo·*del* ist es
 Welches Fabrikat/   **What make/model is it?**
 Modell ist es?

I've lost my car keys.
Ich habe meine   ikh *hah*·be *mai*·ne
Autoschlüssel verloren.   ow·to·shlü·sel fer·*law*·ren

I've locked my keys inside the car.
Ich habe meine Schlüssel   ikh *hah*·be *mai*·ne shlü·sel
im Wagen eingeschlossen.   im *vah*·gen *ain*·ge·shlo·sen

I've run out of petrol.
Ich habe kein Benzin mehr.   ikh *hah*·be kain ben·*tseen* mair

Can you fix it (today)?
Können Sie es (heute)   *ker*·nen zee es (hoy·te)
reparieren?   re·pa·*ree*·ren

When will it be ready?
Wann ist es fertig?   van ist es *fer*·tikh

bicycle

Where can I …?	*Wo kann ich …?*	vaw kan ikh …
buy a second-hand bike	*ein gebrauchtes Fahrrad kaufen*	ain ge·*browkh*·tes fahr·raht *kow*·fen
hire a bicycle	*ein Fahrrad mieten*	ain *fahr*·raht *mee*·ten

How much is it per …?	*Wie viel kostet es für …?*	vee feel *kos*·tel es für …
afternoon	*einen Nachmittag*	*ai*·nen *nahkh*·mi·tahk
day	*einen Tag*	*ai*·nen tahk
hour	*eine Stunde*	ai·ne *shtun*·de
morning	*einen Vormittag*	*ai*·nen *fawr*·mi·tahk

I have a puncture.
Ich habe einen Platten.   ikh *hah*·be *ai*·nen *pla*·ten

local transport

Where's the nearest metro station?

Wo ist der nächste	vaw ist dair *naykhs*·te
U-Bahnhof?	oo·bahn·hawf

Which line goes to (Potsdamer Platz)?

Welche Linie geht zum	*vel*·khe *lee*·ni·e gayt tsum
(Potsdamer Platz)?	(pots·*dah*·mer plats)

day ticket	*Tageskarte* f	*tah*·ges·kar·te
ticket for	*Mehrfach-*	*mair*·fakh·
multiple trips	*fahrkarte* f	fahr·kar·te
tram	*Straßenbahn* f	*shtrah*·sen·bahn
tram stop	*Straßenbahn-*	*shtrah*·sen·bahn·
	haltestelle f	hal·te·shte·le
underground	*U-Bahn* f	*oo*·bahn
underground station	*U-Bahnhof* m	*oo*·bahn·hawf
urban railway	*S-Bahn* f	*es*·bahn
weekly ticket	*Wochenkarte* f	*vo*·khen·kar·te

ticket machines

Buying tickets from machines is very common in Germany, Austria and Switzerland. Some common terms you'll need to know are:

Automat Gibt Rückgeld	**Change Given**
Bitte Wählen	**Please Choose**
Kennzahl Eingeben	**Enter Code**
Korrektur	**Correction**
Taste Drücken	**Press Button**
Zahlbar mit ...	**Pay with ...**

If you can't get the machine to work, you can always try asking someone:

Wie funktioniert das?
  vee foonk·tsywa·*neert* das   **How does this work?**

passport control

I'm here ...	Ich bin hier ...	ikh bin heer ...
in transit	auf der Durchreise	owf dair durkh·rai·ze
on business	auf Geschäftsreise	owt ge·shefts·rai·ze
on holiday	im Urlaub	im oor·lowp
I'm here for ...	Ich bin hier für ...	ikh bin heer für ...
(four) days	(vier) Tage	(feer) lah·ge
(three) weeks	(drei) Wochen	(drai) vo·khen
(two) months	(zwei) Monate	(tsval) maw·na·te

at customs

I have nothing to declare.
  Ich habe nichts   ikh *hah*·be nikhts
  zu verzollen.   tsoo fer·*tso*·len

I have something to declare.
  Ich habe etwas   ikh *hah*·be *et*·vas
  zu verzollen.   tsoo fer·*tso*·len

I didn't know I had to declare it.
  Ich wusste nicht, dass ich   ikh *vus*·te nikht das ikh
  das verzollen muss.   das fer·*tso*·len mus

bureaucabulary

Although Germany has a reputation for being a well-organised country, you may find your spontaneity as a traveller hampered by endless red tape. Learning some of these words can help you get on your way:

Abschrift	*ahb*·shrift	copy/extract
Abstammungs-urkunde	ahb·*shta*·mungs·ur·kun·de	birth certificate
Bekenntnis	be·*kent*·nis	religion
Familienname	fa·*mee*·li·en·nah·me	surname
Familienstand	fa·*mee*·li·en·shtant	marital status
geborene	ge·*baw*·re·ne	maiden name
geboren am	ge·*baw*·ren am	born on
Geburtsdatum	ge·*burts*·da·tum	date of birth
Heirats-urkunde	*hai*·rahts·ur·kun·de	marriage certificate
Staatsange-hörigkeit	shtahts·an·ge·*her*·rikh·kait	citizenship/nationality
Urkunde	*ur*·kun·de	document
Vorname	*for*·nah·me	first name
Wohnort	*vawn*·ort	place of residence

finding accommodation

eine unterkunft finden

Where's a/an ...?	Wo ist ...?	vaw ist ...
bed & breakfast	eine Pension	ai·ne pahng·zyawn
camping ground	ein Campingplatz	ain kem·ping·plats
guesthouse	eine Pension	ai·ne pahng·zyawn
hotel	ein Hotel	ain ho·tel
inn	ein Gasthof	ain gast·hawf
room in a	ein Privalzimmer	ain pri·vahl·tsi·mer
private home		
youth hostel	eine	ai·ne
	Jugendherberge	yoo·gent·her·ber·ge

Can you	Können Sie	ker·nen zee
recommend	etwas ...	et·vas ...
somewhere ...?	empfehlen?	emp·fay·len
cheap	Billiges	bi·li·ges
good	Gutes	goo·tes
luxurious	Luxuriöses	luk·su·ri·er·ses
nearby	in der Nähe	in dair nay·e
romantic	Romantisches	ro·man·ti·shes

What's the address?
Wie ist die Adresse?   vee ist dee a·dre·se

For responses, see **directions**, page 59.

> booking ahead & checking in

I'd like to book a room, please.
Ich möchte bitte ein   ikh merkh·te bi·te ain
Zimmer reservieren.   tsi·mer re·zer·vee·ren

I have a reservation.
Ich habe eine   ikh hah·be ai·ne
Reservierung.   re·zer·vee·rung

My name's ...
  Mein Name ist ...   main *nah*·me ist ...

For (three) nights/weeks.
  Für (drei) Nächte/Wochen.   für (drai) *nekh*·te/*vo*·khen

From (July 2) to (July 6).
  Vom (2. Juli) bis   vom (*tsvai*·ten *yoo*·li) bis
  zum (6. Juli).   tsum (*zeks*·ten *yoo*·li)

How much	*Wie viel kostet*	vee feel *kos*·tet
is it per ...?	*es pro ...?*	es praw ...
night	*Nacht*	nakht
person	*Person*	per·*zawn*
week	*Woche*	*vo*·khe

Do you have	*Haben Sie ein ...?*	*hah*·ben zee ain ...
a ... room?		
double	*Doppelzimmer*	*do*·pel·tsi·mer
	mit einem	mit *ai*·nem
	Doppelbett	*do*·pel·bet
single	*Einzelzimmer*	*ain*·tsel·tsi·mer
twin	*Doppelzimmer*	*do*·pel·tsi·mer
	mit zwei	mit tsvai
	Einzelbetten	*ain*·tsel·be·ten

listen for ...

dair *shlü*·sel ist an dair re·tsep·*tsyawn*
  Der Schlüssel ist   **The key is at reception.**
  an der Rezeption.

ee·ren pas *bi*·te
  Ihren Pass, bitte.   **Your passport, please.**

es toot meer lait veer *hah*·ben *kai*·ne *tsi*·mer frai
  Es tut mir Leid, wir   **I'm sorry, we're full.**
  haben keine Zimmer frei.

für vee *fee*·le *nekh*·te
  Für wie viele Nächte?   **For how many nights?**

Can I see it?
Kann ich es sehen?   kan ikh es zay·en

Is there hot water all day?
Gibt es den ganzen   gipt es dayn gan·tsen
Tag warmes Wasser?   tahk var·mes va·ser

It's fine. I'll take it.
Es ist gut, ich nehme es.   es ist goot ikh nay·me es

Do I need to pay upfront?
Muss ich im Voraus   mus ikh im faw·rows
bezahlen?   be·tsah·len

Can I pay by ...?	*Nehmen Sie ...?*	nay·men zee ...
credit card	*Kreditkarten*	kre·deet·kar·ten
travellers cheque	*Reiseschecks*	rai·ze·sheks

For other methods of payment see **shopping**, page 61.

> requests & queries

When's/Where's breakfast served?
Wann/Wo gibt es Frühstück? van/vaw gipt es frü·shtük

Please wake me at (seven).
Bitte wecken Sie mich   bi·te ve·ken zee mikh
um (sieben) Uhr.   um (zee·ben) oor

Can I use the ...?	*Kann ich ...*	kan ikh ...
	benutzen?	be·nu·tsen
kitchen	*die Küche*	dee kü·khe
laundry	*eine*	ai·ne
	Waschmaschine	vash·ma·shee·ne
telephone	*das Telefon*	das te·le·fawn

Do you have a ...?	*Haben Sie ...?*	hah·ben zee ...
lift (elevator)	*einen Aufzug*	ai·nen owf·tsook
laundry service	*einen*	ai·nen
	Wäscheservice	ve·she·ser·vis
message board	*ein Nachrichten-*	ain nahkh·rikh·ten·
	brett	bret
safe	*einen Safe*	ai·nen sayf
swimming pool	*ein Schwimmbad*	ain shvim·baht

Do you arrange tours here?
Arrangieren Sie hier Touren? · a·rang·zhee·ren zee heer too·ren

Do you change money here?
Wechseln Sie hier Geld? · vek·seln zee heer gelt

Can I leave a message for someone?
Kann ich eine Nachricht für jemanden hinterlassen? · kan ikh ai·ne nahkh·rikht für yay·man·den hin·ter·la·sen

Is there a message for me?
Haben Sie eine Nachricht für mich? · hah·ben zee ai·ne nahkh·rikht für mikh

I'm locked out of my room.
Ich habe mich aus meinem Zimmer ausgesperrt. · ikh hah·be mikh ows mai·nem tsi·mer ows·ge·shpert

signs

Aufzug	owf·tsook	**Lift/Elevator**
Fahrstuhl	fahr·shtool	**Lift/Elevator**
Fernsehzimmer	fern·zay·tsi·mer	**TV Room**
Frühstücksraum	frü·shtüks·rowm	**Breakfast Room**
Notausgang	nawt·ows·gang	**Emergency Exit**

Could I have ... please?	Könnte ich bitte ... haben?	kern·te ikh bi·te ... hah·ben
my key	meinen Schlüssel	mai·nen shlü·sel
a receipt	eine Quittung	ai·ne kvi·tung

It's too ...	Es ist zu ...	es ist tsoo ...
cold	kalt	kalt
dark	dunkel	dung·kel
expensive	teuer	toy·er
light/bright	hell	hel
noisy	laut	lowt
small	klein	klain

PRACTICAL

52

The ... doesn't work.	... funktioniert nicht.	... fungk·tsyo·neert nikht
air-conditioning	Die Klima-anlage	dee klee·ma·an·lah·ge
fan	Der Ventilator	dair ven·ti·lah·tor
toilet	Die Toilette	dee to·a·le·te

The (bathroom) door is locked.

Die (Badezimmer)Tür ist abgeschlossen.	dee (bah·de·tsi·mer·)tür ist ap·ge·shlo·sen

air-conditioning
Klimaanlage f
klee·ma·an·lah·ge

toilet
Toilette f
to·a·le·te

key
Schlüssel m
shlü·sel

bed
Bett n
bet

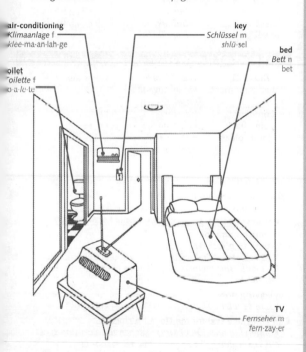

TV
Fernseher m
fern·zay·er

The window won't open/close.
Das Fenster lässt sich   das *fens*·ter lest zikh
nicht öffnen/schließen.   nikht *erf*·nen/*shlee*·sen

Can I get another ...?	*Kann ich noch einen/eine/ein ... bekommen?* m/f/n	kan ikh nokh *ai*·nen/*ai*·ne/ain ... be·*ko*·men
blanket	*Decke* f	*de*·ke
duvet cover	*Bettbezug* m	*bet*·be·tsook
pillow	*Kopfkissen* n	*kopf*·ki·sen
pillowcase	*Kopfkissen-bezug* m	*kopf*·ki·sen·be·tsook
sheet	*Bettlaken* n	*bet*·lah·ken
towel	*Handtuch* n	*hant*·tookh

---

a knock at the door

Who is it?	*Wer ist da?*	vair ist dah
Just a moment.	*Einen Augenblick, bitte!*	*ai*·nen ow·gen·*blik* *bi*·te
Come in.	*Herein!*	he·*rain*
Come back later, please.	*Kommen Sie bitte später noch einmal.*	*ko*·men zee *bi*·te *shpay*·ter nokh *ain*·mahl

---

> checking out

What time is checkout?
Wann muss ich   van mus ikh
auschecken?   *ows*·che·ken

How much extra to stay until (6 o'clock)?
Was kostet es extra, wenn   vas *kos*·tet es *eks*·tra ven
ich bis (6 Uhr) bleiben   ikh bis (zeks oor) *blai*·ben
möchte?   *merkh*·te

I'm leaving now.
Ich reise jetzt ab.   ikh *rai*·ze yetst ap

Can you call a taxi for me (for 11 o'clock)?
Können Sie mir (für 11 Uhr)   *ker*·nen zee meer (für elf oor)
ein Taxi rufen?   ain *tak*·si *roo*·fen

Can I leave my bags here until ...?	Kann ich meine Taschen bis ... hier lassen?	kan ikh *mai*·ne *ta*·shen bis ... heer *la*·sen
next week	nächste Woche	*naykhs*·te vo·khe
tonight	heute Abend	*hoy*·te ah·bent
Wednesday	Mittwoch	*mit*·vokh
Could I have my ... please?	Könnte ich bitte ... haben?	*kern*·te ikh *bi*·te ... *hah*·ben
deposit	meine Anzahlung	*mai*·ne an·tsah·lung
passport	meinen Pass	*mai*·nen pas
valuables	meine Wertsachen	*mai*·ne *vert*·za·khen

There's a mistake in the bill.
Da ist ein Fehler in der Rechnung.
dah ist ain *fay*·ler in dair *rekh*·nung.

I had a great stay, thank you.
Es hat mir hier sehr gut gefallen.
es hat meer heer zair goot ge fa lon

I'll recommend it to my friends.
Ich werde Sie weiterempfehlen.
ikh *ver*·de zee *vai*·ter·emp·fay·len

camping

campen

Where's the nearest ...?	Wo ist der nächste ...?	vaw ist dair *naykhs*·te ...
camp site	Zeltplatz	*tselt*·plats
shop	Laden	*lah*·den
shower facility	Duschraum	*doosh*·rowm
toilet block	Toilettenblock	to·a·*le*·ten·blok
Do you have ...?	Haben Sie ...?	*hah*·ben zee ...
electricity	Strom	shtrawm
shower facilities	Duschen	*doo*·shen
a site	einen Stellplatz	*ai*·nen *shtel*·plats
tents for hire	Zelte zu vermieten	*tsel*·le tsoo fer·*mee*·ten

Is it coin-operated?
Braucht man dafür Münzen? browkht man da·*für mün*·tsen

Is the water drinkable?
Kann man das Wasser trinken? kan man das va·ser *tring*·ken

Who do I ask to stay here?
Wen muss ich fragen, vayn mus ikh *frah*·gen
wenn ich hier zelten ven ikh heer *tsel*·ten
möchte? *merkh*·te

How much do	*Wie viel berechnen*	vee feel be·*rekh*·nen
you charge ...?	*Sie ...?*	zee ...
for a car	*für ein Auto*	für ain *ow*·to
for a caravan	*für einen*	für *ai*·nen
	Wohnwagen	*vawn*·vah·gen
for a tent	*für ein Zelt*	für ain tselt
per person	*pro Person*	praw per·*zawn*
Can I ...?	*Kann ich ...?*	kan ikh ...
camp here	*hier zelten*	heer *tsel*·ten
park next to	*neben meinem*	*nay*·ben *mai*·nem
my tent	*Zelt parken*	tselt *par*·ken
gas cylinder	*Gasflasche* f	*gahs*·fla·she
mallet	*Holzhammer* m	*holts*·ha·mer
peg	*Hering* m	*hay*·ring
rope	*Seil* n	zail
shower token	*Duschmünze* f	*doosh*·mün·tse
sleeping bag	*Schlafsack* m	*shlahf*·zak
spade	*Spaten* m	*shpah*·ten
tent	*Zelt* n	tselt
torch (flashlight)	*Taschenlampe* f	ta·shen·lam·pe

renting

I'm here about the ... for rent.	Ich komme wegen des/der/des zu vermietenden ... m/f/n	ikh ko·me vay·gen des/dair/des tsoo fer·mee·ten·den ...
apartment	Appartement n	a·part·ment
cabin	Hütte f	hü·te
holiday apartment	Ferienwohnung f	fay·ri·en·vaw·nung
house	Haus n	hows
room	Zimmer n	tsi·mer
villa	Villa f	vi·la

furnished	möbliert	mer·bleert
partly furnished	teilmöbliert	tail·mer·bleert
unfurnished	unmöbliert	un·mer·bleert

Do you have a/an ... for rent?
Haben Sie ... hah·ben zee ...
zu vermieten? tsoo fer·mee·ten

How many rooms does it have?
Wie viele vee fee·le
Zimmer hat es? tsi·mer hat es

I want something near the ...	Ich möchte etwas in der Nähe ...	ikh merkh·te et·vas in dair nay·e ...
beach	des Strandes	des shtran·des
city centre	des Stadt-zentrums	des shtat·tsen·trums
shops	der Geschäfte	dair ge·shef·te

How much is it for ...?	Was kostet es für ...?	vas kos·tet es für ...
(one) week	(eine) Woche	(ai·ne) vo·khe
(two) months	(zwei) Monate	(tsvai) maw·na·te

Who is my ...?	Wer ist ...?	vair ist ...
agent	mein Makler	main mahk·ler
contact person	meine Kontaktperson	mai·ne kon·takt·per·zawn

I want to rent it from (July 2) to (July 6).
Ich möchte es vom   ikh *merkh*·te es fom
(2. Juli) bis zum   (*tsvai*·ten *yoo*·li) bis tsum
(6. Juli) mieten.   (*zeks*·ten *yoo*·li) *mee*·ten

Is there a bond?
Gibt es eine Kaution?   gipt es *ai*·ne kow·*tsyawn*

Are bills extra?
Kommen noch   *ko*·men nokh
Nebenkosten dazu?   *nay*·ben·kos·ten da·*tsoo*

staying with locals

<table>
<tr><td>bei einheimischen</td><td>übernachten</td></tr>
</table>

Can I stay at your place?
Kann ich bei Ihnen/dir   kan ikh bai *ee*·nen/deer
übernachten? pol/inf   ü·ber·*nakh*·ten

Is there anything I can do to help?
Kann ich Ihnen/dir   kan ikh *ee*·nen/deer
irgendwie helfen? pol/inf   *ir*·gent·vee *hel*·fen

I have my own ...	*Ich habe ...*	ikh *hah*·be ...
mattress	*meine eigene Matratze*	*mai*·ne *ai*·ge·ne ma·*tra*·tse
sleeping bag	*meinen eigenen Schlafsack*	*mai*·nen *ai*·ge·nen *shlahf*·zak

Can I ...?	*Kann ich ...?*	kan ikh ...
bring anything for the meal	*etwas für das Essen mitbringen*	*et*·vas für das *e*·sen *mit*·bring·en
do the dishes	*abwaschen*	*ap*·va·shen
set/clear the table	*den Tisch decken/ abräumen*	dayn tish *de*·ken/ *ap*·roy·men
take out the rubbish	*den Müll rausbringen*	dayn mül *rows*·bring·en

Thanks for your hospitality.
Vielen Dank für Ihre/deine   *fee*·len dangk für *ee*·re/*dai*·ne
Gastfreundschaft. pol/inf   *gast*·froynt·shaft

See also expressions in **food**, pages 143 & 155.

Where's (a bank)?
Wo ist (eine Bank)? vaw ist (*ai*·ne bangk)

I'm looking for (the cathedral).
Ich suche (den Dom). ikh *zoo*·khe (dayn dawm)

Which way is (a public toilet)?
In welcher Richtung ist in *vel*·kher *rikh*·tung ist
(eine öffentliche Toilette)? (*ai*·ne *er*·fent·li·khe to·a·*le*·te)

listen for ...

es ist ...	*Es ist ...*	It's ...
an dair e·ke	*an der Ecke*	on the corner
dort	*dort*	there
fawr ...	*vor ...*	in front of ...
gay·gen·ü·ber ...	*gegenüber ...*	opposite ...
ge·rah·de·ows	*geradeaus*	straight ahead
heer	*hier*	here
hin·ter ...	*hinter ...*	behind ...
lingks	*links*	left
nah·e	*nahe*	near
nay·ben ...	*neben ...*	next to ...
rekhts	*rechts*	right
vait vek	*weit weg*	far away
bee·gen zee ... ap	*Biegen Sie ... ab.*	Turn ...
an dair e·ke	*an der Ecke*	at the corner
bai dair *am*·pel	*bei der Ampel*	at the traffic lights
lingks/rekhts	*links/rechts*	left/right
es ist ... ent·*fernt*	*Es ist ... entfernt.*	It's ...
(*hun*·dert) *may*·ter	*(100) Meter*	(100) metres
(fünf) mi·*noo*·ten	*(5) Minuten*	(five) minutes
nor·den	*Norden* m	north
zü·den	*Süden* m	south
os·ten	*Osten* m	east
ves·ten	*Westen* m	west

directions

59

How can I get there?
Wie kann ich da hinkommen?   vee kan ikh dah *hin*·ko·men

Can you show me (on the map)?
Können Sie es mir   *ker*·nen zee es meer
(auf der Karte) zeigen?   (owf dair *kar*·te) *tsai*·gen

What's the address?
Wie ist die Adresse?   vee ist dee a·*dre*·se

How far is it?
Wie weit ist es?   vee *vait* ist es

by ...	*mit ...*	mit ...
bus	*dem Bus*	daym *bus*
taxi	*dem Taxi*	daym *tak*·si
train	*dem Zug*	daym *tsook*
on foot	*zu Fuß*	tsoo *foos*
avenue	*Allee* f	a·*lay*
lane	*Gasse* f	*ga*·se
square	*Platz* m	*plats*
street	*Straße/Weg* f/m	*shtrah*·se/*vayk*

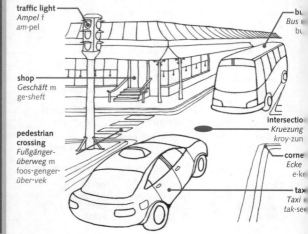

traffic light
Ampel f
am·pel

bus
Bus
bu

shop
Geschäft m
ge·*sheft*

intersection
Kreuzung
kroy·zun

pedestrian
crossing
*Fußgänger-
überweg* m
foos·*genger·
über*·vek

corner
Ecke
e·ke

taxi
Taxi
tak·see

looking for ...

Where's (a/the supermarket)?
Wo ist (ein/der   vaw ist (ain/dair
Supermarkt)?   zoo·per·markt)

Where can I buy ...?
Wo kann ich ... kaufen?   vaw kan ikh ... kow·ten

For phrases on directions, see **directions**, page 59, and for additional shops and services, see the **dictionary**.

making a purchase

I'd like to buy ...
Ich möchte ... kaufen.   ikh merkh·te ... kow·fen

I'm just looking.
Ich schaue mich nur um.   ikh show·e mikh noor um

How much is this?
Wie viel kostet das?   vee feel kos·tet das

Can you write down the price?
Können Sie den Preis   ker·nen zee dayn prais
aufschreiben?   owf·shrai·ben

Do you have any others?
Haben Sie noch andere?   hah·ben zee nokh an·de·re

Can I look at it?
Können Sie es   ker·nen zee es
mir zeigen?   meer tsai·gen

Do you accept ...?	*Nehmen Sie ...?*	nay·men zee ...
credit cards	*Kreditkarten*	kre·deet·kar·ten
debit cards	*Debitkarten*	day·bit·kar·ten
travellers cheques	*Reiseschecks*	rai·ze·sheks

Could I have ... please?	*Könnte ich ... bekommen?*	*kern*·te ikh ... be·ko·men
a bag	*eine Tüte*	*ai*·ne *tü*·te
a receipt	*eine Quittung*	*ai*·ne *kvi*·tung
it wrapped	*es eingepackt*	es *ain*·ge·pakt

Does it have a guarantee?
Gibt es darauf Garantie?   gipt es da·*rowf* ga·ran·*tee*

Can I have it sent overseas?
Kann ich es ins Ausland   kan ikh es ins *ows*·lant
verschicken lassen?   fer·*shi*·ken *la*·sen

Can you order it for me?
Können Sie es für   *ker*·nen zee es für
mich bestellen?   mikh be·*shte*·len

Can I pick it up later?
Kann ich es später   kan ikh es *shpay*·ter
abholen?   *ap*·haw·len

It's faulty/broken.
Es ist fehlerhaft/kaputt.   es ist *fay*·ler·haft/ka·*put*

I'd like ... please.	*Ich möchte bitte ...*	ikh *merkh*·te *bi*·te ...
my change	*mein Wechselgeld*	main *vek*·sel·gelt
my money back	*mein Geld*	main gelt
	zurückhaben	tsu·*rük*·hah·ben
to return this	*dieses*	*dee*·zes
	zurückgeben	tsu·*rük*·gay·ben

local talk

bargain	*Schnäppchen* n	*shnep*·khen
bargain hunter	*Schnäppchenjäger* m	*shnep*·khen·yay·ger
rip-off	*Nepp* m	nep
sale	*Ausverkauf* m	*ows*·fer·kowf
specials	*Sonderangebote* n pl	*zon*·der·an·ge·baw·te

bargaining

That's too expensive.
Das ist zu teuer.   das ist tsoo *toy*·er

Can you lower the price?
Können Sie mit dem   *ker*·nen zee mit dem
Preis heruntergehen?   prais he·*run*·ter·gay·en

Do you have something cheaper?
Haben Sie etwas   *hah*·ben zee *et*·vas
Billigeres?   *bi*·li·ge·res

I'll give you ...
Ich gebe Ihnen ...   ikh *gay*·be ee·nen ...

clothes

Can I try it on?
Kann ich es anprobieren?   kan ikh es *an*·pro·bee·ren

My size is ...
Ich habe Größe ...   ikh *hah*·be *grer*·se ...

It doesn't fit.
Es passt nicht.   es past nikht

repairs

Can I have my ... repaired here?
Kann ich hier mein ...   kan ikh heer main ...
reparieren lassen?   re·pa·*ree*·ren *la*·sen

When will my shoes be ready?
Wann sind meine   van zint *mai*·ne
Schuhe fertig?   *shoo*·e *fer*·tikh

When will my ... be ready?	Wann ist mein/ meine/mein ... fertig? m/f/n	van ist main/ mai·ne/main ... fer·tikh
backpack	Rucksack m	ruk·zak
camera	Kamera f	ka·me·ra
(sun)glasses	(Sonnen)Brille f	(zo·nen·)bri·le

darn holes

buttons	Knöpfe m pl	knerp·fe
needle	Nadel f	nah·del
scissors	Schere f	shair·re
thread	Faden m	fah·den

hairdressing

beim friseur

I'd like (a) ...	Ich möchte ...	ikh merkh·te ...
blow wave	eine Fönwelle	ai·ne fern·ve·le
colour	mir die Haare färben lassen	meer dee hah·re fer·ben la·sen
foils	Folien	faw·li·en
haircut	mir die Haare schneiden lassen	meer dee hah·re shnai·den la·sen
my beard trimmed	mir den Bart stutzen lassen	meer dayn bart shtu·tsen la·sen
shave	mich rasieren lassen	mikh ra·zee·ren la·sen
streaks	Strähnchen	shtrayn·khen
trim	mir die Haare nachschneiden lassen	meer dee hah·re nahkh·shnai·den la·sen

Please use a new blade.
Benutzen Sie bitte   be·nu·tsen zee bi·te
eine neue Klinge.   ai·ne noy·e kling·e

Don't cut it too short.
Schneiden Sie es   shnai·den zee es
nicht zu kurz.   nikht tsoo kurts

Shave it all off!
   Rasieren Sie alles ab!   ra·*zee*·ren zee *a*·les ap

I should never have let you near me!
   Ich hätte Sie nie an mein   ikh *he*·te zee nee an main
   Haar lassen dürfen!   hahr *la*·sen *dür*·fen

For colours, see the **dictionary**.

books & reading

bücher und lesen

Is there a/an (English-language) ...?	*Gibt es ?*	gipt es ...
bookshop	*einen Buch-laden (für englische Bücher)*	*ai*·nen *bookh*·lah·den (für *eng*·li·she *bü*·kher)
section	*eine Abteilung (für englische Bücher)*	*ai*·ne ap·*tai*·lung (für *eng*·li·she *bü*·kher)

Do you have Lonely Planet guidebooks?
   Haben Sie Lonely-Planet-   hah·ben zee *lohn*·li·*ple*·net·
   Reiseführer?   *rai*·ze·fü·rer

Do you have a better phrasebook than this?
   Haben Sie einen besseren   hah·ben zee *ai*·nen *be*·se·ren
   Sprachführer als diesen?   *shprahkh*·fü·rer als *dee*·zen

shopping

music

I'd like (a) ... | *Ich hätte gern ...* | ikh *he*·te gern ...
CD | *eine CD* | *ai*·ne tsay·*day*
blank tape | *eine leere Kassette* | *ai*·ne *lair*·re ka·se·te
headphones | *Kopfhörer* | *kopf*·her·rer

I heard a band called ...
Ich habe eine Band mit | ikh *hah*·be *ai*·ne bent mit
dem Namen ... gehört. | daym *nah*·men ... ge·hert

I heard a singer called ...
Ich habe einen Sänger mit | ikh *hah*·be *ai*·nen *zeng*·er mit
dem Namen ... gehört. | daym *nah*·men ... ge·hert

What's his/her best recording?
Was ist seine/ihre | vas ist *zai*·ne/*ee*·re
beste CD? | *bes*·te tsay·*day*

Can I listen to this?
Kann ich mir das anhören? | kan ikh meer das *an*·her·ren

Is this a pirated copy?
Ist das eine Raubkopie? | ist das *ai*·ne *rowp*·ko·pee

photography

I need a ... film | *Ich brauche einen* | ikh *brow*·khe *ai*·nen
for this camera. | *... für diese* | *... für dee*·ze
| *Kamera.* | *ka*·me·ra
APS | *APS-Film* | ah·pay·*es*·film
B&W | *Schwarzweißfilm* | shvarts·*vais*·film
colour | *Farbfilm* | *farp*·film
slide | *Diafilm* | *dee*·a·film
(200) speed | *(200)-ASA-Film* | (*tsvai*·hun·dert)·
| | ah·za·film

Can you ...?	Können Sie ...?	ker·nen zee ...
develop this film	*diesen Film*	*dee·*zen film
	entwickeln	ent·*vi·*keln
load my film	*mir den Film*	meer dayn film
	einlegen	*ain·*lay·gen

How much is it to develop this film?
Was kostet es, diesen Film   vas *kos·*tet es *dee·*zen film
entwickeln zu lassen?   ent·*vi·*keln tsoo *la·*sen

When will it be ready?
Wann ist er fertig?   van ist air *fer·*tikh

I need a passport photo taken.
Ich möchte ein Passfoto   ikh *merkh·*te ain *pas·*faw·to
machen lassen.   *ma·*khen *la·*sen

I'm not happy with these photos.
Mit diesen Fotos bin   mit *dee·*zen *faw·*tos bin
ich nicht zufrieden.   ikh nikht tsu·*free·*den

I don't want to pay the full price.
Ich möchte nicht den   ikh *merkh·*te *nikht* dayn
vollen Preis bezahlen.   *fo·*len prais be·*tsah·*len

---

cheers for beers & souvenirs

Here's a list of some of the most common souvenirs from Germany, Austria and Switzerland, displayed by region:

Aachen: *Aachener Printen* (gingerbread)

All over Germany: beer steins

Austria: chocolates like *Mozartkugeln* (chocolates filled with marzipan, hazelnuts and nougat) and fruit brandies

Bavarian Forest: crystal glassware

Harz Mountains: puppets and marionettes, especially of witches, also famous for glassware

Lübeck: marzipan

Meissen: modern and antique porcelain

cheers for beers & souvenirs

Nuremberg: toys, especially wooden figures and tin toys; also *Lebkuchen* (gingerbread)

Rhine and Moselle Rivers: renowned for their white wines

Rothenburg ob der Tauber: wooden toys and Christmas decorations

Switzerland: typical souvenirs include cuckoo clocks, chocolate and cow bells – also famous for all kinds of timepieces

The Black Forest: cuckoo clocks, dolls and fruit brandies

Thuringia: wooden figures and Christmas decorations

beer stein	*Bierkrug* m	*beer*·krook
chocolate	*Schokolade* f	sho·ko·*lah*·de
chocolates	*Pralinen* n pl	pra·*lee*·nen
Christmas decorations	*Weihnachts- schmuck* m	*vai*·nakhts· shmuk
clock	*Uhr* f	oor
cow bell	*Kuhglocke* f	*koo*·glo·ke
crystal glassware	*Kristallglas* n	kris·*tal*·glahs
cuckoo clock	*Kuckucksuhr* f	*ku*·kuks·oor
doll	*Puppe* f	*pu*·p e
fruit brandy	*Obstler* m	*awpst*·ler
glassware	*Glaswaren* pl	*glahs*·vah·ren
gingerbread	*Lebkuchen* m	*layp*·koo·khen
marionette	*Marionette* f	ma·ri·o·*ne*·te
marzipan	*Marzipan* n	*mar*·tsi·pahn
porcelain	*Porzellan* n	por·tse·*lahn*
puppet	*Puppe* f	*pu*·pe
tin toys	*Blechspielzeug* n	*blekh*·shpeel·tsoyk
white wine	*Weißwein* m	*vais*·vain
witch	*Hexe* f	*hek*·se
wooden figure	*Holzfigur* f	*holts*·fi·goor
wooden toys	*Holzspielzeug* n	*holts*·shpeel·tsoyk

post office

post

I want to send a ...	*Ich möchte*	ikh *merkh*·te
	... senden.	... *zen*·den
fax	*ein Fax*	ain faks
parcel	*ein Paket*	ain pa·*kayt*
postcard	*eine Postkarte*	ai·ne *post*·kar·te
I want to buy a/an...	*Ich möchte*	ikh *merkh*·te
	... kaufen.	... *kow*·fen
aerogram	*ein Aerogramm*	ain air·ro·*gram*
envelope	*einen Umschlag*	ai·nen *um*·shlahk
stamp	*eine Briefmarke*	ai·ne *breef*·mar·ke

airmail	*Luftpost* f	*luft*·post
customs declaration	*Zollerklärung* f	*tsol*·er·klair·rung
domestic	*Inlands-*	*in*·lants·
express mail	*Expresspost* f	eks·*pres*·post
fragile	*zerbrechlich*	tser·*brekh*·likh
international	*international*	in·ter·na·tsyo·*nahl*
mail box	*Briefkasten* m	*breef*·kas·ten
postcode	*Postleitzahl* f	*post*·lait·tsahl
registered mail	*Einschreiben* n	*ain*·shrai·ben
surface mail	*Landbeförderung* f	*lant*·be·fer·de·rung

Please send it by air/surface mail to …
  Bitte schicken Sie das per   bi·te shi·ken zee das per
  Luftpost/Landbeförderung   luft·post/lant·be·fer·de·rung
  nach …   nahkh …

It contains …
  Es enthält …   es ent·helt …

Where's the poste restante section?
  Wo ist der Schalter für   vaw ist dair shal·ter für
  postlagernde Briefe?   post·lah·gern·de bree·fe

Is there any mail for me?
  Ist Post für mich da?   ist post für mikh dah

listen for …

merkh·ten zee das per eks·pres·post aw·der
nor·mahl·post shi·ken
  Möchten Sie das per   **Would you like to send it**
  Expresspost oder   **express or regular post?**
  Normalpost schicken?

vas ist dah drin
  Was ist da drin?   **What does it contain?**

vaw·hin merkh·ten zee das shi·ken
  Wohin möchten   **Where are you**
  Sie das schicken?   **sending it?**

phone

telefon

I want to make	*Ich möchte …*	ikh merkh·te …
a … (to Singapore).		
call	*(nach Singapur)*	(nahkh zing·a·poor)
	telefonieren	te·le·fo·nee·ren
reverse-charge/	*ein R-Gespräch*	ain air·ge·shpraykh
collect call	*(nach Singapur)*	(nahkh zing·a·poor)
	führen	fü·ren

What's your phone number?
 Wie ist Ihre/deine　　vee ist ee·re/dai·ne
 Telefonnummer? pol/inf　te·le·fawn·nu·mer

Where's the nearest public phone?
 Wo ist das nächste　　vaw ist das naykhs·te
 öffentliche Telefon?　er·fent·li·khe te·le·fawn

I want to buy a phone card.
 Ich möchte eine　　ikh merkh·te ai·ne
 Telefonkarte kaufen.　te·le·fawn·kar·te kow·fen

The number is ...
 Die Nummer ist ...　　dee nu·mer ist ...

What's the area/country code for ...?
 Was ist die Vorwahl für ...?　vas ist dee fawr·vahl für ...

It's engaged.
 Es ist besetzt.　　es ist be·zetst

I've been cut off.
 Ich bin unterbrochen worden.　ikh bin un·ter·bro·khen vor·den

The connection's bad.
 Die Verbindung ist schlecht.　dee fer·bin·dung ist shlekht

Hello.
 Hallo!　　ha·lo

Can I speak to ...?
 Kann ich mit ... sprechen?　kan ikh mit ... shpre·khen

It's ...
 Hier ist ...　　heer ist ...

Can I leave a message?
 Kann ich eine Nachricht　kan ikh ai·ne nahkh·rikht
 hinterlassen?　　hin·ter·la·sen

phone numbers

To avoid confusion with *drei*, three, on the phone,
Germans use *zwo* instead of *zwei*, for two.

communications

71

Please tell him/her I called.
Bitte sagen Sie
ihm/ihr, dass ich
angerufen habe.

bi·te zah·gen zee
eem/eer das ikh
an·ge·roo·fen hah·be

I'll call back later.
Ich rufe später
nochmal an.

ikh roo·fe shpay·ter
nokh·mahl an

What time should I call?
Wann kann ich am
besten anrufen?

van kan ikh am
bes·ten an·roo·fen

My number is …
Meine Nummer ist …

mai·ne nu·mer ist …

I don't have a contact number.
Ich habe keine Nummer,
unter der Sie mich
erreichen können.

ikh hah·be kai·ne nu·mer
un·ter dair zee mikh
er·rai·khen ker·nen

---

listen for …

ai·nen ow·gen·blik bi·te
  Einen Augenblick, bitte.   **One moment, please.**

es toot meer lait (air/zee) ist nikht heer
  Es tut mir Leid, (er/sie)   **I'm sorry, (he/she)**
  ist nicht hier.   **is not here.**

mit vaym merkh·ten zee shpre·khen
  Mit wem möchten   **Who do you want**
  Sie sprechen?   **to speak to?**

toot meer lait zee hah·ben dee fal·she nu·mer
  Tut mir Leid, Sie haben   **Sorry, wrong number.**
  die falsche Nummer.

vair ist am a·pa·raht
  Wer ist am Apparat?   **Who's calling?**

yah (air/zee) ist heer
  Ja, (er/sie) ist hier.   **Yes, (he/she) is here.**

> mobile/cell phone

Where can I find a/an ...?	*Wo kann ich ... finden?*	vaw kan ikh ... fin·den
I'd like a/an ...	*Ich hätte gern ...*	ikh he·te gern ...
adaptor plug	*einen Adapter für die Steckdose*	ai·nen a·dap·ter für dee shtek·daw·ze
charger for my phone	*ein Ladegerät für mein Handy*	ain lah·de·ge·rayt für main hen·di
mobile/cell phone for hire	*ein Miethandy*	ain meet·hen·di
prepaid mobile/ cell phone	*ein Handy mit Prepaidkarte*	ain hen·di mit pree·payd·kar·te
SIM card for your network	*eine SIM-Karte für Ihr Netz*	ai·ne zim·kar·te für eer nets

What are the rates?
Wie hoch sind die Gebühren?
vee hawkh zint dee ge·bü·ren

(30c) per (30) seconds.
(30 Cent) für (30) Sekunden.
(drai·sikh sent) für (drai·sikh) ze·kun·den

the internet

das internet

Where's the local Internet cafe?
Wo ist hier ein Internet-Café?
vaw ist heer ain in·ter·net·ka·fay

I'd like to ...	Ich möchte ...	ikh merkh·te ...
check my email	meine E-Mails checken	mai·ne ee·mayls che·ken
get Internet access	Internetzugang haben	in·ter·net·tsoo·gang hah·ben
use a printer	einen Drucker benutzen	ai·nen dru·ker be·nu·tsen
use a scanner	einen Scanner benutzen	ai·nen ske·ner be·nu·tsen
How much per ...?	Was kostet es ...?	vas kos·tet es ...
(five) minutes	für (fünf) Minuten	für (fünf) mi·noo·ten
hour	pro Stunde	praw shtun·de
page	pro Seite	praw zai·te
Do you have ...?	Haben Sie ...?	hah·ben zee ...
PCs	PCs	pay·tsays
Macs	Macs	meks
a Zip drive	ein Zip-Laufwerk	ain tsip·lowf·verk

I'm attending a ...   *Ich nehme an ... teil.*   ikh *nay*·me an ... tail
    conference   *einer Konferenz*   ai·ner kon·fe·*rents*
    course   *einem Kurs*   ai·nem kurs
    meeting   *einem Meeting*   ai·nem *mee*·ting

I'm visiting a trade fair
Ich besuche eine Messe.   ikh be·*zoo*·khe *ai·ne me·*se

I'm with	*Ich bin*	ikh bin
(company ...)	*bei (Firma ...)*	bai (*fir*·ma ...)
my colleague	*mit meinem*	mit *mai*·nem
	Kollegen hier m	ko·*lay*·gen heer
	mit meiner	mit *mai*·ner
	Kollegin hier f	ko·*lay*·gin heer
my colleagues	*mit meinen*	mit *mai*·nen
	Kollegen hier m pl	ko·*lay*·gen heer
	mit meinen	mit *mai*·nen
	Kolleginnen	ko·*lay*·gi·nen
	hier f pl	heer
(two) others	*mit (zwei)*	mit (tsvai)
	anderen hier	*an*·de·ren heer

I'm alone.
Ich bin allein.   ikh bin a·*lain*

I'm staying at .... room ...
Ich wohne im ..., Zimmer ...   ikh *vaw*·ne im ... *tsi*·mer ...

I'm here for (three) days/weeks.
Ich bin für (drei)   ikh bin für (drai)
Tage/Wochen hier.   *tah*·ge/*vo*·khen heer

Here's my business card.
Hier ist meine Karte.   heer ist *mai*·ne *kar*·te

Where's the ...?	Wo ist ...?	vaw ist ...
business centre	das Tagungs- zentrum	das *tah*·gungks· tsen·trum
conference	die Konferenz	dee kon·fe·*rents*
meeting	das Meeting	das *mee*·ting

I have an appointment with ...
Ich habe einen   ikh *hah*·be *ai*·nen
Termin bei ...   ter·*meen* bai ...

That went very well.
Das war sehr gut.   das vahr zair goot

Shall we go for a drink/meal?
Sollen wir noch etwas   zo·len veer nokh *et*·vas
trinken/essen gehen?   *tring*·ken/*e*·sen gay·en

It's on me.
Ich lade Sie ein.   ikh *lah*·de zee ain

body language

Shaking hands is customary for both men and women
in Germany, Austria and Switzerland. Always give a firm
handshake and look people in the eye. Never keep your
other hand in your pocket, as this is considered impolite.

Where can I ...?	Wo kann ich ...?	vaw kan ikh ...
I'd like to ...	Ich möchte ...	ikh *merkh*·te ...
cash a cheque	einen Scheck einlösen	*ai*·nen shek *ain*·ler·zen
change money	Geld umtauschen	gelt *um*·tow·shen
change some travellers cheques	Reiseschecks einlösen	*rai*·ze·sheks *ain*·ler·zen
get a cash advance	eine Barauszahlung	*ai*·ne *bahr*·ows·tsah·lung
withdraw money	Geld abheben	gelt *ap*·hay·ben

Where's the nearest ...?	Wo ist der/die nächste ...? m/f	vaw ist dair/dee *naykhs*·te ...
automatic teller machine	Geldautomat m	*gelt*·ow·to·maht
foreign exchange office	Geldwechsel·stube f	*gelt*·vek·sel· *shtoo*·be

What time does the bank open?
Wann macht die Bank auf? van makht dee bangk owf

The automatic teller machine took my card.
Der Geldautomat hat meine Karte einbehalten. dair *gelt*·ow·to·maht hat *mai*·ne *kar*·te *ain*·be·hal·ten

I've forgotten my PIN.
Ich habe meine Geheimnummer vergessen. ikh *hah*·be *mai*·ne ge·*haim*·nu·mer fer·*ge*·sen

Can I use my credit card to withdraw money?
Kann ich mit meiner Kreditkarte Geld abheben? kan ikh mit *mai*·ner kre·*deet*·kar·te gelt *ap*·hay·hen

What's the ...?	Wie ...?	vee ...
charge for that	hoch sind die Gebühren dafür	hawkh zint dee ge-bü-ren da-für
commission	hoch ist die Kommission	hawkh ist dee ko-mi-syawn
exchange rate	ist der Wechselkurs	ist dair vek-sel-kurs

Has my money arrived yet?

Ist mein Geld schon angekommen? ist main gelt shawn an-ge-ko-men

How long will it take to arrive?

Wie lange dauert es, bis es da ist? vee lang-e dow-ert es bis es dah ist

---

listen for ...

bi·te shrai·ben zee es owf	
Bitte schreiben Sie es auf.	**Please write it down.**
bi·te un·ter·shrai·ben zee heer	
Bitte unterschreiben Sie hier.	**Please sign here.**
das ker·nen veer nikht ma·khen	
Das können wir nicht machen.	**We can't do that.**
es gipt dah ain pro·blaym mit ee·rem kon·to	
Es gibt da ein Problem mit Ihrem Konto.	**There's a problem with your account.**
eer kon·to ist ü·ber·tsaw·gen	
Ihr Konto ist überzogen.	**You're overdrawn.**
in ai·ner vo·khe	
In einer Woche.	**In one week.**
in (feer) ar·baits·tah·gen	
In (vier) Arbeitstagen.	**In (four) working days.**
kan ikh bi·te ai·nen ows·vais zay·en	
Kann ich bitte einen Ausweis sehen?	**Can I see some ID please?**

I'd like a/an ...	*Ich hätte gern ...*	ikh *he*·te gern ...
audio set	*einen Audioführer*	*ai*·nen ow·di·o·fü·rer
catalogue	*einen Katalog*	*ai*·nen ka·ta·*lawg*
guide	*einen Reiseführer*	*ai*·nen *rai*·ze·fü·rer
guidebook in English	*einen Reiseführer auf Englisch*	*ai*·nen *rai*·ze·fü·rer owf *eng*·lish
(local) map	*eine Karte (von hier)*	*ai*·ne *kar*·te (fon heer)
Do you have information on ... sights?	*Haben Sie Informationen über ... Sehenswürdigkeiten?*	*hah*·ben zee in·for·ma·*tsyaw*·nen *ü*·ber ... *zay*·ens·vür·dikh·kai·ten
cultural	*kulturelle*	kul·tu·*re*·le
local	*örtliche*	*ert*·li·khe
religious	*religiöse*	re·li·*gyer*·ze
unique	*einzigartige*	*ain*·tsikh·ar·ti·ge

We only have (one day).
Wir haben nur (einen Tag).
veer *hah*·ben noor (*ai*·nen tahk)

I'd like to see ...
Ich möchte ... sehen.
ikh *merkh*·te ... *zay*·en

What's that?
Was ist das?
vas ist das

Who made it?
Wer hat das gemacht?   vair hat das ge·*makht*

How old is it?
Wie alt ist es?   vee alt ist es

Could you take a photograph of me?
Könnten Sie ein Foto   *kern*·ten zee ain *faw*·to
von mir machen?   fon meer ma·*khen*

Can I take photographs (of you)?
Kann ich (Sie) fotografieren?   kan ikh (zee) fo·to·gra·*fee*·ren

I'll send you the photograph.
Ich schicke Ihnen das Foto.   ikh *shi*·ke ee·nen das *faw*·to

getting in

What time does it open/close?
Wann macht es auf/zu?   van makht es owf/tsoo

What's the admission charge?
Was kostet der Eintritt?   vas *kos*·tet dair *ain*·trit

It costs ...
Er kostet ...   air *kos*·tet ...

Is there a	Gibt es eine	gipt es *ai*·ne
discount for ...?	Ermäßigung für ...?	er·*may*·si·gung für ...
children	Kinder	*kin*·der
families	Familien	fa·*mee*·li·en
groups	Gruppen	*gru*·pen
pensioners	Rentner	*rent*·ner
students	Studenten	shtu·*den*·ten

tours

When's the next ...?	*Wann ist der/die nächste ...?* m/f	van ist dair/dee naykhs·te ...
boat-trip	*Bootsrundfahrt* f	*bawts*·runt·fahrt
daytrip	*Tagesausflug* m	*tah*·ges·ows·flook
excursion	*Ausflug* m	*ows*·flook
tour	*Tour* f	toor
Is ... included?	*Ist ... inbegriffen?*	ist ... *in*·be·gri·fen
accommodation	*die Unterkunft*	dee *un*·ter·kunft
equipment	*die Ausrüstung*	dee *ows*·rüs·tung
food	*das Essen*	das *e*·sen
transport	*die Beförderung*	dee be·*fer*·de·rung

Can you recommend a ...?
Können Sie ein ... empfehlen?
ker·nen zee ain ... emp·*fay*·len

Do I need to take ... with me?
Muss ich ... mitnehmen?
mus ikh ... *mit*·nay·men

The guide will pay.
Der Reiseleiter bezahlt.   dair *rai*·ze·lai·ter be·*tsahlt*

The guide has paid.
Der Reiseleiter hat bezahlt.   dair *rai*·ze·lai·ter hat be·*tsahlt*

How long is the tour?
Wie lange dauert   vee *lang*·e *dow*·ert
die Führung?   dee *fü*·rung

What time should we be back?
Wann sollen wir   van *zo*·len veer
zurück sein?   tsu·*rük* zain

Be back here at (ten) o'clock.
Seien Sie um (zehn) Uhr zurück.   *zai*·en zee um (tsayn) oor tsu·*rü*.

I'm with them.
Ich gehöre zu ihnen.   ikh ge·*her*·re tsoo *ee*·nen

I've lost my group.
Ich habe meine   ikh *hah*·be *mai*·ne
Gruppe verloren.   *gru*·pe fer·*law*·ren

Have you seen a group of (Australians)?
Haben Sie eine Gruppe   *hah*·ben zee *ai*·ne *gru*·pe
(Australier) gesehen?   (ows·*trah*·li·er) ge·*zay*·en

---

signs

Eingang	*ain*·gang	**Entrance**
Ausgang	*ows*·gang	**Exit**
Offen	*o*·fen	**Open**
Geschlossen	ge·*shlo*·sen	**Closed**
Heiß	hais	**Hot**
Kalt	kalt	**Cold**
Kein Zutritt	kain *tsu*·trit	**No Entry**
Rauchen	*row*·khen	**No Smoking**
Verboten	fer·*baw*·ten	
Verboten	fer·*baw*·ten	**Prohibited**
Toiletten (WC)	to·a·*le*·ten (vee·*tsee*)	**Toilets**
Herren	*hair*·en	**Men**
Damen	*dah*·men	**Women**

disabled travellers
behinderte reisende

I'm disabled.
Ich bin behindert.   ikh bin be·*hin*·dert

I need assistance.
Ich brauche Hilfe.   ikh *brow*·khe *hil*·fe

What services do you have for disabled people?
Was für Leistungen gibt   vas für *lais*·tung·en gipt
es für behinderte Reisende?   es für be·*hin*·der·te *rai*·zen·de

Are there any toilets for the disabled?
Gibt es Toiletten für   gipt es to·a·*le*·ten für
Behinderte?   be·*hin*·der·te

Is there wheelchair access?
Gibt es eine Rollstuhlrampe?   gipt es *ai*·ne *rol*·shtool·ram·pe

How wide are the doors?
Wie breit sind die Türen?   vee brait sind dee *tü*·ren

How many steps are there?
Wieviele Stufen sind es?   vee·*fee*·le *shtoo*·fen sind es

Is there a lift?
Gibt es einen Aufzug?   gipt es *ai*·nen owf·*tsook*

Is there an induction loop for the hard of hearing?
Gibt es eine Induktions-   gipt es *ai*·ne in·duk·*tsyawns*·
schleife für Schwerhörige?   shlai·fe für shver·*her*·ri·ge

I have a hearing aid. Speak more loudly, please.
Ich habe ein Hörgerät.   ikh *hah*·be ain *her*·ge·rayt
Sprechen Sie bitte lauter.   *shpre*·khen zee *bi*·te *low*·ter

I'm deaf.
Ich bin taub. ikh bin towp

Are guide dogs permitted?
Sind Blindenhunde erlaubt? zint *blin*·den·hun·de er·*lowpt*

Could you help me cross this street safely?
Könnten Sie mich sicher *kern*·ten zee mikh *zi*·kher
über diese Straße bringen? *ü*·ber *dee*·ze *shtrah*·se *bring*·en

Braille library	*Blindenbibliothek* f	*blin*·den·bi·bli·o·tayk
disabled man	*Behinderter* m	be·*hin*·der·ter
disabled woman	*Behinderte* f	be·*hin*·der·te
guide dog	*Blindenhund* m	*blin*·den·hunt
wheelchair	*Rollstuhl* m	*rol*·shtool
wheelchair ramp	*Rollstuhlrampe* f	*rol*·shtool·ram·pe
wheelchair space	*Rollstuhlplatz* m	*rol*·shtool·plats

Is there a/an...?	*Gibt es ...?*	gipt es ...
baby change room	*einen Wickelraum*	ai·nen vi·kel·rowm
child-minding service	*einen Babysitter-Service*	ai·nen bay·bi·si·ter·ser·vis
children's menu	*eine Kinderkarte*	ai·ne kin·der·kar·te
(English-speaking) babysitter	*einen (englisch-sprachigen) Babysitter*	ai·nen (eng·lish·shprah·khi·gen) bay·bi·si·ter
family discount	*eine Familien-ermäßigung*	ai·ne fa·mee·li·en·er·may·si·gung
highchair	*einen Kinderstuhl*	ai·nen kin·der·shtool
park	*einen Park*	ai·nen park
playground nearby	*einen Spielplatz in der Nähe*	ai·nen shpeel·plats in dair nay·e
theme park	*einen Freizeitpark*	ai·nen frai·tsait·park

I need a ...	*Ich brauche ...*	Ikh brow·khe ...
baby seat	*einen Babysitz*	ai·nen bay·bi·zits
booster seat	*einen Kindersitz*	ai·nen kin·der·zits
potty	*ein Kindertöpfchen*	ain kin·der·terpf·khen
stroller	*einen Kinderwagen*	ai·nen kin·der·vah·gen

Can I breast-feed here?
Kann ich meinem Kind   kan ikh *mai*·nem kint
hier die Brust geben?   heer dee brust *gay*·ben

Are children allowed?
Sind Kinder erlaubt?   zint *kin*·der er·*lowpt*

Is this suitable for (three) year old children?
Ist das für (drei) Jahre alte   ist das für (drai) *yah*·re *al*·te
Kinder geeignet?   *kin*·der ge·*aig*·net

For children's sicknesses, see **symptoms & conditions**, page 180, and the **dictionary**.

---

signs

When travelling with children, keep an eye out for the following signs:

Junioren bis 5 Jahre frei	**Children up to the age of 5 free**
Junioren bis 15 Jahre halber Preis	**Children up to the age of 15 half price**
Wickeltisch	**Change Room**
Spielplatz	**Playground**

SOCIAL > meeting people
leute treffen

basics

grundlagen

Yes.	*Ja.*	yah
No.	*Nein.*	nain
Please.	*Bitte.*	*bi*·te
Thank you.	*Danke.*	*dang*·ke
Thank you very much.	*Vielen Dank.*	*fee*·len dangk
You're (very) welcome.	*Bitte (sehr)*	*bi*·te (zair)
Excuse me.	*Entschuldigung.*	ent·*shul*·di·gung
Sorry.	*Entschuldigung.*	ent·*shul*·di·gung
Don't worry.	*Macht nichts.*	makht nikhts

greetings

grüsse

Hello.		
(all over Germany)	*Guten Tag.*	*goo*·ten tahk
(in southern Germany)	*Grüß Gott.*	grüs got
(in Switzerland)	*Grüezi.*	*grü*·e·tsi
(in Austria)	*Servus.*	*zer*·vus
Hi.	*Hallo.*	*ha*·lo
Good ...	*Guten ...*	*goo*·ten ...
afternoon	*Tag*	tahk
day	*Tag*	tahk
evening	*Abend*	*ah*·bent
morning	*Morgen*	*mor*·gen
See you later.	*Bis später.*	bis *shpay*·ter
Goodbye.	*Auf Wiedersehen.*	owf *vee*·der·zay·en
Bye.	*Tschüss/Tschau.*	chüs/chow

How are you?
  Wie geht es   vee gayt es
  Ihnen/dir? pol/inf   ee·nen/deer

Fine. And you?
  Danke, gut.   dang·ke goot
  Und Ihnen/dir? pol/inf   unt ee·nen/deer

What's your name?
  Wie ist Ihr Name? pol   vee ist eer *nah*·me
  Wie heißt du? inf   vee haist doo

My name is ...
  Mein Name ist ... pol   main *nah*·me ist ...
  Ich heiße ... inf   ikh *hai*·se ...

I'd like to introduce you to ...
  Darf ich Ihnen/dir   darf ikh ee·nen/dir
  ... vorstellen? pol/inf   ... *fawr*·shte·len

I'm pleased to meet you.
  Angenehm.   an·ge·naym

titles & addressing people

In the past, *Fräulein* was used to address all unmarried women regardless of age but today the term is only used to address girls (and sometimes female waiters). All other women should be addressed using *Frau*. There's no equivalent of the English 'Ms' – use *Frau*. The equivalents of Sir and Madam, *Mein Herr* and *Meine Dame*, are very old-fashioned.

If you want to include academic titles when addressing somebody, these are combined with *Herr* and *Frau*, eg, *Frau Professor* or *Herr Doktor*.

Mr	Herr	her
Mrs	Frau	frow
Miss	Frau/Fräulein	frow/froy·lain

making conversation

Do you live here?
  Wohnen Sie hier? pol   vaw·nen zee heer
  Wohnst du hier? inf   vawnst doo heer

Where are you going?
  Wohin fahren Sie? pol   vaw·hin *fah*·ren zee
  Wohin fährst du? inf   vaw·hin fairst doo

What are you doing?
  Was machen Sie? pol   vas *ma*·khen zee
  Was machst du? inf   vas makhst doo

Are you waiting (for a bus)?
  Warten Sie   var·ten zee
  (auf einen Bus)? pol   (owf *ai*·nen bus)
  Wartest du   var·test doo
  (auf einen Bus)? inf   (owf *ai*·nen bus)

Are you also travelling (on this train)?
  Fahren Sie auch   *fah*·ren zee owkh
  (mit diesem Zug)? pol   (mit *dee*·zem tsook)
  Fährst du auch   fairst doo owkh
  (mit diesem Zug)? inf   (mit *dee*·zem tsook)

Can I have a light?
  Haben Sie Feuer? pol   *hah*·ben zee *foy*·er
  Hast du Feuer? inf   hast doo *foy*·er

Nice day, isn't it?
  Schönes Wetter heute!   *sher*·nes we·ter *hoy*·te

Terrible weather today!
  Furchtbares Wetter heute!   *furkht*·bah·res we·ter *hoy*·te

Just joking!
  Das war nur ein Scherz!   das vahr noor ain sherts

This is my ...	Das ist mein/meine/	das ist main/mai·ne/
	mein ... m/f/n	main ...
child	Kind n	kint
colleague	Kollege/	ko·lay·ge/
	Kollegin m/f	ko·lay·gin
friend	Freund(in) m/f	froynt/froyn·din
husband	Mann m	man
partner	Partner(in) m/f	part·ner/part·ne·rin
(intimate)		
wife	meine Frau f	frow

Do you like it here?
Gefällt es Ihnen/　　　ge·felt es ee·nen/
dir hier? pol/inf　　　deer heer

I love it here.
Mir gefällt es hier sehr gut.　　meer ge·felt es heer zair goot

What do you think (about ...)?
Was denken Sie (über ...)? pol　　vas deng·ken zee (ü·ber ...)
Was denkst du (über ...)? inf　　vas dengkst doo (ü·ber ...)

What's this called?
Wie heißt das?　　　vee haist das

What a beautiful baby!
Was für ein schönes Baby!　　vas für ain sher·nes bay·bi

Can I take a photo (of you)?
Kann ich ein Foto　　　kan ikh ain faw·to
(von Ihnen/dir)　　　(fon ee·nen/deer)
machen? pol/inf　　　ma·khen

That's (beautiful), isn't it?
Ist das nicht (schön)?　　ist das nikht (shern)

Are you here on holiday?
Sind Sie hier im Urlaub? pol　　zint zee heer im oor·lowp
Bist du hier im Urlaub? inf　　bist doo heer im oor·lowp

I'm here ...	*Ich bin hier ...*	ikh bin heer ...
for a holiday	*im Urlaub*	im oor·lowp
on business	*auf Geschäfts-*	owf ge·shefts·
	reise	rai·ze
to study	*zum Studieren*	tsum shtu·dee·ren
with my family	*mit meiner*	mit mai·ner
	Familie	fa·mee·li·e
with my partner	*mit meinem*	mit mai·nem
	Partner m	part·ner
	mit meiner	mit mai·ner
	Partnerin f	part·ne·rin

How long are you here for?
Für wie lange sind	für vee lang·e zint
Sie hier? pol	zee heer
Für wie lange bist	für vee lang·e bist
du hier? inf	doo heer

I'm here for (four) weeks/days.
| *Ich bin für (vier)* | ikh bin für (feer) |
| *Tage/Wochen hier.* | tah·ge/vo·khen heer |

local talk

Hey!	*Hi/Hey!*	hai/hei
Great!	*Toll/Geil!/*	tol/gail/
	Super!/Spitze!	zoo·per/shpi·tse
No problem.	*Kein Problem.*	kain pro·blaym
Sure.	*Klar!*	klahr
Maybe.	*Vielleicht.*	fi·laikht
No way!	*Auf keinen Fall!*	owf kai·nen fal
It's OK.	*Das ist OK.*	das ist o·kay
I'm OK.	*Alles klar.*	a·les klahr
Look!	*Guck mal!*	guk mahl
Listen!	*Hör mal!*	her mahl
Listen to this!	*Hör dir das an!*	her deer das an
I'm ready.	*Ich bin so weit.*	ikh bin zaw vait
Are you ready?	*Bist du so weit?*	bist doo zaw vait
Just a minute.	*Einen Augenblick.*	ai·nen ow·gen·blik

nationalities

Where are you from?
   Woher kommen Sie? pol   vaw·hair ko·men zee
   Woher kommst du? inf   vaw·hair komst doo

I'm from ...   *Ich komme aus ...*   ikh ko·me ows ...
   Australia   *Australien*   ows·trah·li·en
   the US   *den USA*   dayn oo·es·ah
   Wales   *Wales*   waylz

For more countries, see the **dictionary**.

age

How old ...?   *Wie alt ...?*   vee alt ...
   are you   *sind Sie* pol   zint zee
      bist du inf   bist doo
   is your daughter   *ist Ihre/deine*   ist ee·re/dai·ne
      Tochter pol/inf   tokh·ter
   is your son   *ist Ihr/dein*   ist eer/dain
      Sohn pol/inf   zawn

I'm ... years old.
   Ich bin ... Jahre alt.   ikh bin ... yah·re alt

He's/She's ... years old.
   Er/Sie ist ... Jahre alt.   air/zee ist ... yah·re alt

Too old!
   Zu alt!   tsoo alt

I'm younger than I look.
   Ich bin jünger als   ikh bin yüng·er als
   ich aussehe.   ikh ows·zay·e

For your age, see **numbers & amounts**, page 27.

occupations & studies

What's your occupation?

Als was arbeiten Sie? pol	als vas ar·bai·ten zee	
Als was arbeitest du? inf	als vas ar·bai·test doo	

I'm a ... | *Ich bin ein/ eine ... m/f* | ikh bin ain/ ain·e ...

drag queen	*Drag Queen* f	dreg kween
farmer	*Bauer/ Bäuerin* m/f	bow·er/ boy·e·rin
writer	*Schriftsteller/ Schriftstellerin* m/f	shrift·shte·ler/ shrift·shte·le·rin

I work in ... | *Ich arbeite ...* | ikh ar·bai·te ...

administration	*in der Verwaltung*	in dair fer·val·tung
IT	*in der IT-Branche*	in dair ai·tee·brang·she
sales & marketing	*im Verkauf und Marketing*	im fer·kowf unt mar·ke·ting

I'm ... | *Ich bin ...* | ikh bin ...

retired	*Rentner/ Rentnerin* m/f	rent·ner/ rent·ne·rin
self-employed	*selbstständig*	zelpst·shten·dikh
unemployed	*arbeitslos*	ar·baits·laws

What are you studying?

Was studieren Sie? pol	vas shtu·dee·ren zee
Was studierst du? inf	vas shtu·deerst doo

I'm studying ... | *Ich studiere ...* | ikh shtu·dee·re ...

engineering	*Ingenieurwesen*	in·zhe·nyer·vay·zen
German	*Deutsch*	doytsh
medicine	*Medizin*	me·di·tseen

For more occupations and fields of study, see the **dictionary**.

family

Do you have a ...?
Haben Sie einen/eine ...? m/f pol   *hah*·ben zee *ai*·nen/*ai*·ne ...
Hast du einen/eine ...? m/f inf   hast doo *ai*·nen/*ai*·ne ...

I (don't) have a ...
Ich habe (k)einen/   ikh *hah*·be (k)*ai*·nen/
(k)eine ... m/f   (k)*ai*·ne ...

Do you live with (your parents)?
Leben Sie bei   *lay*·ben zee bai
(Ihren Eltern)? pol   (*ee*·ren *el*·tern)
Lebst du bei   laypst doo bai
(deinen Eltern)? inf   (*dai*·nen *el*·tern)

I live with my ...
Ich lebe bei meinem/   ikh *lay*·be bai *mai*·nem/
meiner/meinen ... m/f/pl   *mai*·ner/*mai*·nen ...

This is my ...
Das ist mein/meine ... m/f   das ist main/*mai*·ne ...

Are you married?
Sind Sie verheiratet? pol   zint zee fer·*hai*·ra·tet
Bist du verheiratet? inf   bist doo fer·*hai*·ra·tet

I live with someone.
Ich lebe mit jemandem   ikh *lay*·be mit *yay*·man·dem
zusammen.   tsu·za·men

I'm ...	*Ich bin ...*	ikh bin ...
married	*verheiratet*	fer·*hai*·ra·tet
separated	*getrennt*	ge·*trent*
single	*ledig*	*lay*·dikh

children

When's your birthday?
Wann hast du Geburtstag? van hast doo ge-*burts*-tahk

Do you go to school or kindergarten?
Gehst du in die Schule gayst doo in dee *shoo*-le
oder in den Kindergarten? aw-der in dayn *kin*-der-gar-ten

What grade are you in?
In welcher Klasse bist du? in *vel*-kher *kla*-se bist doo

What do you do after school?
Was machst du vas makhst doo
nach der Schule? nahkh dair *shoo*-le

Do you learn English?
Lernst du Englisch? lernst doo *eng*-lish

I come from very far away.
Ich komme von sehr weit her. ikh *ko*-me fon zair vait hair

Are you lost?
Hast du dich verlaufen? hast doo dikh fer-*low*-ten

farewells

Tomorrow is my last day here.
Morgen ist mein *mor*-gen ist main
letzter Tag hier. *lets*-ter tahk heer

Here's my ...	*Hier ist meine ...*	heer ist *mai*-ne ...
What's your...?	*Wie ist Ihre/*	vee ist *ee*-re/
	deine ...? pol/inf	*dai*-ne ...
address	*Adresse*	a-*dre*-se
email address	*E-mail-Adresse*	ee-*mayl*-a-dre-se
fax number	*Faxnummer*	*faks*-nu-mer
mobile number	*Handynummer*	*hen*-di-nu-mer
pager number	*Pagernummer*	*pay*-dzher-nu-mer
work number	*Nummer bei*	*nu*-mer bai
	der Arbeit	dair *ar*-bait

For addresses, see **directions**, page 59.

If you ever visit (Scotland), come and visit us.

Wenn Sie jemals nach	ven zee *yay*·mahls nahkh
(Schottland) kommen,	(*shot*·lant) *ko*·men
besuchen Sie uns	be·*zoo*·khen zee uns
doch mal. pol	dokh mahl
Wenn du jemals nach	ven doo *yay*·mahls nahkh
(Schottland) kommst,	(*shot*·lant) komst
besuche uns doch mal. inf	be·*zoo*·khe uns dokh mahl

Keep in touch!

Melden Sie sich	*mel*·den zee zikh
doch mal! pol	dokh mahl
Melde dich mal! inf	*mel*·de dikh mahl

It's been great meeting you.

Es war schön, Sie/dich	es vahr shern zee/dikh
kennen zu lernen. pol/inf	*ke*·nen tsoo *ler*·nen

---

local talk

Bless you! (when sneezing)	*Gesundheit!*	ge·*zunt*·hait
Bon voyage!	*Gute Reise!*	*goo*·te *rai*·ze
Cheers!	*Prost!*	prawst
Good luck!	*Viel Glück!*	feel glük
Happy birthday!	*Herzlichen Glückwunsch zum Geburtstag!*	*herts*·li·khen *glük*·vunsh tsum ge·*burts*·tahk
What a pity!	*Schade!*	*shah*·de

common interests

gemeinsame interessen

What do you do in your spare time?

	Was machen Sie in	vas *ma*·khen zee in
	Ihrer Freizeit? pol	ee·rer *frai*·tsait
	Was machst du in	vas makhst doo in
	deiner Freizeit? inf	*dai*·ner *frai*·tsait

Do you like ...?	*Mögen Sie ...?* pol	*mer*·gen zee ...
	Magst du ...? inf	mahkst doo ...
I (don't) like ...	*Ich mag (keine/*	ikh mahk (*kai*·ne/
	keinen) ... m/f	*kai*·nen) ...
music	*Musik* f	*mu*·zeek
sport	*Sport* m	shport

I (don't) like ...	*Ich ... (nicht) gern.*	ikh ... (nikht) gern
dancing	*tanze*	*tan*·tse
drawing	*zeichne*	*tsaikh*·ne
hiking	*wandere*	*van*·de·re
painting	*male*	*mah*·le
photography	*fotografiere*	fo·to·gra·*fee*·re
reading	*lese*	*lay*·ze
travelling	*reise*	*rai*·ze

I (don't) like ...	*Ich ... (nicht) gern ...*	ikh ... (nikht) gern ...
films	*sehe ... Filme*	*zay*·e ... *fil*·me
gardening	*arbeite ...*	ar·*bai*·te ...
	im Garten	im *gar*·ten
shopping	*kaufe ... ein*	*kow*·fe ... ain
socialising	*gehe ... aus*	*gay*·e ... ows

And you?	*Und Sie/du?* pol/inf	unt zee/doo

For types of sport, see **sports**, page 123 and the **dictionary**.

music

Do you like to ...?

listen to music	*Hören Sie gern*	her·ren zee gern
	Musik? pol	mu·zeek
	Hörst du gern	herst doo gern
	Musik? inf	mu·zeek
dance	*Tanzen Sie*	tan·tsen zee
	gern? pol	gern
	Tanzt du gern? inf	tantst doo gern
go to concerts	*Gehen Sie gern*	gay·en zee gern
	in Konzerte? pol	in kon·tser·te
	Gehst du gern	gayst doo gern
	in Konzerte? inf	in kon·tser·te
sing	*Singen Sie*	zing·en zee
	gern? pol	gern
	Singst du gern? inf	zingkst doo gern

Do you play an instrument?

Spielen Sie ein	shpee·len zee ain
Instrument? pol	in·stru·ment
Spielst du ein	shpeelst doo ain
Instrument? inf	in·stru·ment

What ... do	*Welche ... mögen Sie?* pol	vel·khe ... mer·gen zee
you like?	*Welche ... magst du?* inf	vel·khe ... mahkst doo
bands	*Bands*	bents
music	*Art von Musik*	art fon mu·zeek

classical music	klassische Musik f	kla·si·she mu·zeek
electronic music	elektronische Musik f	e·lek·traw·ni·she mu·zeek
jazz	Jazz m	dzhez
metal	Metal m	me·tel
pop	Popmusik f	pop·mu·zeek
punk	Punk m	pangk
rock	Rockmusik f	rok·mu·zeek
R & B	Rhythm'n'Blues m	rithm·n·blooz
traditional music	traditionelle Musik f	tra·di·tsyo·ne·le mu·zeek
world music	Weltmusik f	velt·mu·zeek

Planning to go to a concert? See **going out**, page 108.

cinema & theatre

I feel like going to a ...	Ich hätte Lust, ... zu gehen.	ikh he·te lust ... tsoo gay·en
film	ins Kino	ins kee·no
play	ins Theater	ins te·ah·ter

Did you like it?

| Hat es Ihnen/dir gefallen? pol/inf | hat es ee·nen/deer ge·fa·len |

What's showing at the cinema/theatre tonight?

| Was gibt es heute im Kino/Theater? | vas gipt es hoy·te im kee·no/te·ah·ter |

Is it in English?

| Ist es auf Englisch? | ist es owf eng·lish |

Does it have subtitles?

| Hat es Untertitel? | hat es un·ter·tee·tel |

Are those seats taken?

| Sind diese Plätze besetzt? | zint dee·ze ple·tse be·zetst |

Have you seen ...?

| Haben Sie ... gesehen? pol | hah·ben zee ... ge·zay·en |
| Hast du ... gesehen? inf | hast doo ... ge·zay·en |

interests

99

Who's in it?
Wer spielt da mit?   vair shpeelt dah mit

It stars ...
Es ist mit ...   es ist mit ...

I thought it was ...	*Ich fand es ...*	ikh fant es ...
excellent	*ausgezeichnet*	ows·ge·*tsaikh*·net
long	*lang*	lang
OK	*okay*	o·*kay*

I (don't) like ...	Ich mag ...	ikh mahk ...
action movies	(keine) Actionfilme	(*kai*·ne) *ek*·shen·fil·me
animated films	(keine) Zeichentrickfilme	(*kai*·ne) *tsai*·khen·trik·fil·me
classical theatre	(kein) klassisches Theater	(kain) *kla*·si·shes te·*ah*·ter
comedies	(keine) Komödien	(*kai*·ne) ko·*mer*·di·en
documentaries	(keine) Dokumentarfilme	(*kai*·ne) do·ku·men·*tahr*·fil·me
drama	(keine) Schauspiele	(*kai*·ne) *show*·shpee·le
German cinema	(keine) deutsche(n) Filme	(*kai*·ne) *doyt*·she(n) *fil*·me
horror movies	(keine) Horrorfilme	(*kai*·ne) *ho*·ror·fil·me
period dramas	(keine) Historienfilme	(*kai*·ne) his·*taw*·ri·en·fil·me
realism	(keinen) Realismus	(*kai*·nen) re·a·*lis*·mus
sci-fi	(keinen) Sciencefiction	(*kai*·nen) sai·ens·*fik*·shen
short films	(keine) Kurzfilme	(*kai*·ne) *kurts*·fil·me
war movies	(keine) Kriegsfilme	(*kai*·ne) *kreeks*·fil·me

feelings

gefühle

I'm (not) ...	*Ich bin (nicht) ...*	ikh bin (nikht) ...
Are you ...?	*Sind Sie ...?* pol	zint zee ...
	Bist du ...? inf	bist doo ...
annoyed	*verärgert*	fer·er·gert
disappointed	*enttäuscht*	en·toysht
in a hurry	*in Eile*	in ai·le
sad	*traurig*	trow·rikh
tired	*müde*	mü·de

I'm (not) ...	*Ich habe (kein) ...*	ikh hah·be (kain) ...
Are you ...?	*Haben Sie ...?* pol	hah·ben zee ...
	Hast du ...? inf	hast doo ...
hungry	*Hunger*	hung·er
thirsty	*Durst*	durst

I'm (not) ...	*Mir ist (nicht) ....*	meer ist (nikht) ...
Are you ...?	*Ist Ihnen/*	ist ee·nen/
	dir ...? pol/inf	deer ...
cold	*kalt*	kalt
hot	*heiß*	hais

I'm (not) ...		
embarrassed	*Das ist mir*	das ist meer
	(nicht) peinlich.	(nikht) pain·likh
worried	*Ich mache mir*	ikh ma·khe meer
	(keine) Sorgen.	(kai·ne) zor·gen

Are you ...?

embarrassed	*Ist Ihnen/dir*	ist ee·nen/deer
	das peinlich? pol/inf	das *pain*·likh
worried	*Machen Sie*	*ma*·khen zee
	sich Sorgen? pol	zikh *zor*·gen
	Machst du dir	makhst doo deer
	Sorgen? inf	*zor*·gen

intense feelings

a little	*ein bisschen*	ain *bis*·khen
I'm a little sad.	*Ich bin ein*	ikh bin ain
	bisschen traurig.	*bis*·khen *trow*·rikh
terribly	*furchtbar*	*furkht*·bahr
I'm terribly	*Es tut mir*	es toot meer
sorry.	*furchtbar Leid.*	*furkht*·bahr lait
very	*sehr*	zair
I feel very	*Ich schätze mich*	ikh *she*·tse mikh
lucky.	*sehr glücklich.*	zair *glük*·likh
completely	*völlig*	*fer*·likh
not at all	*überhaupt nicht*	ü·ber·*howpt* nikht
profoundly	*abgrundtief*	*ap*·grun·teef
quite	*ziemlich*	*tseem*·likh
totally	*total*	to·*tahl*

opinions

Did you like it?
Hat es Ihnen/dir   hat es ee·nen/deer
gefallen? pol/inf   ge·*fa*·len

What did you think of it?
Wie hat es Ihnen/dir   vee hat es ee·nen/deer
gefallen? pol/inf   ge·*fa*·len

It is/was ...	*Es ist/war ...*	es ist/vahr ...
awful	*schrecklich*	shrek·likh
beautiful	*schön*	shern
boring	*langweilig*	lang·vai·likh
great	*toll*	tol
interesting	*interessant*	in·tre·sant
OK	*okay*	o·kay
too expensive	*zu teuer*	tsoo toy·er

politics & social issues

politische und soziale fragen

I support the	*Ich unterstütze*	ikh un·ter·shtü·tse
... party.	*die ... Partei.*	dee ... par·tai
communist	*kommunistische*	ko·mu·nis·ti·she
conservative	*konservative*	kon·zer·va·tee·ve
democratic	*demokratische*	de·mo·krah·tish·e
green	*grüne*	grün·e
liberal	*liberale*	li·be·rahl·e
social democratic	*sozial-*	zo·tsyahl·
	demokratische	de·mo·krah·tish·e
socialist	*sozialistische*	zo·tsya·lis·tish·e

I support the labour party.
Ich unterstütze die   ikh un·ter·shtü·tse dee
Arbeiterpartei.   ar·bai·ter·par·tai

Who do you vote for?
Wen wählen Sie? pol   vayn vay·len zee
Wen wählst du? inf   vayn vaylst doo

Did you hear about ...?
Haben Sie von ... gehört? pol   *hah*·ben zee fon ... ge·hert
Hast du von ... gehört? inf   hast doo fon ... ge·hert

Do you agree with it?
Sind Sie damit   zint zee dah·mit
einverstanden? pol   ain·fer·shtan·den
Bist du damit   bist doo dah·mit
einverstanden? inf   ain·fer·shtan·den

feelings & opinions

I (don't) agree with that.
   Ich bin damit (nicht)   ikh bin dah·*mit* (nikht)
   einverstanden.   *ain*·fer·shtan·den

Are you against … ?
   Sind Sie gegen …? pol   zint zee *gay*·gen …
   Bist du gegen …? inf   bist doo *gay*·gen …

Are you in favour of …?
   Sind Sie für …? pol   zint zee für …
   Bist du für …? inf   bist doo für …

How do people feel about …?
   Was denken die   vas *deng*·ken dee
   Leute über …?   *loy*·te ü·ber …

abortion	*Abtreibung* f	*ap*·trai·bung
animal rights	*Tierschutz* m	*teer*·shuts
discrimination	*Diskriminierung* f	dis·kri·mi·*nee*·rung
drugs	*Drogen* f pl	*draw*·gen
the economy	*die Wirtschaft* f	dee *virt*·shaft
education	*Bildung* f	*bil*·dung
the environment	*die Umwelt* f	dee *um*·velt
equal opportunity	*Gleichberech-tigung* f	*glaikh*·be·rekh·ti·gung
euthanasia	*Euthanasie* f	oy·ta·na·*zee*
globalisation	*Globalisierung* f	glaw·ba·li·*zee*·rung
human rights	*Menschenrechte* n pl	*men*·shen·rekh·te
immigration	*Einwanderung* f	*ain*·van·de·rung
racism	*Rassismus* m	ra·*sis*·mus
sexism	*Sexismus* m	sek·*sis*·mus
social welfare	*Wohlfahrtsstaat* m	*vawl*·fahrts·shtaht
unemployment	*Arbeitslosigkeit* f	*ar*·baits·law·zikh·kait

the environment

Is there a ... problem here?

Gibt es hier ein   gipt es heer ain
Problem mit ...?   pro·*blaym* mit ...

What should be done about ...?

Was sollte man   vas *zol*·te man
gegen ... tun?   *gay*·gen ... toon

biodegradable	*biologisch*	bi·o·*law*·gish
	abbaubar	*ap*·bow·bahr
conservation	*Schutz* m	shuts
deforestation	*Abholzung* f	*ap*·hol·tsung
drought	*Trockenheit* f	*tro*·ken·hait
ecosystem	*Ökosystem* n	*er*·ko·züs·taym
endangered species	*gefährdete Arten* f pl	ge·*fair*·de·te *ar*·ten
floods	*Überschwem-*	ü·ber·*shve*·
	mungen f pl	mung·en
genetically	*genmanipuliertes*	*gayn*·ma·ni·pu·*leer*·tes
modified food/	*Essen/Getreide* n/n	e·sen/ge·*trai*·de
crops		
hunting	*Jagd* f	yahkt
hydroelectricity	*Strom* m	shtrawm
	aus Wasserkraft	ows va·ser·kraft
nuclear energy	*Atomenergie* f	a·*tawm*·e·ner·gee
nuclear testing	*Atomtests* m pl	a·*tawm*·tests
nuclear waste	*Atommüll* m	a·*tawm*·mül
ozone layer	*Ozonschicht* f	o·*tsawn*·shikht
pesticides	*Pestizide* n pl	pes·ti·*tsee*·de
pollution	*Umweltver-*	*um*·velt·fer·
	schmutzung f	shmu·tsung
recycling	*Recycling-*	ri·*sai*·kling·
programme	*programm* n	pro·gram
toxic waste	*Giftmüll* m	*gift*·mül
water supply	*Wasserver-*	*va*·ser·for·
	sorgung f	zor·gung

Is this a protected ...?	Ist das ...?	ist das ...
forest	ein geschützter Wald	ain ge·shüts·ter valt
species	eine geschützte Art	ai·ne ge·shüts·te art

the final say

If you'd like to underline your opinions with some colourful language and impress your new German-speaking acquaintances, try your hand at these sayings:

That goes without saying.
Das versteht sich von selbst.
das fer·shtet zikh fon zelbst

That cuts no ice with me.
Damit können Sie bei mir nicht landen.
da·mit ker·nen zee bai meer nikht lan·den

Nobody cares two hoots about it.
Danach kräht kein Hahn.
da·nakh krayt kain han

There's the rub.
Da liegt der Hund begraben.
da leegt dair hunt be·grab·en

Stick to the facts!
Bleiben Sie sachlich!
blai·ben zee zakh·likh

That will get you nowhere.
Das führt zu nichts.
das fürt tsu nikhts

Tell us another one!
Das können Sie uns nicht erzählen!
das kern·en zee uns nikht er·tsay·len

to have the final say
das letze Wort haben
das lets·te vort hab·en

where to go

wohin ausgehen?

What's there to do in the evenings?
Was kann man abends   vas kan man ah·bents
unternehmen?   un·ter·*nay*·men

What's on ...?	*Was ist ... los?*	vas ist ... laws
locally	*hier*	heer
this weekend	*dieses*	dee·zes
	Wochenende	vo·khen·en·de
today	*heute*	hoy·te
tonight	*heute Abend*	hoy·te ah·bent

Where are the ...?	*Wo sind die ...?*	vaw zint dee
clubs	*Klubs*	klups
gay venues	*Schwulen- und*	shvoo·len unt
	Lesbenkneipen	les·ben·knai·pen
places to eat	*Restaurants*	res·to·*rangs*
pubs	*Kneipen*	knai·pen

Is there a local entertainment guide?
Gibt es einen   gipt es ai·nen
Veranstaltungskalender?   fer an·shtal·tungks·ka·len·der

Is there a local gay guide?
Gibt es einen Führer für die   gipt es ai·nen fü·rer für dee
Schwulen- und Lesbenszene?   shvoo·len unt les·bens·tsay·ne

I feel like going	Ich hätte Lust,	ikh *he*·te lust
to a/the ...	... zu gehen.	... tsoo *gay*·en
ballet	zum Ballett	tsum ba·*let*
bar/pub	in eine Kneipe	in *ai*·ne *knai*·pe
cafe	in ein Café	in ain ka·*fay*
concert	in ein Konzert	in ain kon·*tsert*
movies	ins Kino	ins *kee*·no
nightclub	in einen	in *ai*·nen
	Nachtklub	*nakht*·klup
opera	in die Oper	in dee *aw*·per
restaurant	in ein Restaurant	in ain res·to·*rang*
theatre	ins Theater	ins te·*ah*·ter

I feel like going out somewhere.
Ich hätte Lust, auszugehen.   ikh *he*·te *lust* ows·tsu·gay·en

invitations

What are you	Was machst	vas makhst
doing (...)?	du (...)?	doo (...)
right now	jetzt gerade	jetst ge·*rah*·de
this evening	heute Abend	*hoy*·te *ah*·bent
this weekend	am Wochenende	am *vo*·khen·en·de

Would you like	Möchtest du	*merkh*·test doo
to go (for a) ...?	... gehen?	... *gay*·en
coffee	einen Kaffee	*ai*·nen ka·*fay*
	trinken	*tring*·ken
dancing	tanzen	*tan*·tsen
drink	etwas trinken	*et*·vas *tring*·ken
meal	essen	e·sen

Do you want to come to the ... concert with me?
Möchtest du mit mir   *merkh*·test doo mit meer
zum ...-konzert gehen?   tsum ...·kon·*tsert* *gay*·en

We're having a party.
Wir machen eine Party.   veer *ma*·khen *ai*·ne *par*·ti

Would you like to come?
Hättest du Lust zu kommen?   *he*·test doo lust tsoo *ko*·men

responding to invitations

auf einladungen reagieren

Sure!	*Klar!*	klahr
Yes, I'd love to.	*Ja, gerne.*	yah *ger*·ne
That's very kind of you.	*Das ist sehr nett von dir/euch.* sg/pl	das ist zair net fon deer/oykh
Where shall we go?	*Wo sollen wir hingehen?*	vaw zo·len veer *hin*·gay·en
No, I'm afraid I can't.	*Nein, es tut mir Leid, aber ich kann nicht.*	nain es toot meer lait *ah*·ber ikh kan nikht
What about tomorrow?	*Wie wäre es mit morgen?*	vee *vair*·te es mit *mor*·gen

local talk

There's nothing going on there.
Da ist nichts los.   dah ist nikhts laws

It's a hole.
Da ist tote Hose.   dah ist *taw*·te *haw*·ze
(lit: there is dead trousers)

It's all happening there.
Da ist die Sau los.   da ist dee zow laws
(lit: there is the sow loose)
Da boxt der Papst.   dah bokst dair pahpst
(lit: there boxes the pope)

arranging to meet

einen treffpunkt verabreden

Where/When shall we meet?		
Wo/Wann sollen wir uns treffen?	vaw/van zo·len veer uns *tre*·fen	
Let's meet at ...	*Wir treffen uns ...*	veer *tre*·fen uns ...
(eight) o'clock	*um (acht) Uhr*	um (akht) oor
the (entrance)	*am (Eingang)*	am (*ain*·gang)

OK!
Okay! .... o·kay

I'll see you then.
Bis dann! .... bis dan

I'll pick you up.
Ich hole dich ab. .... ikh *haw*·le dikh ap

I'll be coming later. Where will you be?
Ich komme später. .... ikh *ko*·me *shpay*·ter
Wo wirst du sein? .... vaw virst doo zain

If I'm not there by (nine), don't wait for me.
Wenn ich bis (neun) .... ven ikh bis (noyn)
Uhr nicht da bin, ... oor nikht dah bin
warte nicht auf mich. .... *var*·te nikht owf mikh

See you later/tomorrow.
Bis später/morgen. .... bis *shpay*·ter/*mor*·gen

I'm looking forward to it.
Ich freue mich darauf. .... ikh *froy*·e mikh da·*rowf*

Sorry I'm late.
Es tut mir Leid, dass .... es toot meer lait das
ich zu spät komme. .... ikh tsoo shpayt *ko*·me

Never mind.
Macht nichts. .... makht nikhts

drugs

drogen

I don't take drugs.
Ich nehme keine Drogen. .... ikh *nay*·me *kai*·ne *draw*·gen

I take ... occasionally.
Ich nehme ab und zu ... . ikh *nay*·me ap unt tsoo ...

Do you want to have a smoke?
Wollen wir einen .... *vo*·len veer *ai*·nen
Joint rauchen? .... dzhoynt *row*·khen

I'm high.
Ich bin high. .... ikh bin hai

asking someone out

sich verabreden

Would you like to do something ...?	Hättest du Lust, ... was zu unternehmen?	he·test doo lust ... vas tsoo un·ter·nay·men
Where would you like to go ...?	Wo würdest du ... gerne hingehen?	vaw vür·dest doo ... ger·ne hin·gay·en
tomorrow	morgen	mor·gen
tonight	heute Abend	hoy·te ah·bent
on the weekend	am Wochenende	am vo·khen·en·de

Yes, I'd love to.
Ja, gerne.   yah ger·ne
Sure, thanks.
Klar! Das wäre nett.   klahr das vair·re net
I'm busy.
Ich habe keine Zeit.   ikh hah·be kai·ne tsait
Forget it!
Vergiss es!   fer·gis es

local talk

He's/She's a ...	Er/Sie ist ...	air/zee ist ...
babe	eine Schönheit	ai·ne shern·hait
bitch	eine Zicke	ai·ne tsi·ke
hot guy	ein heißer Typ	ain hai·ser tüp
hot girl	eine heiße Frau	ai·ne hai·se frow
prick	ein Depp	ain dep

He/She looks really great.
Er/Sie sieht echt geil aus.   air/zee zeet ekht gail ows

He/She gets around.
Er/Sie lässt nichts anbrennen.   air/zee lest nikhts an·bre·nen
(lit: he/she lets nothing burn)

pick-up lines

Haven't we met before?
Kennen wir uns nicht   ke·nen veer uns nikht
von irgendwoher?   fon ir·gent·vo·hair

Would you like a drink?
Möchtest du etwas trinken?   merkh·test doo et·vas tring·ken

What star sign are you?
Was für ein Sternzeichen   vas für ain shtern·tsai·khen
bist du?   bist doo

Shall we get some fresh air?
Sollen wir ein bisschen an   zo·len veer ain bis·khen an
die frische Luft gehen?   dee fri·she luft gay·en

You have a beautiful personality.
Du hast eine wundervolle   doo hast ai·ne vun·der·vo·ler
Persönlichkeit.   per·zern·likh·kait

You have (a) beautiful ...	*Du hast ...*	doo hast ...
body	*einen schönen Körper*	ai·nen sher·nen ker·per
eyes	*schöne Augen*	sher·ne ow·gen
hands	*schöne Hände*	sher·ne hen·de
laugh	*ein schönes Lachen*	ain sher·nes la·khen

rejections

I'm here with ...	*Ich bin mit ... hier.*	ikh bin mit ... heer
my boyfriend	*meinem Freund*	mai·nem froynt
my girlfriend	*meiner Freundin*	mai·ner froyn·din

Excuse me, I have to go now.
Tut mir Leid, ich   toot meer lait ikh
muss jetzt gehen.   mus yetst gay·en

No, thank you.
Nein, danke. — nain *dang*·ke

I'd rather not.
Lieber nicht. — *lee*·ber nikht

Perhaps some other time.
Vielleicht ein andermal. — fi·*laikht* ain *an*·der·mahl

Before this goes any further, I must be upfront.
I'm (an accountant).
Bevor wir uns näher — be·*fawr* veer uns *nay*·er
kennen lernen, muss — *ke*·nen *ler*·nen mus
ich etwas klarstellen. — ikh *et*·vas *klahr*·shte·len
Ich bin (Buchhalter/ — ikh bin (*bookh*·hal·ter/
Buchhalterin). m/f — *bookh*·hal·te·rin)

Your ego is out of control.
Du leidest wohl unter — doo *lai*·dest vawl *un*·ter
Größenwahn. — *grer*·sen·wahn

---

local talk

I'd rather you left me alone.
Es wäre mir lieber, — es *vair*·re meer *lee*·ber
du würdest mich in — doo *vür*·dest mikh in
Frieden lassen. — *free*·den *la*·sen

Leave me alone!
Lass mich zufrieden! — las mikh tsu·*free*·den

You're (really) getting on my nerves!
Du nervst (echt — doo nerfst (ekht
verstärkt)! — fer·*shterkt*)

Piss off!
Verpiss dich! — fer·*pis* dikh

I'm not interested
Ich bin nicht interessiert. — ikh bin nikht in·tre·*seert*

getting closer

Will you take me home?
*Kannst du mich nach
Hause bringen?*
kanst doo mikh nahkh
how·ze *bring*·en

Do you want to come inside for a while?
*Möchtest du noch
kurz mit reinkommen?*
merkh·test doo nokh
kurts mit *rain*·ko·men

You're very nice.
Du bist sehr nett.
doo bist zair net

I like you very much.
Ich mag dich sehr.
ikh mahk dikh zair

Do you like me too?
Magst du mich auch?
mahkst doo mikh owkh

You're very attractive.
Du bist sehr attraktiv.
doo bist zair a·trak·*teef*

I'm interested in you.
Ich interessiere mich für dich.
ikh in·tre·*see*·re mikh für dikh

You're great.
Du bist toll.
doo bist tol

sex

Kiss me.	*Küss mich.*	küs mikh
I want you.	*Ich will dich.*	ikh vil dikh
I want to make love to you.	*Ich möchte mit dir schlafen.*	ikh *merkh*·te mit deer *shlah*·fen
Take this off.	*Zieh das aus!*	tsee das ows
Touch me here.	*Berühr mich hier!*	be·*rür* mikh heer
Do you like this?	*Magst du das?*	mahkst doo das

SOCIAL

Let's go to bed!
Gehen wir ins Bett! — gay·en veer ins bet

Do you have (a condom)?
Hast du (ein Kondom)? — hast doo (ain kon·*dawm*)

Let's use a (condom).
Lass uns (ein Kondom) — las uns (ain kon·*dawm*)
benutzen. — be·*nu*·tsen

I won't do it without protection.
Ohne Kondom mache — *aw*·ne kon·*dawm* ma·khe
ich es nicht. — ikh es nikht

I (don't) like that.
Das mag ich (nicht). — das mahk ikh (nikht)

Please (don't) stop!
Bitte hör (nicht) auf. — *bi*·te her (nikht) owf

I think we should stop now.
Ich denke, wir sollten — ikh *deng*·ke veer *zol*·ten
jetzt aufhören. — yetst owf·her·ren

I can't get it up – sorry.
Ich krieg ihn nicht — ikh kreek een nikht
hoch – tut mir Leid! — hawkh toot meer lait

harder	*härter*	*her*·ter
faster	*schneller*	*shne*·ler
softer	*sanfter*	*zanf*·ter
slower	*langsamer*	*lang*·zah·mer

Oh yeah!	*Oh ja!*	aw yah
That's great.	*Das ist geil.*	das ist gail
Easy tiger!	*Sachte!*	*zakh*·te
It's my first time.	*Das ist mein*	das ist main
	erstes Mal.	*ers*·tes mahl
Don't worry,	*Gib dir keine*	geep deer *kai*·ne
I'll do it myself.	*Mühe, ich mach*	*mü*·e ikh makh
	es mir selbst.	es meer zelpst

It helps to have a sense of humour.
Mit Humor geht — mit hu·*mawr* gayt
alles besser. — *a*·les be·ser

AIDS	AIDS n	aydz
contraception	Empfängnis-	emp·*feng*·nis·
	verhütung f	fer·hü·tung
dental dam	Dental Dam m	*den*·tel dem
HIV	HIV n	hah·ee·*fow*
IUD	Intrauterin-	in·tra·u·te·*reen*·
	pessar m	pe·sahr
the Pill	die Pille f	dee *pi*·le
spermicide	Spermizid n	shper·mi·*tseet*

> afterwards

That was ...	Das war ...	das vahr ...
amazing	fantastisch	fan·*tas*·tish
weird	seltsam	*zelt*·zahm

Can I ...?	Kann ich ...?	kan ikh ...
call you	dich anrufen	dikh *an*·roo·fen
meet you	dich morgen	dikh *mor*·gen
tomorrow	treffen	*tre*·fen
see you again	dich wiedersehen	dikh *vee*·der·zay·en
stay over	hier übernachten	heer ü·ber·*nakh*·ten

I'll ...	Ich ...	ikh ...
call you	rufe dich	*roo*·fe dikh
tomorrow	morgen an	*mor*·gen an
see you tomorrow	sehe dich morgen	*zay*·e dikh *mor*·gen
never forget	werde das nie	*ver*·de das nee
	vergessen	fer·*ge*·sen

love

I love you.
Ich liebe dich. — ikh *lee*·be dikh

I think we're good together.
Ich glaube, wir passen — ikh *glow*·be veer *pa*·sen
gut zueinander. — goot tsu·ai·*nan*·der

Will you ...? — *Willst du ...?* — vilst doo ...
  go out with me — *mit mir gehen* — mil meer *gay*·en
  live with me — *mit mir* — mit meer
  — *zusammenleben* — tsu·za·men·*lay*·ben
  marry me — *mich heiraten* — mikh *hai*·ra·ten

problems

Are you seeing someone else?
Gibt es da einen — gipt es dah *ai*·nen
anderen/eine andere? m/f — an·de·ren/*ai*·ne an·de·re

I never want to see you again.
Ich will dich nie — ikh vil dikh nee
mehr wiedersehen. — mair vee·der·*zay*·en

We'll work it out.
Wir finden schon — veer *fin*·den shawn
eine Lösung. — *ai*·ne *ler*·zung

He's/She's just a friend.
Er/Sie ist nur ein — air/zee ist noor ain
Freund/eine — froynt/*ai*·ne
Freundin. m/f — *troyn*·din

I want to ... — *Ich möchte ...* — ikh *merkh*·te ...
  end the — *Schluss* — shlus
    relationship — *machen* — *ma*·khen
  stay friends — *dass wir Freunde* — das veer *froyn*·de
    — *bleiben* — *blai*·ben

romance

117

leaving

I have to leave tomorrow.
Ich muss morgen los.   ikh mus *mor*·gen laws

I'll ...	*Ich ...*	ikh ...
come and	*komme dich*	*ko*·me dikh
visit you	*besuchen*	be·*zoo*·khen
miss you	*werde dich*	*ver*·de dikh
	vermissen	fer·*mi*·sen

on heat

Some German expressions might seem similar to English expressions, but have a very different meaning – beware of the following:

Ich bin heiss.   ikh bin hais
(lit: I am hot)
  I'm feeling sexy.

Ich bin kalt.   ikh bin kalt
(lit: I am cold)
  I'm frigid/I have an unfriendly personality.

To say you're feeling physically hot or cold, use:

Mir ist heiss.   mir ist hais
(lit: to me is hot)
  I'm hot.

Mir ist kalt.   mir ist kalt
(lit: to me is cold)
  I'm cold.

Similarly, be careful not to mix up these:

Ich bin voll.   ikh bin fol
(lit: I am full)
  I'm drunk.

Ich bin satt.   ikh bin zat.
(lit: I am full)
  I've had enough to eat.

religion

religion

What's your religion?
Was ist Ihre/deine vas ist ee·re/dai·ne
Religion? pol/inf re·li·gyawn

I'm (not) religious.
Ich bin (nicht) religiös. ikh bin (nikht) re·li·gyers

I'm (not) ...	*Ich bin (kein/*	ikh bin (kain/
	keine) ... m/f	kai·ne) ...
agnostic	*Agnostiker(in)* m/f	a·gnos·ti·ker/
		a·gnos·ti·ke·rin
Buddhist	*Buddhist(in)* m/f	bu·dist/bu·dis·tin
Catholic	*Katholik(in)* m/f	ka·to·leek/
		ka·to·lee·kin
Christian	*Christ(in)* m/f	krist/kris·tin
Hindu	*Hindu* m&f	hin·du
Jewish	*Jude/Iüdin* m/f	yoo·de/yü·din
Muslim	*Moslem/*	mos·lem/
	Moslime m/f	mos·lee·me
practising	*praktizierender/*	prak·ti·tsee·ren·der/
	praktizierende m/f	prak·ti·tsee·ren·de
Protestant	*Protestant(in)* m/f	pro·tes·tant/
		pro·tes·tan·tin

I (don't)	*Ich glaube*	ikh glow·be
believe in ...	*(nicht) an ...*	(nikht) an ...
God	*Gott*	got
destiny/fate	*das Schicksal*	das shik·zahl

Where can I ...?	Wo kann ich ...?	vaw kan ikh ...
attend mass	eine Messe	ai·ne me·se
	besuchen	be·zoo·khen
attend service	einen	ai·nen
	Gottesdienst	go·tes·deenst
	besuchen	be·zoo·khen
make confession	(auf Englisch)	(owf eng·lish)
(in English)	beichten	baikh·ten
pray	beten	bay·ten
receive	das Abendmahl	das ah·bent·mahl
communion	empfangen	emp·fang·en
worship	meine Andacht	mai·ne an·dakht
	verrichten	fer·rikh·ten

cultural differences

kulturelle unterschiede

Is this a local or national custom?

Ist das ein örtlicher oder landesweiter Brauch?

ist das ain ert·li·kher aw·der lan·des·vai·ter browkh

I'm not used to this.

Das ist ganz ungewohnt für mich.

das ist gants un·ge·vawnt für mikh

I don't mind watching, but I'd rather not join in.

Ich sehe gerne zu, würde aber lieber nicht selbst mitmachen.

ikh zay·e ger·ne tsoo vür·de ah·ber lee·ber nikht zelpst mit·ma·khen

I'll try it.

Ich versuche es.

ikh fer·zoo·khe es

I'm sorry, I didn't mean to do anything wrong.

Es tut mir Leid, ich wollte nichts Falsches tun.

es toot meer lait ikh vol·te nikhts fal·shes toon

I'm sorry, it's against my ...	Es tut mir Leid, das ist gegen meine ...	es toot meer lait das ist gay·gen mai·ne ...
beliefs	Anschauungen	an·show·ung·en
culture	Kultur	kul·toor
religion	Religion	re·li·gyawn

Where's (the museum)?
  Wo ist (das Museum)? vaw ist (das mu·*zay*·um)

When's (the gallery) open?
  Wann hat (die Galerie) van hat (dee ga·le·*ree*)
  geöffnet? ge·*erf*·net

What kind of art are you interested in?
  Für welche Art von Kunst für *vel*·khe art fon kunst
  interessieren Sie sich? pol in·tre·*see*·ren zee zikh
  Für welche Art von Kunst für *vel*·khe art fon kunst
  interessierst du dich? inf in·tre·*seerst* doo dikh

What's in the collection?
  Was gibt es in der vas gipt es in dair
  Sammlung? *zam*·lung

What do you think of ...?
  Was halten Sie von ...? pol vas *hal*·ten zee fon ...
  Was hältst du von ...? inf vas heltst doo fon ...

artistic styles

art nouveau	*Jugendstil*	yoo·*gent*·shteel
baroque art	*barocke Kunst*	ba·*ro*·ke kunst
Bauhaus art	*Bauhaus-Kunst*	*bow*·hows·kunst
expressionist art	*expressionistische Kunst*	eks·pre·syo·*nis*·ti·she kunst
Gothic art	*gotische Kunst*	*gaw*·ti·she kunst
impressionist art	*impressionistische Kunst*	im·pre·syo·*nis*·ti·she kunst
modernist art	*moderne Kunst*	mo·*der*·ne kunst
performance art	*Performance Art*	pe·*faw*·mens aht
Renaissance art	*Renaissance-Kunst*	re·ne·*sangs*·kunst
Romanesque art	*romanische Kunst*	ro·*mah*·ni·she kunst

It's a/an ... exhibition.
Es ist eine ...-Ausstellung.   es ist *ai*·ne ...·ows·shte·lung

I'm interested in ...
Ich interessiere mich für ...   ikh in·tre·*see*·re mikh für ...

I like the works of ...
Ich mag die Arbeiten von ...   ikh mahk dee *ar*·bai·ten fon ...

It reminds me of ...
Es erinnert mich an ...   es er·*i*·nert mikh an ...

tongue twisters

If you're feeling pretty comfortable with the language and want to impress the locals, try these tongue twisters:

Blaukraut bleibt Blaukraut und Brautkleid bleibt Brautkleid.
blow·krowt blaipt *blow*·krowt unt *browt*·klait blaipt *browt*·klait
('Red cabbage remains red cabbage and a wedding dress remains a wedding dress.')

Der Potsdamer Postkutscher putzt den Potsdamer Postkutschkasten.
dair *pots*·dah·mer *post*·ku·cher putst dayn *pots*·dah·mer *post*·kuch·kah·sten
('The Potsdam mailcoach driver cleans the Potsdam mailcoach postboxes.')

Der Dachdecker deckt dein Dach, drum dank dem Dachdecker, der dein Dach deckt.
dair *dakh*·de·ker dekt dain dakh drum dank daym *dakh*·de·ker dair dain dakh dekt
('The roofer roofs your roof, for that thank the roofer, who roofs your roof.')

sporting interests

sportarten

What sport do you play?
Was für Sport treiben Sie? pol   vas für shport *trai*·ben zee
Was für Sport treibst du? inf   vas für shport traipst doo

What sport do you follow?
Für welche Sportarten   für *vel*·khe shport·ar·ten
interessieren Sie sich? pol   in·tre·*see*·ren zee zikh
Für welche Sportarten   für *vel*·khe shport·ar·ten
interessierst du dich? inf   in·tre·*seerst* doo dikh

I play ...	*Ich spiele ...*	ikh *shpee*·le ...
I do ...	*Ich mache ...*	ikh *ma*·khe ...
I follow ...	*Ich interessiere*	ikh in·tre·*see*·re
	mich für ...	mikh für ...
athletics	*Leichtathletik*	laikht·at·lay·tik
basketball	*Basketball*	bahs·ket·bal
football (soccer)	*Fußball*	foos·bal
handball	*Handball*	hant·bal
ice hockey	*Eishockey*	ais·ho·ki
skiing	*Skifahren*	shee·fah·ren
tennis	*Tennis*	te·nis

For more types of sport, see the **dictionary**.

Do you like (sport)?
Mögen Sie (Sport)? pol   mer·gen zee (shport)
Magst du (Sport)? inf   mahkst doo (shport)

Yes, very much.
Ja, sehr.   yah zair

Not really.
Nicht besonders.   nikht be·*zon*·ders

I like watching it.
Ich sehe es mir gerne an.   ikh *zay*·e es meer *ger*·ne an

Only as a spectator.
Nur als Zuschauer.   noor als *tsoo*·show·er

Who's your favourite sportsperson?
Wer ist Ihr/dein   vair ist eer/dain
Lieblingssportler? pol/inf   *leep*·lingks·shport·ler

Who's your favourite team?
Was ist Ihre/deine   vas ist *ee*·re/*dai*·ne
Lieblingsmannschaft? pol/inf   *leep*·lingks·man·shaft

Can you play (soccer)?
Spielen Sie (Fußball)? pol   *shpee*·len zee (*foos*·bal)
Spielst du (Fußball)? inf   shpeelst doo (*foos*·bal)

going to a game

zu einem spiel gehen

Would you like to go to a game?
Möchten Sie zu einem   *merkh*·ten zee tsoo *ai*·nem
Spiel gehen? pol   shpeel *gay*·en
Möchtest du zu einem   *merkh*·test doo tsoo *ai*·nem
Spiel gehen? inf   shpeel *gay*·en

Who are you supporting?
Wen unterstützen Sie? pol   vayn un·ter·*shtü*·tsen zee
Wen unterstützt du? inf   vayn un·ter·*shtütst* doo

Who's ...?	*Wer ...?*	vair ...
playing	*spielt*	speelt
winning	*gewinnt*	ge·*vint*

---

sports talk

What a ...!	*Was für ...!*	vas für ...
goal	*ein Tor*	ain tawr
hit	*ein Treffer*	ain *tre*·fer
kick	*ein Schuss*	ain shus
pass	*ein Pass*	ain pas
performance	*eine Leistung*	*ai*·ne *lais*·tung

What was the final score?
Was war das Endergebnis? vas vahr das *ent·er·gayp·*nis

It was a draw.
Es ging unentschieden aus. es ging *un·*ent·shee·den ows

That was a	*Das war ein*	das vahr ain
... game!	*... Spiel!*	... shpeel
bad	*schlechtes*	*shlekh·*tes
boring	*langweiliges*	*lang·*vai·li·ges
great	*tolles*	*to·*les

scoring

What's the score?	*Wie steht es?*	vee shtayt es
draw/even	*unentschieden*	*un·*ent·shee·den
love (zero)	*null*	nul
match-point	*Matchball*	*mech·*bal
nil (zero)	*null*	nul
3–1	*3:1 (drei zu eins)*	drai tsoo ains

playing sport

Do you want to play?
Möchten Sie mitspielen? pol *merkh·*ten zee *mit·*shpee·len
Möchtest du mitspielen? inf *merkh·*test doo *mit·*shpee·len

Can I join in?
Kann ich mitspielen? kan ikh *mit·*shpee·len

Yes, that'd be great.
Ja, das wäre toll. yah das *vair·*re tol

I'm sorry, I can't.
Es tut mir Leid, es toot meer lait
ich kann nicht. ikh kan nikht

I have an injury.
Ich habe eine Verletzung. ikh *hah·*be *ai·*ne fer·*le·*tsung

sports

125

Your point.
Ihr/Dein Punkt. pol/inf   eer/dain pungkt

My point.
Mein Punkt.   main pungkt

Kick/Pass it to me!
Hierher!   heer·hair

You're a good player.
Sie sind   zee zint
ein guter Spieler/   ain goo·ter shpee·ler/
eine gute Spielerin. m/f pol   ai·ne goo·te shpee·le·rin

You're a good player.
Du bist   doo bist ...
ein guter Spieler/   ain goo·ter shpee·ler/
eine gute Spielerin. m/f inf   ai·ne goo·te shpee·le·rin

Thanks for the game.
Vielen Dank für das Spiel.   fee·len dangk für das shpeel

Where's the best place to jog/run around here?
Wo kann man hier am   vaw kan man heer am
besten joggen/laufen?   bes·ten dzho·gen/low·fen

Where's the   *Wo ist ...?*   vaw ist ...
nearest ...?

gym	*das nächste*	das naykhs·te
	Fitness-Studio	fit·nes·shtoo·di·o
swimming pool	*das nächste*	das naykhs·te
	Schwimmbad	shvim·baht
tennis court	*der nächste*	dair naykhs·te
	Tennisplatz	te·nis·plats

Do I have to be a member to attend?
Muss ich Mitglied sein,   mus ikh mit·gleet zain
um mitzumachen?   um mit·tsu·ma·khen

Is there a women-only session?

	Gibt es eine Session	gipt es *ai*·ne ses·yawn
	nur für Frauen?	noor für *frow*·en

Is there a women-only pool?

	Gibt es ein Schwimmbecken	gipt es ain shvim·be·ken
	nur für Frauen?	noor für *frow*·en

Where are the change rooms?

	Wo sind die	vaw zint dee
	Umkleideräume?	*um*·klai·de·roy·me

What's the	*Wie viel kostet*	vee feel *kos*·tet
charge per ...?	*es pro ...?*	es praw ...
day	*Tag*	tahk
game	*Spiel*	shpeel
hour	*Stunde*	shtun·de
visit	*Besuch*	be·zookh

Can I hire a ...?	*Kann ich ...?*	kan ikh ...
ball	*einen Ball leihen*	*ai*·nen bal lai·en
bicycle	*ein Fahrrad leihen*	ain fahr·raht lai·en
court	*einen Platz*	*ai*·nen plats
	mieten	mee·ten
racquet	*einen Schläger*	*ai*·nen shlay·ger
	leihen	lai·en

cycling

radsport

Where does the race finish?

Wo endet das Rennen?	vaw *en*·det das *re*·nen

Where does the race pass through?

Wo führt das Rennen lang?	vaw fürt das *re*·nen lang

Who's winning?

Wer gewinnt?	vair ge·*vint*

Is today's leg very hard?

Ist die Etappe heute	ist dee e·ta·pe hoy·te
sehr schwer?	zair shvair

How many kilometres is today's (leg)?

Wie viel Kilometer ist	vee feel ki·lo·*may*·ter ist
(die Etappe) heute?	(dee e·*ta*·pe) *hoy*·te

My favourite cyclist is …

Mein Lieblings-	main *leep*·lings·
radfahrer ist …	*raht*·fah·rer ist …

climbing stage	*Bergetappe* f	*berk*·e·ta·pe
cyclist	*Radfahrer(in)* m/f	*raht*·fah·rer/
		raht·fah·re·rin
the (yellow) jersey	*das (gelbe) Trikot* n	das (*gel*·be) tri·*kaw*
leg (in race)	*Etappe* f	e·*ta*·pe
	(des Rennens)	(des *re*·nens)
racing cyclist	*Radrenn-*	*raht*·ren·fah·rer/
	fahrer(in) m/f	*raht*·ren·fah·re·rin
time trial	*Zeitfahren* n	*tsait*·fah·ren
winner	*Sieger(in)* m/f	*zee*·ger/zee·ge·rin
winner of a leg	*Etappen-*	e·*ta*·pen·zee·ger/
	sieger(in) m/f	e·*ta*·pen·zee·ge·rin

For words and phrases on getting around by bicycle, see **transport**, page 45.

extreme sports

Are you sure this is safe?

Sind Sie sicher, dass das	zint zee zi·*kher* das das
ungefährlich ist? pol	*un*·ge·fair·likh ist
Bist du sicher, dass das	bist doo zi·*kher* das das
ungefährlich ist? inf	*un*·ge·fair·likh ist

Is the equipment secure?

Ist die Ausrüstung sicher?	ist dee *ows*·rüs·tung zi·*kher*

This is insane.

Das ist verrückt!	das ist fer·*rükt*

SOCIAL

128

abseiling	*Abseilen* n	*ap·zai·len*
bungy-jumping	*Bungyjumping* n	*ban·dzhi·dzham·ping*
caving	*Höhlenerforschung* f	*her·len·er·for·shung*
hanggliding	*Drachenfliegen* n	*dra·khen·flee·gen*
mountain biking	*Mountainbiken* n	*mown·ten·bai·ken*
parachuting	*Fallschirmspringen* n	*fal·shirm·shpring·en*
parasailing	*Parasailing* n	*pah·ra·say·ling*
rock-climbing	*Klettern* n	*kle·tern*
skydiving	*Skydiving* n	*skai·dai·ving*
snowboarding	*Snowboarden* n	*snoh·bor·den*
white-water rafting	*Wildwasser-fahrten* f pl	*vilt·va·ser·fahr·ten*

soccer

Who plays for (Bayern München)?
Wer spielt für (Bayern München)?
vair shpeelt für (*bai*·ern *mün*·khen)

What a terrible team!
Was für eine furchtbare Mannschaft!
vas für *ai*·ne *furkht*·bah·re *man*·shaft

Which team is at the top of the league?
Welcher Verein steht an der Tabellenspitze?
vel·kher fer·*ain* shtayt an dair ta·*be*·len·shpi·tse

She's a great player.
Sie ist eine tolle Spielerin.
zee ist ain·e *to*·le *shpee*·ler·in

He played brilliantly in the match against (Italy).
Im Spiel gegen (Italien) hat er fantastisch gespielt.
im shpeel gay·gen (i·*tah*·li·en) hat air fan·*tas*·tish ge·*shpeelt*

She scored (three) goals.
Sie hat (drei) Tore geschossen.
zee hat (drai) *taw*·re ge·*sho*·sen

corner	*Ecke* f	*e·ke*
free kick	*Freistoß* m	*frai·shtaws*
goalkeeper	*Torhüter(in)* m/f	*tawr·hü·ter/*
		tawr·hü·te·rin
offside	*Abseits* n	*ap·zaits*
penalty	*Strafstoß* m	*shtrahf·shtaws*

skiing

skifahren

How much is a pass?
Was kostet ein Skipass? vas *kos·tet* ain *shee·pas*

Can I take lessons?
Kann ich Unterricht nehmen? kan ikh *un·ter·rikht nay·men*

I'd like to hire ...	*Ich möchte ...*	ikh *merkh·te ...*
	leihen.	*lai·en*
boots	*Skistiefel*	*shee·shtee·fel*
goggles	*eine Skibrille*	*ai·ne shee·bri·le*
poles	*Skistöcke*	*shee·shter·ke*
skis	*Skier*	*shee·er*
a ski suit	*einen*	*ai·nen*
	Skianzug	*shee·an·tsook*
Is it possible to	*Kann man*	kan man
go ... here/there?	*hier/da ...?*	heer/dah ...
Alpine skiing	*Abfahrtsski*	*ap·fahrts·shee*
	fahren	*fah·ren*
cross-country	*Skilanglauf*	shee·*lang·*lowf
skiing	*machen*	*ma·*khen
snowboarding	*snowboarden*	*snoh·bor·den*
tobogganing	*Schlitten fahren*	*shli·ten fah·ren*

What are the	*Wie sind die*	vee zint dee
skiing conditions	*Schneebeding-*	shnay·be·ding·
like …?	*ungen …?*	ung·en …
at (Lauberhorn)	*am (Lauberhorn)*	am (*low*·ber·horn)
on that run	*an dieser Abfahrt*	an *dee*·zer *ap*·fahrt
higher up	*weiter oben*	*vai*·ter *aw*·ben

What level is that slope?
Wie schwierig ist — vee *shvee*·rikh ist
dieser Hang? — *dee*·zer hang

Which are the	*Welches sind*	*vel*·khes zint
… slopes?	*die …?*	dee …
beginner	*Anfängerhänge*	an·feng·er·heng·e
intermediate	*mittelschweren*	*mi*·tel·shvair·ren
	Hänge	heng·e
advanced	*Fortgeschrittenen*	fort·ge·shri·te·nen·
	hänge	heng·e

cable car	*Seilbahn* f	*zail*·bahn
chairlift	*Sessellift* m	*ze*·sel·lift
instructor	*Skilehrer* m	*shee*·lair·rer
resort	*Ort* m	ort
ski-lift	*Skilift* m	*shee*·lift
sled	*Schlitten* m	*shli*·ten

tennis

Would you like to play tennis?
Möchten Sie Tennis — *merkh*·ten zee *te*·nis
spielen? pol — *shpee*·len
Möchtest du Tennis — *merkh*·test doo *te*·nis
spielen? inf — *shpee*·len

Can we play at night?
Können wir abends spielen? — *ker*·nen veer *ah*·bents *shpee*·len

ace	*Ass* n	as
advantage	*Vorteil* m	*fawr*·tail
clay court	*Sandplatz* m	*zant*·plats
fault	*Fehler* m	*fay*·ler
game, set, match	*Spiel, Satz und Sieg*	shpeel *zats* unt zeek
grass court	*Rasenplatz* m	*rah*·zen·plats
hard court	*Hartplatz* m	*hart*·plats
play doubles	*ein Doppel spielen*	ain *do*·pel shpee·len
serve	*Aufschlag* m	*owf*·shlahk
set	*Satz* m	zats

könig fußball

The king of German amateur and professional sports is '*König Fußball*' (king football). Football (or soccer as it's known in the US and Australia) is played at thousands of amateur clubs known as *Fußballvereine*. Germans are passionate about the game and professional games draw an average 25,000 fans. One of the longest words in the German language belongs to the football sphere. Try getting your tongue around *Fußballweltmeisterschafts-qualifikationsspiel* (World Cup Soccer qualifying game).

hiking

wandern

Where can I ...?	*Wo kann ich ...?*	vaw kan ikh ...
buy supplies	*Vorräte einkaufen*	fawr·ray·te ain·kow·fen
find out about hiking trails	*Informationen über Wanderwege bekommen*	in·for·ma·tsyaw·nen ü·ber van·der·vay·ge be·ko·men
find someone who knows this area	*jemanden finden, der die Gegend kennt*	yay·man·den fin·den dair dee gay·gent kent
get a map	*eine Karte bekommen*	ai·ne kar·te be·ko·men
hire hiking gear	*Wanderausrüstung leihen*	van·der·ows·rüs·tung lai·en
Do we need to take ...?	*Müssen wir ... mitnehmen?*	mü·sen veer ... mit·nay·men
bedding	*Bettzeug*	bet·tsoyk
food	*Essen*	e·sen
water	*Wasser*	va·ser

How long is the trail?
Wie lang ist der Weg? — vee lang ist dair vayk

How high is the climb?
Wie hoch führt die Klettertour hinauf? — vee hawkh fürt dee kle·ter·toor hi·nowf

Do we need a guide?
Brauchen wir einen Führer? — brow·khen veer ai·nen fü·rer

Are there guided treks?
Gibt es geführte Wanderungen? — gipt es ge·für·te van·de·rung·en

Is it safe?
Ist es ungefährlich? — ist es un·ge·fair·likh

Is there a hut there?
Gibt es dort eine Hütte? — gipt es dort ai·ne hü·te

When does it get dark?
Wann wird es dunkel? — van virt es dung·kel

Is the track ...?	*Ist der Weg ...?*	ist dair vayk ...
(well-)marked	*(gut) markiert*	(goot) mar·keert
open	*offen*	o·fen
scenic	*schön*	shern

Which is the ...?	*Welches ist die ...?*	vel·khes ist dee ...
shortest route	*kürzeste Route*	kür·tses·te roo·te
easiest route	*einfachste Route*	ain·fakhs·te roo·te

Where's a/the ...?	*Wo ...?*	vaw ...
camp site	*ist ein Zeltplatz*	ist ain tselt·plats
nearest village	*ist das nächste Dorf*	ist das naykhs·te dorf
showers	*sind (die) Duschen*	zint (dee) doo·shen
toilets	*sind (die) Toiletten*	zint (dee) to·a·le·ten

Where have you come from?
Wo kommen Sie
gerade her? pol
vaw *ko*-men zee
ge-*rah*-de hair

How long did it take?
Wie lange hat
das gedauert?
vee *lang*-e hat
das ge-*dow*-ert

Does this path go to ...?
Führt dieser Weg nach ...?
fürt *dee*-zer vayk nahkh ...

Can we go through here?
Können wir hier
durchgehen?
ker-nen veer heer
durkh-gay-en

Is the water OK to drink?
Kann man das
Wasser trinken?
kan man das
va-ser *tring*-ken

I'm lost.
Ich habe mich verlaufen.
ikh *hah*-be mikh fer-*low*-fen

at the beach

Where's the ...	Wo ist der ...	vaw ist dair ...
beach?	Strand?	shtrant
best	beste	*bes*-te
nearest	nächste	*naykhs*-te
nudist	FKK-	ef-kah-*kah*-
public	öffentliche	er-*fent*-li-khe

Is it safe to dive/swim here?
Kann man hier gefahrlos   kan man heer ge-*fahr*-laws
tauchen/schwimmen?   *tow*-khen/*shvi*-men

What time is high/low tide?
Wann ist Flut/Ebbe?   van ist floot/*e*-be

Do we have to pay?
Müssen wir bezahlen?   *mü*-sen veer be-*tsah*-len

listen for ...

akh-ten zee owf dayn zawk
  Achten Sie auf den Sog.   **Be careful of the undertow.**

es ist ge-*fair*-likh
  Es ist gefährlich!   **It's dangerous!**

zee *mü*-sen *ai*-ne *koor*-tak-se be-*tsah*-len
  Sie müssen eine   **You have to pay a health**
  Kurtaxe bezahlen.   **resort visitor's tax.**

How much for a/an ...?	*Was kostet ein ...?*	vas *kos*-tet ain ...
canopied wicker beach-chair	*Strandkorb*	*shtrant*-korp
chair	*Stuhl*	shtool
hut	*Hut*	hoot
umbrella	*Schirm*	shirm

SOCIAL

136

weather

What's the weather like?
Wie ist das Wetter?   vee ist das ve·ter

It's ...	Es ist ...	es ist ...
Will it be ...	Wird es morgen	virt es mor·gen
tomorrow?	... sein?	... zain
cloudy	wolkig	vol·kikh
cold	kalt	kalt
freezing	eiskalt	ais·kalt
hot	heiß	hais
raining	regnerisch	rayg·ne·rish
sunny	sonnig	zo·nikh
warm	warm	varm
windy	windig	vin·dikh

Where can I	Wo kann ich	vaw kan ikh
buy a/an ...?	... kaufen?	... kow·fen
rain jacket	eine	ai·ne
	Regenjacke	ray·gen·ya·ke
umbrella	einen	ai·nen
	Regenschirm	ray·gen·shirm

flora & fauna

flora und fauna

What ... is that?	Wie heißt ...?	vee haist ...
animal	dieses Tier	dee·zes teer
flower	diese Blume	dee·ze bloo·me
plant	diese Pflanze	dee·ze pflan·tse
tree	dieser Baum	dee·zer bowm

Is it ...?	Ist es ...?	ist es ...
common	weit verbreitet	vait fer·brai·tet
dangerous	gefährlich	ge·fair·likh
endangered	vom Aussterben	fom ows·shter·ben
	bedroht	be·drawt
protected	geschützt	ge·shütst

What's it used for?
   Wofür wird es benutzt?   vaw·*für* virt aes be·*nutst*

Can you eat it?
   Kann man es essen?   kan man es e·sen

For geographical and agricultural terms and names of animals and plants, see the **dictionary**.

anyone for a dip?

Aquatic pursuits are popular in Germany and it's hard to find a town that doesn't have a public *Schwimmbad* (swimming pool). Often there's a *Hallenbad* (indoor pool) alongside the *Freibad* (outdoor pool). Spas are popular too, with people seeking to cure a variety of conditions. The most famous spa town in Germany is called *Baden Baden*. This double-barrelled name represents both the name of the surrounding region and the German word for bathing.

key language

		wichtige wörter
breakfast	Frühstück n	frü·shtük
lunch	Mittagessen n	mi·tahk·e·sen
dinner	Abendessen n	ah·bent·e·sen
snack	Snack m	snek
eat	essen	e·sen
drink	trinken	tring·ken
Please.	Bitte.	bi·te
Thank you.	Danke.	dang·ke
I'd like ...	Ich möchte ...	ikh merkh·te ...
I'm starving!	Ich bin am	ikh bin am
	Verhungern!	fer·hung·ern

finding a place to eat

ein restaurant suchen

Can you	Können Sie ...	ker·nen zee ...
recommend a ...	empfehlen? pol	emp·fay·len
	Kannst du ...	kanst doo ...
	empfehlen? inf	emp·fay·len
bar/pub	eine Kneipe	ai·ne knai·pe
cafe	ein Café	ain ka·fay
coffee bar	eine Espressobar	ai·ne es·pre·so·bahr
restaurant	ein Restaurant	ain res·to·rang
Where would	Wo kann man	vaw kan man
you go for (a) ...?	hingehen, um ...?	hin·gay·en um
celebration	etwas zu feiern	et·vas tsoo fai·ern
cheap meal	etwas Billiges	et·vas bi·li·ges
	zu essen	tsoo e·sen
local specialities	örtliche	ert·li·khe
	Spezialitäten	shpe·tsya·li·tay·ten
	zu essen	tsoo e·sen

eating out

139

I'd like to reserve a table for ...	Ich möchte einen Tisch für ... reservieren.	ikh merkh·te ai·nen tish für ... re·zer·vee·ren
(two) people	(zwei) Personen	(tsvai) per·zaw·nen
(eight) o'clock	(acht) Uhr	(akht) oor
I'd like ..., please.	Ich hätte gern ..., bitte.	ikh he·te gern ... bi·te
a table for (five)	einen Tisch für (fünf) Personen	ai·nen tish für (fünf) per·zaw·nen
the smoking section	einen Rauchertisch	ai·nen row·kher·tish
the non-smoking section	einen Nichtrauchertisch	ai·nen nikht·row·kher·tish
Do you have ...?	Haben Sie ...?	hah·ben zee ...
children's meals	Kinderteller	kin·der·te·ler
a menu in English	eine englische Speisekarte	ai·ne eng·li·she shpai·ze·kar·te

listen for ...

es toot meer lait veer *hah*·ben ge·*shlo*·sen
Es tut mir Leid, wir haben geschlossen. — **Sorry, we're closed.**

veer zint fol *ows*·ge·bookht
Wir sind voll ausgebucht. — **We're fully booked.**

veer *hah*·ben *kai*·nen tish frai
Wir haben keinen Tisch frei. — **We have no free tables.**

vaw *merkh*·ten zee *zi*·tsen
Wo möchten Sie sitzen? — **Where would you like to sit?**

merkh·ten zee et·vas *tring*·ken *vair*·rent zee *var*·ten
Möchten Sie etwas trinken, während Sie warten? — **Would you like a drink while you wait?**

vas darf ikh ee·nen *bring*·en
Was darf ich Ihnen bringen? — **What can I get for you?**

bi·te
Bitte! — **Here you go!**

Are you still serving food?
Gibt es noch etwas zu essen? gipt es nokh et·vas tsoo e·sen

How long is the wait?
Wie lange muss man warten? vee lang·e mus man var·ten

at the restaurant

I'd like ...,	*Ich hätte gern ...,*	ikh he·te gern ...
please.	*bitte*	bi·te
the drink list	*die Getränke-*	dee ge·treng·ke·
	karte	kar·te
the menu	*die Speisekarte*	dee shpai·ze·kar·te

What would you recommend?
Was empfehlen Sie? vas emp·fay·len zee

I'll have what they're having.
Ich nehme das   ikh nay·me das
gleiche wie sie.   glai·khe vee zee

I'd like a local speciality.
Ich möchte etwas   ikh merkh·te et·vas
Typisches aus der Region.   tü·pi·shes ows dair re·gyawn

What's in that dish?
Was ist in diesem Gericht? vas ist in dee·zem ge·rikht

eating out

141

Does it take long to prepare?
Dauert das lange? — dow·ert das lang·e

Is it self-serve?
Ist das Selbstbedienung? — ist das zelpst·be·dee·nung

Is service included in the bill?
Ist die Bedienung — ist dee be·dee·nung
inbegriffen? — in·be·gri·fen

Are these complimentary?
Sind die gratis? — zint dee grah·tis

We're just having drinks.
Wir möchten nur — veer merkh·ten noor
etwas trinken. — et·vas tring·ken

For more on special diets, see **vegetarian & special meals**, page 159.

---

look for ...

Vorspeisen	fawr·shpai·zen	appetisers/entrees
Suppen	zu·pen	soups
Salate	za·lah·te	salads
Hauptgerichte	howpt·ge·rikh·te	main courses
Beilagen	bai·lah·gen	side dishes
Nachspeisen	nahkh·shpai·zen	desserts
Aperitifs	a·pe·ri·teefs	aperitifs
Alkoholfreie	al·ko·hawl·frai·e	soft drinks
Getränke	ge·treng·ke	
Spirituosen	shpi·ri·tu·aw·zen	spirits
Bier	beer	beers
Schaumweine	showm·vai·ne	sparkling wines
Weißweine	vais·vai·ne	white wines
Rotweine	rawt·vai·ne	red wines
Dessertweine	de·sair·vai·ne	dessert wines
Digestifs	di·zhes·teefs	digestifs

For more words you might see on a menu, see the **culinary reader**, page 163.

at the table

Please bring ...	*Bitte bringen Sie ...*	bi·te bring·en zee ...
the bill	*die Rechnung*	dee rekh·nung
a cloth	*eine Tischdecke*	ai·ne tish·de·ke
a glass	*ein Glas*	ain (vain·)glahs

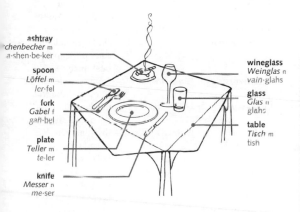

ashtray
chenbecher m
a·shen·be·ker

spoon
Löffel m
ler·fel

fork
Gabel f
gah·bel

plate
Teller m
te·ler

knife
Messer n
me·ser

wineglass
Weinglas n
vain·glahs

glass
Glas n
glahs

table
Tisch m
tish

talking food

I love this dish.
Ich mag dieses Gericht.
ikh mahk dee·zes ge·rikht

I love the local cuisine.
Ich mag die regionale Küche.
ikh mahk dee re·gyo·nah·le kü·khe

That was delicious!
Das hat hervorragend geschmeckt!
das hat her·fawr·rah·gent ge·shmekt

One of Germany's favourite and most famous foods is the not-so-humble *Wurst* (sausage). There are over 1500 types, some of the more common of which are listed below:

Blutwurst f	*bloot·*vurst	blood sausage
Bockwurst f	*bok·*vurst	pork sausage
Bratwurst f	*braht·*vurst	fried pork sausage
Bregenwurst f	*bray·*gen·vurst	brain sausage
Cervelatwurst f	ser·ve·*laht·*vurst	sausage made of a spicy pork and beef mixture
Katenwurst f	*kah·*ten·vurst	country-style smoked sausage
Knackwurst f	*knak·*vurst	mildly garlic-flavoured sausage
Krakauer f	*krah·*kow·er	thick, paprika-spiced sausage of Polish origin
Landjäger m	*lant·*yay·ger	thin, long, hard spicy sausage
Leberwurst f	*lay·*ber·vurst	liver sausage
Regensburger m	*ray·*gens·bur·ger	highly spiced smoked sausage
Rotwurst f	*rawt·*vurst	black pudding
Thüringer f	*tü·*ring·er	long, thin spicy sausage
Wiener Würstchen n	*vee·*ner *vürst·*khen	frankfurter (small smoked sausage)
Weißwurst f	*vais·*vurst	veal sausage
Würstchen n	*vürst·*khen	small sausage
Zwiebelwurst f	*tsvee·*bel·vurst	liver and onion sausage

This is ...	Das ist ...	das ist ...
(too) cold	*(zu) kalt*	(tsoo) kalt
spicy	*scharf*	sharf
superb	*exzellent*	ek·se·lent

My compliments to the chef.
Mein Kompliment   main kom·pli·*ment*
an den Koch.   an dayn kokh

I'm full.
Ich bin satt.   ikh bin zat

meals

> breakfast

What's a typical breakfast in (Bavaria)?
Was ißt man in (Rayern)   vas ist man in (*bai*·ern)
normalerweise zum   nor·*mah*·ler·vai·ze tsum
Frühstück?   frü·shtük

---

when is a roll not a roll?

Bread rolls can be called many different things, depending on which area you're in. Below are five of the most common terms and where you'll hear them used:

Brölchen n	brert·khen	in Germany
Schrippe f	shri·pe	in Berlin
Semmel f	ze·mel	in Bavaria
Wecken m&f	ve·ken	in southern Germany and Austria
Weggli n	veg·li	in Switzerland

---

bread	Brot n	brawt
butter	Butter f	bu·ter
cereal	Frühstücksflocken f pl	frü·shtüks·flo·ken
cheese	Käse m	kay·ze
coffee	Kaffee m	ka·fay
cold cuts of	Wurst/	vurst/
meat/sausage	Aufschnitt f/m	owf·shnit
croissant	Hörnchen n	hern·khen
egg/eggs	Ei/Eier n sg/pl	ai/ai·er
boiled egg	gekochtes Ei n	ge·kokh·tes ai
scrambled eggs	Rührei n	rür·ai
fried egg	Spiegelei n	shpee·gel·ai
poached egg	pochiertes Ei	po·sheer·tes ai
honey	Honig m	haw·nikh
jam	Marmelade f	mar·me·lah·de
omelette	Omelette n	om·let
orange juice	Orangensaft m	o·rang·zhen·zaft
milk	Milch f	milkh
muesli	Müsli n	müs·li
spreads	Brotaufstrich m	brawt·owf·shtrikh
tea	Tee m	tay
toast	Toast m	tawst

For other breakfast items see the **culinary reader**, page 163, and the **dictionary**.

> light meals

What's that called?	Wie heißt das?	vee haist das
I'd like	Ich hätte gern	ikh he·te gern
..., please	..., bitte.	... bi·te
one slice	eine Scheibe	ai·ne shai·be
a piece	ein Stück	ain shtük
a sandwich	ein Sandwich	ain sent·vich
that one	dieses da	dee·zes dah
two	zwei	tsvai

> condiments

Is there any ...?	Gibt es ...?	gipt es ...
chilli sauce	Chilisauce f	chi·li·zaw·se
ketchup	Ketchup m	ket·chap
pepper	Pfeffer m	pfe·fer
salt	Salz n	zalts
tomato sauce	Tomaten-	to·mah·ten·
	ketchup n	ket·chap
vinegar	Essig m	e·sikh

For additional items, see the **culinary reader**, page 163, and the **dictionary**.

methods of preparation

zubereitungsarten

I'd like it ...	Ich hätte es gern ...	ikh he·te es gern ...
I don't want it ...	Ich möchte	ikh merkh·te
	es nicht ...	es nikht ...
boiled	gekocht	ge·kokht
broiled	gegrillt	ge·grilt
deep-fried	frittiert	fri·teert
fried	gebraten	ge·brah·ten
grilled	gegrillt	ge·grilt
mashed	püriert	pü·reert
medium	halb durch	halp durkh
rare	englisch	eng·lish
re-heated	aufgewärmt	owf·ge·vermt
steamed	gedämpft	ge·dempft
well-done	gut durch-	goot durkh·
	gebraten	ge·brah·ten
with the dressing on the side	mit dem Dressing daneben	mit daym dre·sing da·nay·ben
without ...	ohne ...	aw·ne ...

in the bar

Excuse me!	*Entschuldigung!*	ent·*shul*·di·gung
I'm next.	*Ich bin dran.*	ikh bin dran
I'll have ...	*Ich hätte gern ...*	ikh *he*·te gern ...

Same again, please.
Dasselbe nochmal, bitte. das·*zel*·be nokh·*mahl* *bi*·te

No ice, thanks.
Kein Eis, bitte. kain ais *bi*·te

I'll buy you a drink.
Ich gebe Ihnen/dir ikh *gay*·be *ee*·nen/deer
einen aus. pol/inf *ai*·nen ows

What would you like?
Was möchten Sie? pol vas *merkh*·ten zee
Was möchtest du? inf vas *merkh*·test doo

It's my round.
Diese Runde geht auf mich. dee·ze *run*·de gayt owf mikh

---

listen for ...

vas *merkh*·ten zee (*tring*·ken)
Was möchten Sie **What are you having**
(trinken)? pol **(to drink)?**

ikh *glow*·be zee ha·ten ge·*nook*
Ich glaube, Sie hatten **I think you've**
genug. pol **had enough.**

loy·te vee zee be·*dee*·nen veer heer *nikht*
Leute wie Sie bedienen **We don't serve**
wir hier nicht. pol **your type in here.**

You can get the next one.
Sie können die nächste zee *ker*·nen dee *naykhs*·te
Runde bestellen. pol *run*·de be·*shte*·len
Du kannst die nächste doo kanst dee *naykhs*·te
Runde bestellen. inf *run*·de be·*shte*·len

Do you serve meals here?
Gibt es hier auch etwas zu essen?

gipt es heer owkh *et*·vas tsoo *e*·sen

nonalcoholic drinks

alkoholfreie getränke

soft drink	*Softdrink* m	*soft*·dringk
coffee	*Kaffee* m	ka·*fay*
tea	*Tee* m	tay
... with (milk)	*... mit (Milch)*	... mit (milkh)
... without (sugar)	*... ohne (Zucker)*	... *aw*·ne (*tsu*·ker)
water	*Wasser* n	va·ser
boiled water	*heißes Wasser* n	*hai*·ses va·ser
mineral water	*Mineralwasser* n	mi·ne·*rahl*·va·ser

what's in a name?

In Germany, *Softdrink* (soft drink) only designates sweet fizzy drinks, such as lemonade or cola. Mineral water is not known as *ein Softdrink*, but as *ein alkoholfreies Getränk* (a nonalcoholic drink).

alcoholic drinks

beer	Bier n	beer
light beer	Leichtbier n	laikht·beer
nonalcoholic beer	alkoholfreies Bier n	al·ko·hawl·frai·es beer
pilsner/lager	Pils n	pils
wheat beer	Weißbier n	vais·beer
brandy	Weinbrand m	vain·brant
(French) champagne	Champagner m	sham·pan·yer
cocktail	Cocktail m	kok·tayl
sparkling wine	Sekt m	zekt
a shot of ...	einen ...	ai·nen ...
gin	Gin	dzhin
rum	Rum	rum
tequila	Tequila	te·kee·la
vodka	Wodka	vot·ka
whisky	Whisky	vis·ki
a bottle of ... wine	eine Flasche ...	ai·ne fla·she ...
a glass of ... wine	ein Glas ...	ain glahs ...
dessert	Dessertwein	de·sair·vain
mulled	Glühwein	glü·vain
red	Rotwein	rawt·vain
rose	Rosé	ro·zay
sparkling	Sekt	zekt
white	Weißwein	vais·vain
a ... (of) beer	ein ... Bier	ain ... beer
glass	Glas	glahs
large	großes	graw·ses
pint	halbes	halb·es
small	kleines	klai·nes
a beer on tap	ein Bier vom Fass	ain beer fom fas

grape varieties

Germany is famous for its wines. There are three basic wine categories – *trocken* (dry), *halbtrocken* (medium-dry), and *lieblich* (sweet). Some of the more well-known grape varieties are listed below:

> white
Gewürztraminer m ge·*vürts*·tra·mee·ner
very spicy with an intense bouquet

Müller-Thurgau m mü·ler·*toor* gow
early-ripening grape with a slight muscat flavour. Also called *Rivaner*, this wine is less acidic than *Riesling* and is best when young.

Riesling m rees·ling
late-ripening grape with a fragrant, fruity bouquet, this wine can be drunk young or old

Rulander/ roo·len·der/
Grauburgunder m grow·bur·gun·der
robust, soft and full-bodied. Also known as *pinot gris* or *pinot grigio*.

Silvaner m zil·*vah*·ner
full-bodied, mildly acidic wine with a neutral nose. Should be drunk young.

> red
Portugieser m por·tu·*gee*·zer
light, mild red wine originally from Austria (not Portugal)

Spätburgunder m shpayt·bur·gun·der
also known as Pinot Noir. A velvety and full-bodied wine – the best have an almond taste.

Trollinger m *tro*·ling·er
hearty, full-bodied wine with a fragrant nose. *Trollinger* grapes ripen late and are only grown in Württemberg.

Alkoholfreies Bier n   al·ko·*hawl*·frai·es beer
  nonalcoholic beer

Alster(wasser) n   *als*·ter(·va·ser)
  mixture of pilsner and orange lemonade

Alt(bier) n   *alt*(·beer)
  amber-coloured speciality beer from Düsseldorf, with
  a strong taste of hops

Altbierbowle f   *alt*·beer·baw·le
  Altbier with strawberries or other fruit

Alt-Schuss n   alt·*shus*
  Altbier with a shot of syrup or *Malzbier*

Berliner Weiße f   ber·*lee*·ner *vai*·se
  slightly fizzy and cloudy, often served with a shot of
  raspberry (*rot*) or woodruff (*grün*) syrup

Bockbier n   *bok*·beer
  light or dark beer with a high alcohol content

Eisbock m   *ais*·bok
  Bockbier from which water has been extracted by
  freezing thus increasing its alcoholic potency

Export n   eks·*port*
  lager

Gose f   *gaw*·ze
  wheat beer from Leipzig

Hefeweizen n   *hay*·fe·vai·tsen
  cloudy wheat beer (with some yeast still in the
  bottle) – comes in light (*hell*) or dark (*dunkel*) varieties

Helles n   *he*·les
  lager (Bavaria)

Kölsch n   kerlsh
  yellow-golden coloured beer from Cologne

Kräusen n   *kroy*·zen
  unfiltered beer, gold-coloured or dark

Krefelder n   *kray*·fel·der
  Altbier mixed with cola

Kristallweizen n   kris·*tal*·vai·tsen
  clear light (*hell*) or dark (*dunkel*) wheat beer

beer reader

Leichtbier n   *laikht·beer*
beer with half the alcohol content of normal beer

Maibock m   *mai·bok*
special *Bockbier* brewed in May

Malzbier n   *malts·beer*
nonalcoholic malt beer

Märzen n   *mer·tsen*
special Bavarian beer brewed at the end of winter

Pils/Pils(e)ner n   *pils/pil·z(e·)ner*
pilsner, similar to lager

Radler n   *raht·ler*
mixture of pilsner or lager and sweet lemonade

Rauchbier n   *rowkh·beer*
smoky-flavoured beer from Bamberg

Schwarzbier n   *shvarts·beer*
stout (lit: black beer)

Weizenbier/Weißbier n   *vai·tsen·beer/vais·beer*
wheat beer

one too many?

einen über den durst?

Cheers!
Prost!   prawst

Thanks, but I don't feel like it.
Nein danke, ich möchte   nain *dang·ke ikh merkh·te*
jetzt nichts.   yetst nikhts

I don't drink alcohol.
Ich trinke keinen Alkohol.   ikh *tring·ke kai·nen al·ko·hawl*

This is hitting the spot.
Das kommt jetzt echt gut.   das komt yetst ekht goot

I'm tired, I'd better go home.
Ich bin müde, ich sollte   ikh bin *mü·de* ikh zol·te
besser nach Hause gehen.   be·ser nahkh how·ze gay·en

I'm feeling drunk.
Ich glaube, ich bin betrunken.   ikh *glow*·be ikh bin be·*trung*·ken

I feel fantastic!
Ich fühle mich fantastisch!   ikh *fü*·le mikh fan·*tas*·tish

I really, really love you.
Ich liebe dich echt total.   ikh *lee*·be dikh ekht to·*tahl*

I think I've had one too many.
Ich glaube, ich habe ein   ikh *glow*·be ikh *hah*·be ain
bisschen zu viel getrunken.   bis·khen tsoo feel ge·*trung*·ken

Can you call a taxi for me?
Können Sie mir ein   *ker*·nen zee meer ain
Taxi rufen? pol   *tak*·si roo·fen
Kannst du mir ein   kanst doo meer ain
Taxi rufen? inf   *tak*·si roo·fen

I don't think you should drive.
Ich glaube, Sie sollten   ikh *glow*·be zee zol·ten
nicht mehr fahren. pol   nikht mair *fah*·ren
Ich glaube, du solltest   ikh *glow*·be doo zol·test
nicht mehr fahren. inf   nikht mair *fah*·ren

There's still room for another!
Zwischen Leber und Milz   tsvi·shen *lay*·ber unt milts
ist noch Platz für ein Pils.   ist nokh plats für ain pils
(lit: between liver and spleen
is still room for a beer)

Let's have a second drink.
Auf einem Bein steht   owf *ai*·nem bain shtayt
man schlecht.   man shlekht
(lit: on one leg
stands one badly)

Where's the toilet?
Wo ist die Toilette?   vaw ist dee to·a·*le*·te

I'm pissed.	*Ich bin blau.*	ikh bin blow
	(lit: I am blue)	
I feel ill.	*Mir ist schlecht.*	meer ist shlekht
I've got a	*Ich habe einen Kater.*	ikh *hah*·be *ai*·nen *kah*·ter
hangover.	(lit: I have a tomcat)	

key language

wichtige wörter

cooked	gekocht	ge·kokht
dried	getrocknet	ge·trok·net
fresh	frisch	frish
frozen	eingefroren	ain·ge·fraw·ren
raw	roh	raw
A piece.	Ein Stück.	ain shtük
A slice.	Eine Scheibe.	ai·ne shai·be
That one.	Dieses da.	dee·zes dah
This.	Dieses	dee·zes
A bit more.	Ein bisschen mehr.	ain bis·khen mair
Less.	Weniger.	vay·ni·ger
Enough.	Genug.	ge·nook

dining tips

The main meal of the day in the German-speaking countries is *das Mittagsessen* or lunch.

It's good manners to say *Guten Appetit* or *Mahlzeit* (Enjoy your meal) to your fellow diners. Observing German table etiquette is easy – it's enough to eat in a basically civilized manner. It's customary, however, to keep your hands on the table at all times.

To say you've really enjoyed your meal say *Das hat geschmeckt*.

To get the attention of a waiter call out *Herr Ober* (to a man) or *Fräulein* (to a woman). To indicate that you want to pay your bill say *Zahlen bitte!*

Germans are fond of toasts. If they break out the drink, wait until everyone is served. Then raise your glasses in unison, look your fellow toasters in the eye and give a hearty *Prost!* or *Zum Wohl!*

buying food

How much?
Wie viel?   vee feel

How much is (a kilo of cheese)?
Was kostet (ein Kilo Käse)?   vas kos·tet (ain kee·lo kay·ze)

What's the local speciality?
Was ist eine örtliche   vas ist ai·ne ert·li·khe
Spezialität?   shpe·tsya·li·tayt

What's that?
Was ist das?   vas ist das

Can I taste it?
Kann ich das probieren?   kan ikh das pro·bee·ren

Can I have a bag, please?
Könnte ich bitte eine   kern·te ikh bi·te ai·ne
Tüte haben?   tü·te hah·ben

I'd like ...	Ich möchte ...	ikh merkh·te ...
(three) pieces	*(drei) Stück*	(drai) shtük
(six) slices	*(sechs) Scheiben*	(zeks) shai·ben
some ...	*etwas ...*	et·vas ...
(two) kilos	*(zwei) Kilo*	(tsvai) kee·lo
(200) grams	*(200) Gramm*	(tsvai·hun·dert) gram

Do you have ...?	Haben Sie ...?	hah·ben zee ...
anything cheaper	*etwas Billigeres*	et·vas bi·li·ge·res
other kinds	*andere Sorten*	an·de·re zor·ten

Where can I find the ... section?	Wo kann ich die ... finden?	vaw kan ikh dee ... fin·den
dairy	Abteilung für Milchprodukte	ap·tai·lung für milkh·pro·duk·te
frozen goods	Abteilung für Tiefkühlprodukte	ap·tai·lung für teef·kül·pro·duk·te
fruit and vegetable	Obst- und Gemüse- abteilung	awpst· unt ge·mü·ze· ap·tai·lung
meat	Fleischabteilung	flaish·ap·tai·lung
poultry	Geflügel- abteilung	ge·flü·gel· ap·tai·lung

For food items see the **culinary reader** page 163 and the **dictionary**.

listen for ...

kan ikh ee·nen hel·fen
Kann ich Ihnen helfen? Can I help you?

vas merkh·ten zee?
Was möchten Sie? What would you like?

das ist (ai·ne brat·vurst)
Das ist (eine Bratwurst). That's (a bratwurst).

das ist ows
Das ist aus. There's none left.

das hah·ben veer nikht
Das haben wir nicht. I don't have any.

merkh·ten zee nokh et·vas
Möchten Sie noch etwas? Would you like anything else?

das kos·tet (fünf oy·ro)
Das kostet (fünf Euro). That's (five euros).

cooking utensils

Could I please borrow a ...?	Könnte ich bitte ... ausleihen?	kern·te ikh bi·te ... ows·lai·en
bottle opener	einen Flaschenöffner	ai·nen fla·shen·erf·ner
bowl	eine Schüssel	ai·ne shü·sel
can opener	einen Dosenöffner	ai·nen daw·zen·erf·ner
chopping board	ein Schneidebrett	ain shnai·de·bret
corkscrew	einen Korkenzieher	ai·nen kor·ken·tsee·er
cup	eine Tasse	ai·ne ta·se
fork	eine Gabel	ai·ne gah·bel
frying pan	eine Bratpfanne	ai·ne braht·pfa·ne
glass	ein Glas	ain glahs
knife	ein Messer	ain me·ser
plate	einen Teller	ai·nen te·ler
saucepan	einen Kochtopf	ai·nen kokh·topf
spoon	einen Löffel	ai·nen ler·fel
toaster	einen Toaster	ai·nen taws·ter
fridge	Kühlschrank m	kül·shrank
microwave	Mikrowelle f	mi·kro·ve·le
oven	Ofen m	aw·fen
stove	Kochplatte f	kokh·pla·te

vegetarian & special meals
vegetarische und besondere gerichte

ordering

bestellen

Is there a (vegetarian) restaurant near here?
Gibt es ein (vegetarisches) gipt es ain vege·*tar*·ish·shes
Restaurant hier in der Nähe? res·to·*rang* heer in dair *nay*·e

Do you have	*Haben Sie*	*hah*·ben zee
... food?	*... Essen?*	*... e*·sen
halal	*Halal-*	ha·*lal·*
kosher	*koscheres*	*kaw*·she·res
vegetarian	*vegetarisches*	ve·ge·*tah*·ri·shes

Is it cooked	*Ist es in/mit*	ist es in/mit
in/with ...?	*... zubereitet?*	... *tsoo*·be·rai·tet
butter	*Butter*	*bu*·ter
eggs	*Eiern*	*ai*·ern
meat stock	*Fleischbrühe*	*flaish*·brü·e

I don't eat ...
Ich esse kein ... ikh *e*·se kain ...

Does this dish have ... in it?
Enthält dieses Gericht ...? ent·*helt* dee·zes ge·*rikht* ...

Can I get this without ... in it?
Kann ich das ohne ... kan ikh das *aw*·ne ...
bekommen? be·*ko*·men

Could you prepare a meal without ...?
Können Sie ein Gericht *ker*·nen zee ain ge·*rikht*
ohne ... zubereiten? *aw*·ne ... *tsoo*·be·rai·ten

Is this ...?	Ist das ...?	ist das ...
free of animal produce	*ohne tierische Produkte*	aw·ne *tee*·ri·she pro·*duk*·te
free-range	*von freilaufenden Tieren*	fon *frai*·low·fen·den *tee*·ren
genetically modified	*genmanipuliert*	gayn·ma·ni·pu·leert
gluten-free	*glutenfrei*	*gloo*·ten·frai
halal	*nach den Vorschriften des Koran zubereitet*	nahkh dayn *fawr*·shrif·ten des ko·*rahn* *tsoo*·be·rai·tet
kosher	*koscher*	*kaw*·sher
low in sugar	*zuckerarm*	*tsu*·ker·arm
low-fat	*fettarm*	*fet*·arm
organic	*organisch*	or·*gah*·nish
salt-free	*ohne Salz*	*aw*·ne zalts

FOOD

160

special diets & allergies

spezielle diäten und allergien

I'm (a) ...	Ich bin ...	ikh bin ...
Buddhist	Buddhist(in) m/f	bu·dist/bu·dis·tin
Hindu	Hindu	hin·du
Jewish	Jude/Jüdin m/f	yoo·de/yü·din
Muslim	Moslem/	mos·lem/
	Moslime m/f	mos·lee·me
vegan	Veganer(in) m/f	ve·gah·ner/
		ve·gah·ne·rin
vegetarian	Vegetarier(in) m/f	ve·ge·tah·ri·er/
		ve·ge·tah·ri·e·rin

I'm allergic to ...	Ich bin allergisch gegen ...	ikh bin a·lair·gish gay·gen ..
animal products	Tierprodukte	teer·pro·duk·te
caffeine	Koffein	ko·fe·een
dairy produce	Milchprodukte	milkh·pro·duk·te
eggs	Eier	ai·er
fish	Fisch	fish
gelatin	Gelatine	zhe·la·tee·ne
genetically modified food	genmanipulierte Speisen	gayn·ma·ni·pu·leer·te shpai·zen
gluten	Gluten	gloo·ten
honey	Honig	haw·nikh
MSG	Natrium- glutamat	nah·tri·um- glu·ta·maht
nuts	Nüsse	nü·se
pork	Schweinefleisch	shvai·ne·flaish
poultry	Geflügelfleisch	ge·flü·gel·flaish
red meat	Rind- und Lammfleisch	rint· unt lam·flaish
seafood	Meeresfrüchte	mair·res·frükh·te
shellfish	Schaltiere	shahl·tee·re

I'm on a special diet.
Ich bin auf einer Spezialdiät.
ikh bin owf *ai*·ner shpe·*tsyahl*·di·et

I can't eat it because I'm allergic.
Ich kann es nicht essen wiel ich allergisch bin.
ikh kan es nikht *ess*·en vail ikh a·*lair*·gish bin

I can't eat it for ...	*Ich kann es nicht essen aus ...*	ikh kan es nikht *ess*·en ows ...
health reasons	*Gesundheits-gründen*	ge·*zunt*·haits·grün·den
religious reasons	*religiösen Gründen*	re·li·*gyer*·zen *grün*·den
philosophical reasons	*philosophischen Gründen*	fi·lo·*zaw*·fi·shen *grün*·den

A

Aachener Printen pl *ah·khe·ner prin·ten cakes with chocolate, nuts, fruit peel, honey & spices*

Aal ⓜ *ahl eel*
  —**suppe** ⓕ *ahl·zu·pe eel soup*
  geräucherter Aal ⓜ *ge·roy·kher·ter ahl smoked eel*

Alpzirler ⓜ *alp·tsir·ler cow's milk cheese from Austria*

Apfel ⓜ *ap·fel apple*
  —**strudel** ⓜ *ap·fel·shtroo·del apple strudel*

Apfelsine ⓕ *ap·fel·zee·ne orange*

Aprikose ⓕ *a·pri·kaw·ze apricot*
  —**nmarmelade** ⓕ *a·pri·kaw·zen mar·me·lah·de apricot jam*

Artischocke ⓕ *ar·ti·sho·ke artichoke*

Auflauf ⓜ *owf·lowf souffle • casserole*

Auster ⓕ *ows·ter oyster*

B

Bäckerofen ⓜ *be·ker·aw·fen 'baker's oven' – pork & lamb bake from Saarland*

Backhähnchen ⓝ *bak·hayn·khen fried chicken*

Backobst ⓝ *bak·awpst dried fruit*

Backpflaume ⓕ *bak·pflow·me prune*

Banane ⓕ *ba·nah·ne banana*

Barsch ⓜ *barsh perch*

Bauern
  —**brot** ⓝ *bow·ern·brawt 'farmer's bread' – rye or wholemeal bread*
  —**frühstück** ⓝ *bow·ern·frü·shtük 'farmer's breakfast' – scrambled eggs, bacon, cooked diced potatoes, onions & tomatoes*

  —**schmaus** ⓜ *bow·ern·shmows 'farmer's feast' – sauerkraut garnished with bacon, smoked pork, sausages & dumpling or potatoes*
  —**suppe** ⓕ *bow·ern·zu·pe 'farmer's soup' – made from cabbage & sausage*

Bayrisch Kraut ⓝ *bai·rish krowt shredded cabbage cooked with sliced apples, wine & sugar*

Beefsteak ⓝ *beef·slayk hamburger patty*

Berliner ⓜ *ber·lee·ner Jam doughnut*

Beuschel ⓝ *boy·chel heart, liver & kidney of a calf or lamb in a slightly sour sauce*

Bienenstich ⓜ *bee·nen·shtikh cake baked on a tray with a coating of almonds & sugar*

Birne ⓕ *bir·ne pear*

Bischofsbrot ⓝ *bi·shofs·brawt fruit & nut cake*

Blaubeere ⓕ *blow·bair·re bilberry • blueberry*

Blaukraut ⓝ *blow·krowt red cabbage*

Blumenkohl ⓜ *bloo·men·kawl cauliflower*

Blutwurst ⓕ *bloot·vurst blood sausage*

Dockwurst ⓕ *bok·vurst pork sausage*

Bohnen ⓕ pl *baw·nen beans*

Brat
  —**huhn** ⓝ *braht·hoon roast chicken*
  —**kartoffeln** ⓕ pl *braht·kar·to·feln fried potatoes*
  —**wurst** ⓕ *braht·vurst fried pork sausage*

Bregenwurst ⓕ *bray·gen·vurst brain sausage, found mainly in Lower Saxony & Western Saxony-Anhalt*

Brezel ⓕ *bray·tsel pretzel*

Brokkoli ⓜ pl *bro·ko·li broccoli*
Brombeere ⓕ *brom·bair·re blackberry*
Brot ⓝ *brawt bread*
  belegtes Brot ⓝ *be·layk·tes brawt
  open sandwich*
Brötchen ⓝ *brert·khen roll*
Brühwürfel ⓜ *brü·vür·fel stock cube*
Bulette ⓕ *bu·le·te meatball (Berlin)*
Butter ⓕ *bu·ter butter*

C

Cervelatwurst ⓕ *ser·ve·laht·vurst
spicy pork & beef sausage*
Christstollen ⓜ *krist·shto·len spiced
loaf with candied peel, traditionally
eaten at Christmas*
Cremespeise ⓕ *kraym·shpai·ze mousse*

D

Damenkäse ⓜ *dah·men·kay·ze
soft, buttery cheese*
Dampfnudeln ⓕ pl *dampf·noo·deln
hot yeast dumplings with vanilla sauce*
Dattel ⓕ *da·tel date*
Dorsch ⓜ *dorsh cod*
Dotterkäse ⓜ *do·ter·kay·ze cheese
made from skimmed milk & egg yolk*

E

Ei ⓝ *ai egg*
  gekochte Eier ⓝ pl *ge·kokh·te ai·er
  boiled eggs*
Eierkuchen ⓜ *ai·er·koo·khen pancake*
Eierschwammerln ⓜ pl
*ai·er·shva·merln chanterelle mush-
rooms (Austria)*
Eierspeispfandl ⓝ *ai·er·shpais·pfandl
special Viennese omelette (Austria)*
Eintopf ⓜ *ain·topf stew*
Eis ⓝ *ais ice cream*
Eisbein ⓝ *ais·bain pickled pork knuckles*
Emmentaler ⓜ *e·men·tah·ler Swiss
Emmental, whole-milk hard cheese*
Ennstaler ⓜ *ens·tah·ler blue cheese
produced from mixed milk*

Ente ⓕ *en·te duck*
Erbse ⓕ *erp·se pea*
Erbsensuppe ⓕ *erp·sen·zu·pe pea soup*
Erdäpfel ⓜ pl *ert·ep·fel potatoes*
  —gulasch ⓝ *ert·ep·fel·goo·lash
  spicy sausage & potato stew*
  —knödel ⓜ pl *ert·ep·fel·kner·del
  potato & semolina dumplings*
  —nudeln ⓜ pl *ert·ep·fel·noo·deln
  boiled potato balls fried & tossed in
  fried breadcrumbs*
Erdbeere ⓕ *ert·bair·re strawberry*
Erdbeermarmelade ⓕ
ert·bair·mar·me·lah·de strawberry jam
Erdnuss ⓕ *ert·nus peanut*
Essig ⓜ *e·sikh vinegar*

F

Falscher Hase ⓜ *fal·sher hah·ze
'false hare' – baked mince meatloaf*
Fasan ⓜ *fa·zahn pheasant*
Feige ⓕ *fai·ge fig*
Filet ⓝ *fi·lay fillet*
Fisch ⓜ *fish fish*
Fladen ⓜ *flah·den round, flat dough
cake*
Flädle ⓝ pl *flayt·le thin strips of
pancake, added to soup*
Fledermaus ⓕ *flay·der·mows 'bat' –
boiled beef in horseradish cream
browned in the oven*
Fleisch ⓝ *flaish meat*
  —brühe ⓕ *flaish·brü·e bouillon*
  —pflanzerl ⓝ *flaish·pflan·tserl
  meatballs, a Bavarian speciality*
  —sülze ⓕ *flaish·zül·tse aspic*
Fondue ⓝ *fon·dü melted cheese with
wine served with bread for dipping*
Forelle ⓕ *fo·re·le trout*
  — blau *fo·re·le blow steamed trout
  with potatoes & vegetables*
  — Müllerin *fo·re·le mü·le·rin
  trout fried in batter with almonds*
  geräucherte Forelle ⓕ *ge·roy·kher·te
  fo·re·le smoked trout*

Frankfurter Kranz ⑩ frank·fur·ter
krants *sponge cake with rum, butter,
cream & cherries (from Frankfurt)*
Frikadelle ① fri·ka·de·le *meatball*
Frischling ⑩ frish·ling *young wild boar*
Frucht ① frukht *fruit*
Frühlingssuppe ① frü·lings·zu·pe
vegetable soup
Frühstücksspeck ⑩ frü·shtüks·shpek
bacon

G

Gans ① gans *goose*
Garnele ① gar·nay·le *shrimp • prawn*
Gebäck ⑩ ge·bek *pastries*
Geflügel ⑩ ge·flü·gel *poultry*
gekocht ge·kokht *boiled • cooked*
Gemüse ⑩ ge·mü·ze *vegetables*
　　—suppe ① ge·mü·ze·zu·pe *vegetable
soup*
geräuchert ge·roy·khert *smoked*
Geschnetzeltes ⑩ ge·shne·tsel·tes
small slices of meat
　　Züricher Geschnetzeltes ⑩ tsü·ri·kher
ge·shne·tsel·tes *sliced veal with
mushrooms & onions cooked in a
white wine & cream sauce*
Gitziprägol ⑩ gi·tsi·pray·gel *baked
rabbit in batter (Switzerland)*
Graf Görz ⑩ grahf gerts *Austrian
soft cheese*
Granat ⑩ gra·naht *shrimp*
Granatapfel ⑩ gra·naht·ap·fel
pomegranate
Gratin ⑩ gra·teng *a dish topped with
cheese & baked in the oven*
Graupensuppe ① grow·pen·zu·pe
barley soup
Greyerzer ⑩ grai·er·tser *Gruyère,
a smooth, rich cheese*
Grießklößchensuppe ①
grees·klers·khen·zu·pe *soup with
semolina dumplings*
Gröstl ⑩ grerstl *grated fried potatoes
with meat (Tyrol)*
grüner Salat ⑩ grü·ner zä·laht
green salad

Grünkohl ⑩ **mit Pinkel** grün·kawl
mit ping·kel *cabbage with sausages
(Bremen)*
Güggeli ⑩ gü·ge·lee *spring chicken
(Switzerland)*
Gurke ① gur·ke *cucumber • gherkin*

H

Hack
　　—braten ⑩ hak·brah·ten *meatloaf*
　　—fleisch ⑩ hak·flaish *minced meat*
Haferbrei ⑩ hah·fer·brai *porridge*
Hähnchen ⑩ hayn·khen *chicken*
Hämchen ⑩ hem·khen *pork or hock
shank, served with sauerkraut &
potatoes (Cologne)*
Handkäs ⑩ **mit Musik** hant·kays mit
mu·zeek *spicy cheese, marinated in
vinegar & white wine*
Hartkäse ⑩ hart·kay·ze *hard cheese*
Hase ⑩ hah·ze *hare*
　　—nläufe ⑩ pl **in Jägerrahmsauce**
hah·zen·loy·fe in yay·ger·rahm·zaw·se
*hare thigh in dark cream sauce of
mushroom, shallots, white wine &
parsley*
　　—npfeffer ⑩ hah·zen·pfe·fer *hare
stew with mushrooms & onions*
Haselnuß ① hah·zel·nus *hazelnut*
Haxe ① hak·se *knuckle*
Hecht ⑩ hekht *pike*
Heidelbeere ① hai·del·bair·re
bilberry • blueberry
Heidelbeermarmelade ① hai·del·bair·
mar·me·lah·de *blueberry/bilberry jam*
Heilbutt ⑩ hail·but *halibut*
Hering ⑩ hay·ring *herring*
　　—sschmaus ⑩ hay·rings·shmows
herring in creamy sauce
　　—ssalat ⑩ hay·rings·za·laht
salad with herring & beetroot
Himbeere ① him·bair·re *raspberry*
Himmel und Erde hi·mel unt er·de
*'Heaven & Earth' – mashed
potatoes & apple sauce, sometimes
served with slices of black pudding*
Hirsch ⑩ hirsh *male deer*

Holsteiner Schnitzel ⑩ *hol·shtai·ner shni·tsel* veal schnitzel with fried egg, accompanied by seafood

Honig ⑩ *haw·nikh* honey

Hörnchen ⑩ *hern·khen* croissant

Hühnerbrust ① *hü·ner·brust* chicken breast

Hühnersuppe ① *hü·ner·zu·pe* chicken soup

Hummer ⑩ *hu·mer* lobster

Husarenfleisch ⑩ *hu·zah·ren·flaish* braised beef, veal & pork fillets with sweet peppers, onions & sour cream

Hutzelbrot ⑩ *hu·tsel·brawt* bread made of prunes & other dried fruit

I

Ingwer ⑩ *ing·ver* ginger

italienischer Salat ⑩ *i·tal·yay·ni·sher za·laht* finely sliced veal, salami, anchovies, tomatoes, cucumber & celery in mayonnaise

J

Joghurt ⑩ *yaw·gurt* yogurt

K

Kabeljau ⑩ *kah·bel·yow* cod

Kaiserschmarren ⑩ *kai·zer·shmar·ren* 'emperor's pancakes' – fluffy pancakes with raisins, served with fruit compote or chocolate sauce

Kaisersemmeln ① pl *kai·zer·ze·meln* 'emperor's rolls' – Austrian bread rolls

Kalbfleisch ⑩ *kalp·flaish* veal

Kalbsnierenbraten ⑩ *kalps·nee·ren·brah·ten* roast veal stuffed with kidneys

Kaninchen ⑩ *ka·neen·khen* rabbit

Kapern ① pl *kah·pern* capers

Karotte ① *ka·ro·te* carrot

Karpfen ⑩ *karp·fen* carp

Kartoffel ① *kar·to·fel* potato

—auflauf ⑩ *kar·to·fel·owf·lowf* potato casserole

—brei ⑩ *kar·to·fel·brai* mashed potatoes

—püree ⑩ *kar·to·fel·pü·ray* mashed potatoes

—salat ⑩ *kar·to·fel·za·laht* potato salad

Käse ⑩ *kay·ze* cheese

—fondue ⑩ *kay·ze·fon·dü* melted cheese flavoured with wine & kirsch, into which bread is dipped

Kasseler ⑩ *kas·ler* smoked pork

— Rippe ① **mit Sauerkraut** *kas·ler ri·pe mit zow·er·krowt* smoked pork rib with sauerkraut

Katenwurst ① *kah·ten·vurst* country-style smoked sausage

Katzenjammer ⑩ *ka·tsen·ya·mer* cold slices of beef in mayonnaise with cucumbers or gherkin

Keule ① *koy·le* leg • haunch

Kieler Sprotten ① pl *kee·ler shpro·ten* small smoked herring

Kirsche ① *kir·she* cherry

Kirtagssuppe ① *kir·tahks·zu·pe* soup with caraway seed, thickened with potato

Klöße ⑩ pl *kler·se* dumplings

Knackwurst ① *knak·vurst* sausage lightly flavoured with garlic

Knoblauch ⑩ *knawp·lowkh* garlic

Knödel ⑩ *kner·del* dumpling

—beignets ⑩ pl *kner·del·ben·yays* fruit dumplings

Kohl ⑩ *kawl* cabbage

—rabi ⑩ *kawl·rah·bi* kohlrabi

—roulade ① *kawl·ru·lah·de* cabbage leaves stuffed with minced meat

Kompott ⑩ *kom·pot* stewed fruit

Königsuppe ① *ker·ni·gin·zu·pe* creamy chicken soup with pieces of chicken breast

Königsberger Klopse ⑩ pl *ker·niks·ber·ger klop·se* meatballs in a sour cream & caper sauce

Königstorte ① *ker·niks·tor·te* rum-flavoured fruit cake

Kopfsalat ⓜ *kopf*·za·laht lettuce
Kotelett ⓝ kot·*let* chop
Krabbe ⓕ *kra*·be crab
Krakauer ⓜ *krah*·kow·er thick, paprika-spiced sausage of Polish origin
Kraut ⓝ krowt cabbage
　—salat ⓜ *krowt*·za·laht coleslaw
Kräuter ⓝ pl *kroy*·ter herbs
Krebs ⓜ krayps crab • crayfish
Kren ⓜ krayn horseradish
　(Bavaria & Austria)
Krokette ⓕ kro·*ke*·te croquette
Kuchen ⓜ *koo*·khen cake
Kümmel ⓜ *kü*·mel caraway (seeds)
Kürbis ⓜ *kür*·bis pumpkin
Kutteln ⓝ pl *ku*·teln tripe

L

Labskaus ⓜ *laps*·kows thick
　meat & potato stew
Lachs ⓜ laks salmon
　geräucherter Lachs ⓜ ge·*roy*·kher·ter
　laks smoked salmon
Lamm ⓝ lam
　—fleisch ⓝ *lam*·flaish lamb
　—keule ⓕ *lam*·koy·le leg of lamb
Landjäger ⓜ *lant*·yay·ger thin, long,
　hard, spicy sausage
Languste ⓕ lan·*gus*·te crayfish
Lappenpickert ⓜ *la*·pen·pi·kert pan-sized potato pancake usually served
　with jam or salted fish (Westphalia)
Lauch ⓜ lowkh leek
Leber ⓕ *lay*·ber liver
　—käse ⓜ *lay*·ber·kay·ze
　seasoned meatloaf made of minced
　liver, pork & bacon
　—knödel ⓜ *lay*·ber·kner·del liver
　dumpling
　—knödelsuppe ⓕ *lay*·ber·kner·del·
　zu·pe hot broth with liver dumplings
　—wurst ⓕ *lay*·ber·vurst liver sausage
Lebkuchen ⓝ *layp*·koo·khen
　gingerbread
Leckerli ⓝ *le*·ker·lee
　honey-flavoured ginger biscuit

Leipziger Allerlei ⓝ *laip*·tsi·ger a·ler·lai
　mixed vegetable stew (Leipzig)
Lende ⓕ *len*·de loin
Limburger ⓜ *lim*·bur·ger strong cheese
　flavoured with herbs
Linsen ⓕ pl *lin*·zen lentils
　— mit Spätzle mit *shpets*·le lentil
　stew with noodles & sausages
　—suppe ⓕ *lin*·zen·zu·pe lentil soup
Linzer Torte ⓕ *lin*·tser tor·te
　latticed tart with jam topping
Lorbeerblätter ⓝ pl *lor*·bair·ble·ter
　bay leaves
Lübecker Marzipan ⓝ *lü*·be·ker
　mar·tsi·pahn marzipan (Lübeck)
Lucullus-Eier ⓝ pl lu·*ku*·lus·ai·er
　poached, boiled or scrambled eggs
　with goose liver, truffle & other
　garnishes, served with a sauce

M

Mais ⓜ mais sweet corn
Majonäse ⓕ *mai*·yo·nay·ze
　mayonnaise
Makrele ⓕ ma·*kray*·le mackerel
Mandarine ⓕ man·da·*ree*·ne
　mandarine • tangerine
Mandel ⓕ *man*·del almond
Marmelade ⓕ mar·me·*lah*·de jam
Matjes ⓜ *mat*·yes young herring
Maultasche ⓕ *mowl*·ta·she filled pasta
　(Swabia)
Meeresfrüchte ⓝ pl *mair*·res·frükh·te
　seafood
Meerrettich ⓜ *mair*·re·tikh horseradish
Mehl ⓝ mayl flour
Mett ⓜ met lean minced pork
Mettentchen ⓝ *met*·ent·khen beer
　stick
Milch ⓕ milkh milk
　—rahmstrudel ⓜ
　milkh·rahm·shtroo·del strudel filled
　with egg custard & soft cheese
Mohnbrötchen ⓝ *mawn*·brert·khen
　bread roll with poppy seeds
Möhre ⓕ *mer*·re carrot

Muschel ① mu·shel clam • mussel
Muskat ⑩ mus·kaht nutmeg
Müesli ⑩ mü·es·li muesli
Müsli ⑪ müs·li muesli

N

Nelken ① pl nel·ken cloves
Niere ① nee·re kidney
Nockerl ⑪ no·kerl small dumpling (Austria)
Nudeln ① pl noo·deln noodles
Nudelauflauf ⑩ noo·del·owf·lowf pasta casserole
Nürnberger Lebkuchen ⑩ nürn·ber·ger layp·koo·khen cakes with chocolate, nuts, fruit peel, honey & spices

O

Obatzter ⑩ aw·bats·ter Bavarian soft cheese mousse
Obst ⑪ awpst fruit
　　—**salat** ⑩ awpst·za·laht fruit salad
Ochsenschwanz ⑩ ok·sen·shvants oxtail
　　—**suppe** ① ok·sen·shvants·zu·pe oxtail soup
Öl ⑪ erl oil
Orangenmarmelade ① o·rahng·zhen·mar·me·lah·de marmelade

P

Palatschinken ⑩ pa·lat·shing·ken pancake, usually filled with jam or cheese, sometimes served with a hot chocolate & nut topping
Pampelmuse ① pam·pel·moo·ze grapefruit
Paprika ⑩ pap·ri·kah sweet pepper
Pastetchen ⑩ pas·tayt·khen filled puff-pastry case
Pastete ① pas·tay·te pastry • pie
Pellkartoffeln ① pl pel·kar·to·feln small jacket potatoes served in their skins, often served with quark
Petersilie ① pay·ter·zee·li·e parsley
Pfälzer Saumagen ⑩ pfel·tser zow·mah·gen stuffed stomach of pork

Pfannkuchen ⑩ pfan·koo·khen pancake
Pfeffer ⑩ pfe·fer pepper
Pfifferling ⑩ pfi·fer·ling chanterelle mushroom
Pfirsich ⑩ pfir·zikh peach
Pflaume ① pflow·me plum
Pilz ⑩ pilts mushroom
Pichelsteiner ⑩ pi·khel·shtai·ner meat & vegetable stew
Pökelfleisch ⑪ per·kel·flaish marinated meat
Pomeranzensoße ① po·me·ran·tsen·zaw·se sauce made of bitter oranges, wine & brandy, usually served with duck
Pommes Frites pl pom frit French fries
Porree ⑩ por·ray leek
Preiselbeere ① prai·zel·bair·re cranberry
Printe ① prin·te honey-flavoured biscuit
Pumpernickel ⑩ pum·per·ni·kel very dark bread made with coarse wholemeal rye flour
Putenbrust ① poo·ten·brust turkey breast
Puter ⑩ poo·ter turkey

Q

Quargel ⑩ kvar·gel small, round, salty & slightly acidic cheese
Quark ⑩ kvark quark (curd cheese)
Quitte ① kvi·te quince

R

Radieschen ⑪ ra·dees·khen radish
Ragout ⑪ ra·goo stew
Rahm ⑩ rahm cream
Rebhuhn ⑪ rayp·hoon partridge
Regensburger ⑩ ray·gens·bur·ger highly spiced smoked sausage
Reh ⑪ ray venison
　　—**pfeffer** ⑩ ray·pfe·fer jugged venison, fried & braised in its marinade, served with sour cream
　　—**rücken** ⑩ ray·rü·ken saddle of venison

Reibekuchen ⓜ *rai*·be·koo·khen *potato cake*

Reis ⓜ rais *rice*

Remouladensauce ⓕ re·mu·*lah*·den·zaw·se *mayonnaise sauce with mustard, anchovies, capers, gherkins, tarragon & chervil*

Rettich ⓜ re·tikh *radish*

Rhabarber ⓜ ra·*bar*·ber *rhubarb*

Rheinischer Sauerbraten ⓜ **mit Kartoffelklößen** *rai*·ni·sher zow·er·*brah*·ten mit kar·*to*·fel·*kler*·sen *roasted marinated meat, slightly sour, often served with potato dumpling*

Rindfleisch ⓝ rint·flaish *beef*

Rippenspeer ⓜ *ri*·pen·shpair *spare ribs*

Rogen ⓜ *raw*·gen *roe*

Roggenbrot ⓝ ro·gen·brawt *rye bread*

Rohkost ⓕ raw·kost *uncooked vegetables • vegetarian food*

Rollmops ⓜ *rol*·mops *pickled herring fillet rolled around chopped onions or gherkins*

Rosenkohl ⓜ *raw*·zen·kawl *Brussels sprouts*

Rosinen ⓕ pl ro·*zee*·nen *raisins*

Rosmarin ⓜ *raws*·ma·reen *rosemary*

Rost
—**braten** ⓜ rost·brah·ten *roast*
—**brätl** ⓜ rost·braytl *grilled meat*
—**hähnchen** ⓝ rost·hayn·khen *roast chicken*

Rösti pl rers·tee *grated, fried potatoes (Switzerland)*

rot rawt *red*
—**e Beete** ⓕ raw·te bay·te *beetroot*
—**e Grütze** ⓕ raw·te grü·tse *fruit pudding of cooked & sweetened berries, thickened & put in moulds*
—**e Johannisbeere** ⓕ raw·te yo·ha·nis·bair·re *redcurrant*
—**kohl** ⓜ rawt·kawl *red cabbage*
—**e Rüben** ⓕ pl raw·te rü·ben *beetroot*
—**wurst** ⓕ rawt·vurst *black pudding*

Roulade ⓕ ru·*lah*·de *collared beef – thin slices of beef stuffed with onion, bacon and dill pickles then rolled & braised*

Rühreier ⓝ pl *rür*·ai·er *scrambled eggs*

Russische Eier ⓝ pl *ru*·si·she ai·er 'Russian eggs' – eggs with mayonnaise

S

Sahne ⓕ *zah*·ne *cream*

Salat ⓜ za·*laht* *salad*
grüner Salat ⓜ grü·ner za·*laht* *green salad*
italienischer Salat ⓜ i·tal·yay·ni·sher za·*laht* *finely sliced veal, salami, anchovies, tomatoes, cucumber & celery in mayonnaise*

Salbei ⓜ *zal*·bai *sage*

Salz ⓝ zalts *salt*

Salzburger Nockerln ⓝ pl zalts·bur·ger *nö*·kerln *Austrian dessert of sweet dumplings poached in milk & served with warm vanilla sauce*

Salzkartoffeln ⓕ pl zalts·kar·to·feln *boiled potatoes*

Sauerbraten ⓜ zow·er·*brah*·ten *marinated roasted beef served with a sour cream sauce*

Sauerkraut ⓝ zow·er·krowt *pickled cabbage*

Schafskäse ⓜ shahfs·kay·ze *sheep's milk feta*

Schellfisch ⓜ shel·fish *haddock*

Schinken ⓜ shing·ken *ham*
gekochter Schinken ⓜ ge·kokh·ter shing·ken *cooked ham*
geräucherter Schinken ⓜ ge·roy·kher·ter shing·ken *gammon*

Schlachtplatte ⓕ shlakht·pla·te *selection of pork & sausage*

Schmalzbrot ⓝ shmalts·brawt *slice of bread with dripping*

Schmorbraten ⓜ shmawr·brah·ten *beef pot roast*

Schnitte ⓕ shni·te *slice of bread • small square piece of cake*

Schnittlauch ⓜ *shnit·lowkh chives*
Schnitzel ⓝ *shni·tsel pork, veal or chicken breast pounded flat, covered in breadcrumbs & pan-fried*
  Holsteiner Schnitzel ⓝ *hol·shtai·ner shni·tsel veal schnitzel with fried egg, accompanied by seafood*
  Wiener Schnitzel ⓝ *vee·ner shni·tsel crumbed veal*
Scholle ⓕ *sho·le plaice*
schwarze Johannisbeere ⓕ *shvar·tse yo·ha·nis·bair·re blackcurrant*
Schwarzwälder Kirschtorte ⓕ *shvarts·vel·der kirsh·tor·te Black Forest cake (chocolate layer cake filled with cream & cherries)*
Schwein ⓝ *shvain pork*
  —ebraten ⓜ *shvai·ne·brah·ten roast pork*
  —efleisch ⓝ *shvai·ne·flaish pork*
  —shaxe ⓕ *shvains·hak·se crispy leg of pork served with dumplings*
Seezunge ⓕ *zay·tsung·e sole*
Seidfleisch ⓝ *zait·flaish boiled meat*
Sekt ⓜ *zekt German champagne*
Selchfleisch ⓝ *zelkh·flaish smoked pork*
Sellerie ⓜ *ze·le·ree celery*
Semmel ⓕ *ze·mel bread roll (Austria & Bavaria)*
  —knödel ⓜ pl *ze·mel·kner·del dumplings made of dry rolls dunked in milk (Bavaria)*
Senf ⓜ *zenf mustard*
Sonnenblumenkerne ⓜ pl *zo·nen·bloo·men·ker·ne sunflower seeds*
Soße ⓕ *zaw·se sauce • gravy*
  spanische Soße ⓕ *shpah·ni·she zaw·se brown sauce with herbs*
Spanferkel ⓝ *shpahn·fer·kel suckling pig*
Spargel ⓜ *shpar·gel asparagus*
Spätzle pl *shpets·le thick noodles*
Speck ⓜ *shpek bacon*
Spekulatius ⓜ *shpe·ku·lah·tsi·us almond biscuits*

Spiegelei ⓝ *shpee·gel·ai fried egg*
Spinat ⓜ *shpi·naht spinach*
Sprossenkohl ⓜ *shpro·sen·kawl Brussels sprouts*
Sprotten ⓕ pl *shpro·ten sprats (small herring-like fish)*
Steckrübe ⓕ *shtek·rü·be turnip*
Steinbuscher ⓜ *shtain·bu·sher semi-hard, creamy cheese with a strong, slightly bitter flavour*
Steinbutt ⓜ *shtain·but turbot (flatfish)*
Stelze ⓕ *shtel·tse knuckle of pork*
Sterz ⓜ *shterts Austrian polenta*
Stollen ⓜ *shto·len spiced loaf with candied peel, traditionally eaten at Christmas*
Strammer Max ⓜ *shtra·mer maks sandwich with ham (or sausage or spiced minced pork), served with fried eggs & sometimes onions*
Streichkäse ⓜ *shtraikh·kay·ze any kind of soft cheese spread*
Streuselkuchen ⓜ *shtroy·zel·koo·khen coffee cake topped with a mixture of butter, sugar, flour & cinnamon*
Strudel ⓜ *shtroo·del loaf-shaped pastry filled with something sweet or savoury*
Suppe ⓕ *zu·pe soup*

T

Tascherl ⓝ *ta·sherl pastry turnover with meat, cheese or jam filling*
Tatarenbrot ⓝ *ta·tah·ren·brawt open sandwich topped with raw spiced minced beef*
Teigwaren pl *taik·vah·ren pasta*
Thunfisch ⓜ *toon·fish tuna*
Thüringer ⓕ *tü·ring·er long, thin, spiced sausage*
Thymian ⓜ *tü·mi·ahn thyme*
Toast ⓜ *tawst toast*
Tomate ⓕ *to·mah·te tomato*
  —nketchup ⓜ *to·mah·ten·ket·chap tomato sauce*
  —nsuppe ⓕ *to·mah·ten·zu·pe tomato soup*

Topfen ⓜ top·fen curd cheese (Austria)
Törtchen ⓝ tert·khen small tart or cake
Torte ⓕ tor·te layer cake
Truthahn ⓜ troot·hahn turkey
Tunke ⓕ tung·ke sauce • gravy

V

Vollkornbrot ⓝ fol·korn·brawt wholemeal bread
Voressen ⓝ fawr·e·sen meat stew

W

Wachtel ⓕ vakh·tel quail
Walnuss ⓕ val·nus walnut
Wecke ⓕ ve·ke bread roll (Austria & southern Germany)
Weichkäse ⓜ vaikh·kay·ze soft cheese
Weinbergschnecken ⓟ pl vain·berk·shne·ken snails
Weinkraut ⓝ vain·krowt white cabbage, braised with apples & simmered in wine
Weintraube ⓕ vain·trow·be grape
Weißbrot ⓝ vais·brawt white bread
Weißwurst ⓕ vais·vurst veal sausage, found mainly in southern Germany
Westfälischer Schinken ⓜ vest·fay·li·sher shing·ken variety of cured & smoked ham
Wiener vee·ner in the Viennese style
— **Würstchen** ⓝ vee·ner vürst·khen frankfurter (sausage)
— **Schnitzel** ⓝ vee·ner shni·tsel crumbed veal

Wiezenbrot ⓝ vai·tsen·brawt wheat bread
Wild ⓝ vilt game
— **braten** ⓜ vilt·brah·ten roast venison
— **ente** ⓕ vilt·en·te wild duck
— **schwein** ⓝ vilt·shvain wild boar
Wilstermarschkäse ⓜ vils·ter·marsh·kay·ze semi-hard cheese
Wurst ⓕ vurst sausage
Würstchen ⓝ vürst·khen small sausage
Wurstplatte ⓕ vurst·pla·te cold cuts

Z

Ziege ⓕ tsee·ge goat
Zimt ⓜ tsimt cinnamon
Zitrone ⓕ tsi·traw·ne lemon
Zucker ⓜ tsu·ker sugar
Zunge ⓕ tsung·e tongue
Zwetschge ⓕ tsvetsh·ge plum
— **ndatschi** ⓜ tsvetsh·gen·dat·shi damson plum tart
Zwieback ⓜ tsvee·bak rusk
Zwiebel ⓕ tsvee·bel onion
— **fleisch** ⓝ tsvee·bel·flaish beef sauteed with onion
— **kuchen** ⓜ tsvee·bel·koo·khen onion quiche, often served with Federweißer (new wine)
— **suppe** ⓕ tsvee·bel·zu·pe onion soup
— **wurst** ⓕ tsvee·bel·vurst liver & onion sausage
Zwischenrippenstück ⓝ tsvi·shen·ri·pen·shtük rib eye steak

emergencies

notfälle

Help!	*Hilfe!*	*hil·*fe
Stop!	*Halt!*	halt
Go away!	*Gehen Sie weg!*	*gay·*en zee vek
Thief!	*Dieb!*	deeb
Fire!	*Feuer!*	*foy·*er
Watch out!	*Vorsicht!*	for·*zikht*

signs

Unfallstation	un·fal·sta·*tsyawn*	**Casualty**
Polizei	po·li·*tsai*	**Police**
Polizeirevier	po·li·*tsai·*re·veer	**Police Station**

It's an emergency!
Es ist ein Notfall! — es ist ain *nawt·*fal

Call the police!
Rufen Sie die Polizei! — *roo·*fen zee dee po·li·*tsai*

Call a doctor!
Rufen Sie einen Arzt! — *roo·*fen zee *ai·*nen artst

Call an ambulance!
Rufen Sie einen
Krankenwagen! — *roo·*fen zee *ai·*nen
*krang·*ken·vah·gen

I'm ill.
Ich bin krank. — ikh bin krank

My friend is ill.
Mein Freund/Meine — main froynd/*mai·*ne
Freundin ist krank. m/f — *froyn·*din ist krank

Could you please help me/us?
Könnten Sie mir/ — *kern·*ten zee meer/
uns bitte helfen? — uns *bi·*te hel·fen

I have to use the telephone.
Ich muss das Telefon benutzen.
ikh mus das te·le·*fawn* be·*nu*·tsen

I'm lost.
Ich habe mich verirrt.
ikh *hah*·be mikh fer·*irt*

police

Where's the police station?
Wo ist das Polizeirevier?
vaw ist das po·li·*tsai*·re·veer

I want to report an offence.
Ich möchte eine Straftat melden.
ikh *merkh*·te *ai*·ne *shtrahf*·taht *mel*·den

My ... was/ were stolen.	*Man hat mir ... gestohlen.*	man hat meer ... ge·*shtaw*·len
I've lost my...	*Ich habe ... verloren.*	ikh *hah*·be ... fer·*law*·ren
backpack	*meinen Rucksack*	*mai*·nen *ruk*·zak
bags	*meine Reisetaschen*	*mai*·ne *rai*·ze·ta·shen
credit card	*meine Kreditkarte*	*mai*·ne kre·*deet*·karte
handbag	*meine Handtasche*	*mai*·ne *hant*·ta·she
jewellery	*meinen Schmuck*	*mai*·nen shmuk
money	*mein Geld*	main gelt
papers	*meine Papiere*	*mai*·ne pa·*pee*·re
travellers cheques	*meine Reiseschecks*	*mai*·ne *rai*·ze·sheks
passport	*meinen Pass*	*mai*·nen pas
purse	*mein Portemonnaie*	main port·mo·*nay*
wallet	*meine Brieftasche*	*mai*·ne *breef*·ta·she
She/He tried to ... me.	*Sie/Er hat versucht, mich zu ...*	zee/air hat fer·*zookht* mikh tsoo ...
assault	*überfallen*	*an*·ge·gri·fen
rape	*vergewaltigen*	fer·ge·*val*·ti·gen
rob	*bestehlen*	be·*shtay*·len

I've been ...	Ich bin ... worden.	ikh bin ... vor·den
He/She	Er/Sie ist ...	air/zee ist ...
has been ...	worden.	vor·den
assaulted	angegriffen	an·ge·gri·fen
raped	vergewaltigt	fer·ge·val·tikht
robbed	bestohlen	be·shtaw·len

I have insurance.
Ich bin versichert.   ikh bin fer·zi·khert

I apologise.
Entschuldigen Sie bitte.   ent·shul·di·gen zee bi·te

I didn't realise I was doing anything wrong.
Ich war mir nicht bewusst,	ikh vahr meer nikht be·vust
etwas Unrechtes getan	et·vas un·rekh·tes ge·tahn
zu haben.	tsoo hah·ben

I didn't do it.
Das habe ich nicht getan.   das hah·be ikh nikht ge·tahn

I'm innocent.
Ich bin unschuldig.   ikh bin un·shul·dikh

Can I call someone?
| Kann ich jemanden | kan ikh yay·man·den |
| anrufen? | an·roo·fen |

Can I call a lawyer?
| Kann ich einen | kan ikh ai·nen |
| Rechtsanwalt anrufen? | rekhts·an·valt an·roo·fen |

Can I have a lawyer who speaks English?
| Kann ich einen Rechtsanwalt | kan ikh ai·nen rekhts·an·valt |
| haben, der Englisch spricht? | hah·ben dair eng·lish shprikht |

Is there a fine we can pay to clear this?
| Können wir eine Geldbuße | ker·nen veer ai·ne gelt·boo·se |
| dafür bezahlen? | da·für be·tsah·len |

I want to	Ich möchte	ikh merkh·te
contact my ...	mich mit ... in	mikh mit ... in
	Verbindung setzen.	fer·bin·dung ze·tsen
consulate	meinem Konsulat	mai·nem kon·zu·laht
embassy	meiner Botschaft	mai·ner bawt·shatt

This drug is for personal use.

Diese Droge ist für meinen   dee·ze *draw*·ge ist für *mai*·nen
persönlichen Gebrauch.   per·*zern*·li·khen ge·*browkh*

I have a prescription for this drug.

Ich habe ein Rezept für   ikh *hah*·be ain re·*tsept* für
dieses Medikament.   *dee*·zes me·di·ka·*ment*

I (don't) understand.

Ich verstehe (nicht).   ikh fer·*shtay*·e (nikht)

I know my rights.

Ich kenne meine Rechte.   ikh *ke*·ne *mai*·ne *rekh*·te

What am I accused of?

Wessen werde ich   *ve*·sen *ver*·de ikh
beschuldigt?   be·*shul*·dikht

---

the police may say ...

You'll be charged with ...	*Sie werden ... beschuldigt.*	zee *ver*·den ... be·*shul*·dikht
She/He will be charged with ...	*Sie/Er wird ... beschuldigt.*	zee/air virt ... be·*shul*·dikht
assault	*des Überfalls*	des *ü*·ber·fals
possession (of illegal substances)	*des Besitzes (illegaler Substanzen)*	des be·*zi*·tses (*i*·le·gah·ler zup·*stan*·tsen)
not having a visa	*der Einreise ohne Visum*	dair *ain*·rai·ze *aw*·ne vee·zum
overstaying your visa	*der Überschreitung der Gültigkeitsdauer Ihres Visums*	dair *ü*·ber·*shrai*·tung dair *gül*·tikh·kaits·dow·er *ee*·res vee·zums
shoplifting	*des Ladendiebstahls*	des *lah*·den·deep·shtahls
speeding	*der Geschwindigkeitsüberschreitung*	dair ge·*shvin*·dikh·kaits·ü·ber·shrai·tung

Where's the nearest ...?	Wo ist der/die/das nächste ...? m/f/n	vaw ist dair/dee/das naykhs·te ...
chemist	Apotheke f	a·po·tay·ke
dentist	Zahnarzt m	tsahn·artst
doctor	Arzt m	artst
hospital	Krankenhaus n	krang·ken·hows
optometrist	Augenoptiker m	ow·gen·op·ti·ker

I need a doctor (who speaks English).
Ich brauche einen Arzt (der Englisch spricht).
ikh brow·khe ai·nen artst (dair eng·lish shprikht)

Could I see a female doctor?
Könnte ich von einer Ärztin behandelt werden?
kern·te ikh fon ai·ner erts·tin be·han·delt ver·den

Could the doctor come here?
Könnte der Arzt hierher kommen?
kern·te dair artst heer·hair ko·men

Is there a (night) chemist nearby?
Gibt es in der Nähe eine (Nacht)Apotheke?
gipt es in dair nay·e ai·ne (nakht·)a·po·tay·ke

I don't want a blood transfusion.
Ich möchte keine Bluttransfusion.
ikh merkh·te kai·ne bloot·trans·fu·zyawn

Please use a new syringe.
Bitte benutzen Sie eine neue Spritze.
bi·te be·nu·tsen zee ai·ne noy·e shpri·tse

I have my own syringe.
Ich habe meine eigene Spritze.
ikh hah·be mai·ne ai·ge·ne shpri·tse

I've been vaccinated for ...	*Ich bin gegen ... geimpft worden.*	ikh bin *gay*·gen ... ge·*impft vor*·den
He's/She's been vaccinated for ...	*Er/Sie ist gegen ... geimpft worden.*	air/zee ist *gay*·gen ... ge·*impft vor*·den
... fever	*...Fieber*	...*fee*·ber
hepatitis A/B/C	*Hepatitis A/B/C*	he·pa·*tee*·tis ah/bay/tsay
tetanus	*Tätanus*	*tay*·ta·nus
typhoid	*Typhus*	*tü*·fus
I need new ...	*Ich brauche ...*	ikh *brow*·khe ...
contact lenses	*neue Kontaktlinsen*	*noy*·e kon·*takt*·lin·zen
glasses	*eine neue Brille*	*ai*·ne *noy*·e *bri*·le

I've run out of my medication.
Ich habe keine Medikamente mehr. ikh *hah*·be *kai*·ne me·di·ka·*men*·te mair

My prescription is ...
Mein Rezept ist ... main re·*tsept* ist ...

Can I have a receipt for my insurance?
Kann ich eine Quittung für meine Versicherung bekommen? kan ikh *ai*·ne *kvi*·tung für *mai*·ne fer·*zi*·khe·rung be·*ko*·men

the doctor may say ...

What's the problem?
vas faylt *ee*·nen
Was fehlt Ihnen?

Where does it hurt?
vaw toot es vay
Wo tut es weh?

Do you have a temperature?
hah·ben zee *fee*·ber
Haben Sie Fieber?

How long have you been like this?
zait van *hah*·ben zee *dee*·ze be·*shver*·den
Seit wann haben Sie diese Beschwerden?

Have you had this before?
ha·ten zee das
shawn *ain*·mahl
*Hatten Sie das
schon einmal?*

How long are you travelling for?
vee *lang*·e *dow*·ert
ee·re *rai*·ze
*Wie lange dauert
Ihre Reise?*

Are you on medication?
nay·men zee *ir*·gent·vel·khe
me·di·ka·*men*·te
*Nehmen Sie irgendwelche
Medikamente?*

Are you allergic to anything?
zint zee *gay*·gen be·*shtim*·te
shto·fe a·*lair*·gish
*Sind Sie gegen bestimmte
Stoffe allergisch?*

Do you ...?

drink	*tring*·ken zee	*Trinken Sie?*
smoke	*row*·khen zee	*Rauchen Sie?*
take drugs	*nay*·men	*Nehmen*
	zee *draw*·gen	*Sie Drogen?*

Are you sexually active?
zint zee zek·su·el ak·*teef*
Sind Sie sexuell aktiv?

Have you had unprotected sex?
ha·ten zee un·ge·*shüts*·ten
ge·*shlekhts*·fer·kair
*Hatten Sie ungeschützten
Geschlechtsverkehr?*

You need to be admitted to hospital.
zee *mü*·sen in ain
krang·ken·hows
ain·ge·vee·zen ver·den
*Sie müssen in ein
Krankenhaus
eingewiesen werden.*

You should have it checked when you go home.
zee *zol*·ten es tsoo *how*·ze
un·ter·*zoo*·khen *la*·sen
*Sie sollten es zu Hause
untersuchen lassen.*

You should return home for treatment.
zee *zol*·ten nahkh *how*·ze
fah·ren um zikh
be·*han*·deln tsoo *la*·sen
*Sie sollten nach Hause
fahren, um sich
behandeln zu lassen.*

symptoms & conditions

I'm sick.
Ich bin krank. — ikh bin krangk

My friend is sick.
Mein Freund/Meine — main froynt/*mai*·ne
Freundin ist krank. m/f — *froyn*·din ist krangk

It hurts here.
Es tut hier weh. — es toot heer *vay*

I've been vomiting.
Ich habe mich übergeben. — ikh *hah*·be mikh *ü*·ber·*gay*·ben

I can't sleep.
Ich kann nicht schlafen. — ikh kan nikht *shlah*·fen

I feel ...

anxious	*Ich habe Ängste.*	ikh *hah*·be *engs*·te
better	*Ich fühle*	ikh *fü*·le
	mich besser.	mikh *be*·ser
depressed	*Ich bin deprimiert.*	ikh bin de·pri·*meert*
dizzy	*Mir ist*	meer ist
	schwindelig.	*shvin*·de·likh
hot and cold	*Mir ist*	meer ist
	abwechselnd	*ap*·vek·selnt
	heiß und kalt	hais unt kalt
nauseous	*Mir ist übel.*	meer ist *ü*·bel
shivery	*Mich fröstelt.*	mikh *frers*·telt
strange	*Mir ist komisch.*	meer ist *kaw*·mish
weak	*Ich fühle mich*	ikh *fü*·le mikh
	schwach.	shvakh
worse	*Ich fühle mich*	ikh *fü*·le mikh
	schlechter.	*shlekh*·ter

I have (a) ... — *Ich habe ...* — ikh *hah*·be ...

diarrhoea	*Durchfall*	*durkh*·fal
fever	*Fieber*	*fee*·ber
headache	*Kopfschmerzen*	*kopf*·shmer·tsen
pain	*Schmerzen*	*shmer*·tsen

I've noticed a lump here.
Ich habe hier einen   ikh *hah*·be heer *ai*·nen
Knoten bemerkt.   *knaw*·ten be·*merkt*

I've recently had ...
Ich hatte vor kurzem ...   ikh *ha*·te fawr *kur*·tsem ...

He's/She's recently had ...
Er/Sie hatte vor kurzem ...   air/zee *ha*·te fawr *kur*·tsem ...

There's a history of ...
Es gibt eine   es gipt *ai*·ne
Vorgeschichte mit ...   *fawr*·ge·shikh·te mit ...

I'm on medication for ...
Ich nehme   ikh *nay*·me
Medikamente gegen ...   me·di·ka·*men*·te *gay*·gen ...

He's/She's on medication for ...
Er/Sie nimmt   air/zee nimt
Medikamente gegen ...   me·di·ka·*men*·te *gay*·gen ...

asthma	*Asthma* n	*ast*·ma
heart condition	*Herzbeschwerden* f	*herts*·be·shver·den
venereal disease	*Geschlechts-*	ge·*shlekhts*·
	krankheit f	krangk·hait

For more symptoms and conditions, see the **dictionary**.

women's health

gesundheit bei frauen

(I think) I'm pregnant.
(Ich glaube,) Ich bin   (ikh *glow*·be) ikh bin
schwanger.   *shvang*·er

I'm on the Pill.
Ich nehme die Pille.   ikh *nay*·me dee *pi*·le

I haven't had my period for ... weeks.
Ich habe seit ...   ikh *hah*·be zait ...
Wochen meine   *vo*·khen *mai*·ne
Periode nicht   pe·ri·*aw*·de nikht
gehabt.   ge·*hahpt*

Are you using contraception?
be·*nu*·tsen zee
fer·*hü*·tungks·mi·tel — *Benutzen Sie Verhütungsmittel?*

Are you menstruating?
hah·ben zee *ee*·re
pe·ri·*aw*·de — *Haben Sie Ihre Periode?*

Are you pregnant?
zint zee *shvang*·er — *Sind Sie schwanger?*

When did you last have your period?
van *ha*·ten zee
ee·re *lets*·te pe·ri·*aw*·de — *Wann hatten Sie Ihre letzte Periode?*

You're pregnant.
zee zint *shvang*·er — *Sie sind schwanger.*

allergies

allergien

I have a skin allergy.
Ich habe eine Hautallergie.   ikh *hah*·be *ai*·ne howt·a·ler·gee

I'm allergic to ...	*Ich bin allergisch gegen ...*	ikh bin a·*lair*·gish *gay*·gen ...
He/She's allergic to ...	*Er/Sie ist allergisch gegen ...*	air/zee ist a·*lair*·gish *gay*·gen ...
antibiotics	*Antibiotika*	an·ti·bi·*aw*·ti·ka
anti-inflammatories	*entzündungs-hemmende Mittel*	en·*tsün*·dungks-he·men·de *mi*·tel
aspirin	*Aspirin*	as·pi·*reen*
bees	*Bienen*	*bee*·nen
codeine	*Kodein*	ko·de·*een*
penicillin	*Penizillin*	pe·ni·tsi·*leen*
pollen	*Pollen*	*po*·len
inhaler	*Inhalator* m	in·ha·*lah*·tor
injection	*Injektion* f	in·yek·*tsyawn*
antihistamines	*Antihistamine* n pl	an·ti·his·ta·*mee*·ne

For food-related allergies, see **special diets & allergies**, page 161.

parts of the body

My ... hurts.
 *Mir tut der/die/
 das ... weh.* m/f/n
 meer toot dair/dee/
 das ... vay

I can't move my ...
 *Ich kann meinen/meine/
 mein ... nicht bewegen.* m/f/n
 ikh kan *mai*·nen/*mai*·ne/
 main ... nikht be·*vay*·gen

I have a cramp In my ...
 *Ich habe einen Krampf in
 meinem/meiner/
 meinem ...* m/f/n
 ikh *hah*·be *ai*·nen krampf in
 mai·nem/*mai*·ner/
 mai·nem ...

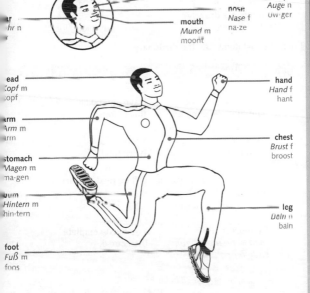

eye
Auge n
ow·ger

nose
Nase f
na·ze

mouth
Mund m
moont

ead
Kopf m
Kopf

arm
Arm m
arm

stomach
Magen m
ma·gen

bum
Hintern m
hin·tern

foot
Fuß m
foos

hand
Hand f
hant

chest
Brust f
broost

leg
Bein n
bain

My ... is swollen.
Mein/Meine/Mein ... ist main/*mai*·ne/main ... ist
geschwollen. m/f/n ge·*shvo*·len

For other body parts, see the **dictionary**.

chemist

die apotheke

I need something for ...
Ich brauche etwas gegen ... ikh *brow*·khe *et*·vas *gay*·gen ...

Do I need a prescription for ...?
Brauche ich für ... ein Rezept? *brow*·khe ikh für ... ain re·*tsept*

How many times a day?
Wie oft am Tag? vee oft am tahk

Will it make me drowsy?
Macht es müde? makht es *mü*·de

For chemist items, see the **dictionary**.

---

listen for ...

hah·ben zee das shawn *ain*·mahl *ain*·ge·no·men
Haben Sie das schon **Have you taken**
einmal eingenommen? **this before?**

tsvai·mahl am tahk (tsum *e*·sen)
Zweimal am Tag **Twice a day**
(zum Essen). **(with food).**

zee *ker*·nen es in (*tsvan*·tsikh mi·*noo*·ten) *ap*·haw·len
Sie können es in (zwanzig **It'll be ready to pick up**
Minuten) abholen. **in (20 minutes).**

zee *mü*·sen dee me·di·ka·*men*·te bis tsum *en*·de
ain·nay·men
Sie müssen die **You must complete**
Medikamente bis zum **the course.**
Ende einnehmen.

dentist

der zahnartz

I have a ...	Ich habe...	ikh *hah*·be ...
broken tooth	einen abgebro-chenen Zahn	*ai*·nen *ap*·ge·bro·khe·nen tsahn
cavity	ein Loch	ain lokh
toothache	Zahnschmerzen	*tsahn*·shmer·tsen

I need ...	Ich brauche ...	ikh *brow*·khe ...
an anaesthetic	eine Betäubung	*ai*·ne be·*toy*·bung
a filling	eine Füllung	*ai*·ne *fü*·lung

listen for ...

bai·sen zee heer drowf
Beißen Sie hier drauf. **Bite down on this.**

be·*vay*·gen zee zikh nikht
Bewegen Sie sich nicht. **Don't move.**

bi·te dayn munt vait *erf*·nen
Bitte den Mund weit öffnen. **Open wide.**

das toot fi·*laikht* ain *bis*·khen vay
Das tut vielleicht **This might hurt a little.**
ein bisschen weh.

das toot gar nikht vay
Das tut gar nicht weh. **This won't hurt a bit.**

ko·men zee tsu·*rük* ikh bin nokh nikht *fer*·tikh
Kommen Sie zurück, **Come back,**
ich bin noch nicht fertig! **I haven't finished!**

shpu·len
Spülen. **Rinse.**

I've lost a filling.
Ich habe eine
Füllung verloren.

ikh *hah*·be ai·ne
fü·lung fer·*law*·ren

My dentures are broken.
Mein Gebiss ist zerbrochen.

main ge·*bis* ist tser·*bro*·khen

My gums hurt.
Das Zahnfleisch
tut mir weh.

das *tsahn*·flaish
toot meer vay

I don't want it extracted.
Ich will ihn nicht
ziehen lassen.

ikh vil een nikht
tsee·en *la*·sen

Ouch!
Au!

ow

SUSTAINABLE TRAVEL

As the climate change debate heats up, the matter of sustainability becomes an important part of the travel vernacular. In practical terms, this means assessing our impact on the environment and local cultures and economies – and acting to make that impact as positive as possible. Here are some basic phrases to get you on your way …

communication & cultural differences

I'd like to learn some words and phrases from the local dialect.
Ich möchte ein paar Wörter und Ausdrücke aus dem lokalen Dialekt lernen.
ikh *merkh*·te ain pahr ver·ter unt ows·drü·ke ows daym law·kah·len dee·a·*lekt* lair·nen

Would you like me to teach you some English?
Möchten Sie, dass ich Ihnen ein bisschen Englisch beibringe?
merkh·ten zee das ikh ee·nen ain *bis*·khen *eng*·lish *bai*·bring·e

Is this a local or national custom?
Ist dies ein lokaler oder landesweiter Brauch?
ist dees ain lo·*kah*·ler aw·der lan·des·vai·ter browkh

I respect your customs.
Ich respektiere Ihre Bräuche.
ikh res·pek·*tee*·re ee·re broy·khe

community benefit & involvement

What sorts of issues is this community facing?
Welche Probleme gibt es hier?
vel·khe pro·*blay*·me gipt es heer

aging population	*Überalterung* f	*ü·ber·al·te·rung*
climate change	*Klimawandel* m	*klee·ma·van·del*

globalisation	*Globalisierung* f	glaw·bah·li·zee·rung
integration of immigrants	*Integration von Einwanderern* f	in·tay·gra·tsyawn fon ain·van·de·rern
racism	*Rassismus* m	ra·sis·mus
unemployment	*Arbeitslosigkeit* f	ar·baits·law·zikh·kait

I'd like to volunteer my skills.
Ich möchte meine Mitarbeit als Freiwilliger anbieten.
ikh *merkh*·te *mai*·ne *mit*·ar·bait als *frai*·vi·li·ger *an*·bee·ten

Are there any volunteer programs available in the area?
Gibt es hier in der Region irgendwelche Freiwilligenprogramme?
gipt es heer in dair re·*gyawn* *ir*·gent·vel·khe *frai*·vi·li·gen·pro·gra·me

environment

Where can I recycle this?
Wo kann ich das recyceln?
vaw kan ikh das ri·*sai*·keln

transport

Can we get there by public transport?
Können wir mit öffentlichen Verkehrsmitteln dahin kommen?
ker·nen veer mit *er*·fent·li·khen fair·*kairs*·mi·teln dah·*hin* ko·men

Can we get there by bike?
Können wir mit dem Fahrrad dahin kommen?
ker·nen veer mit daym *fah*·raht dah·*hin* ko·men

I'd prefer to walk there.
Ich gehe lieber zu Fuß dahin.
ikh *gay*·e *lee*·ber tsoo foos dah·*hin*

accommodation

Are there any eco-hotels here?
Gibt es hier irgendwelche Öko-Hotels?
gipt es heer *ir*·gent·vel·khe *er*·kaw·ho·tels

I'd like to stay at a locally-run hotel.

Ich möchte in einem Hotel ikh *merkh*·te in *ai*·nem ho·*tel*
übernachten, das ü·ber·*nakh*·ten das
Einheimischen gehört. *ain*·hai·mi·shen ge·*hert*

Can I turn the air conditioning off and open the window?

Kann ich die Klimaanlage kan ikh dee *klee*·ma·an·lah·ge
ausschalten und das *ows*·shal·ten unt das
Fenster öffnen? *fens*·ter erf·nen

There's no need to change my sheets/towels.

Sie brauchen meine zee *brow*·khen *mai*·ne
Bettwäsche/Handtücher *bet*·ve·she/*han*·tü·kher
nicht zu wechseln. nikht tsoo *ve*·kseln

shopping

Where can I buy locally produced goods/souvenirs?

Wo kann ich örtlich vaw kan ikh *ert*·likh
produzierte Waren/ pro·du·*tseer*·te *vah*·ren/
Andenken kaufen? *an*·deng·ken *kow*·fen

Do you sell Fair Trade products?

Verkaufen Sie Produkte fer·*kow*·fen zee pro·*duk*·te
aus fairem Handel? ows *fair*·rem *han*·del

food

Can you tell me which traditional foods I should try?

Können Sie mir sagen, *ker*·nen zee meer *zah*·gen
welche traditionellen *vel*·khe tra·di·tsyo·*ne*·len
Speisen ich probieren sollte? *shpai*·zen ikh pro·*bee*·ren *zol*·te

Do you sell ...?	Verkaufen Sie ...?	fer·*kow*·fen zee ...
locally produced food	*örtlich produzierte Lebensmittel*	*ert*·likh pro·du·*tseer*·te *lay*·bens·mi·tel
organic produce	*Bioprodukte*	*bee*·o·pro·*duk*·te

sightseeing

Does your company hire local guides?
Beschäftigt Ihre Firma be·*shef*·tikht ee·re *fir*·ma
Führer von hier? *fü*·rer fon heer

Does your company donate money to charity?
Spendet Ihre Firma Geld *shpen*·det ee·re *fir*·ma gelt
für wohltätige Zwecke? für *vawl*·tay·ti·ge *tsve*·ke

Does your company visit local businesses?
Besucht Ihre Firma be·*zookht* ee·re *fir*·ma
örtliche Betriebe? *ert*·li·khe be·*tree*·be

Are cultural tours available?
Gibt es Kulturtouren? gipt es kul·*toor*·too·ren

Does the guide speak the local dialect?
Spricht der Führer den shprikht dair *fü*·rer dayn
örtlichen Dialekt? *ert*·li·khen dee·a·*lekt*

Bavarian	*Bairisch* n	*bai*·rish
Low German	*Plattdeutsch* n	*plat*·doytsh
Saxonian	*Sächsisch* n	ze·ksish
Swabian	*Schwäbisch* n	*shvay*·bish
Swiss German	*Schwyzerdütsch* n	*shvee*·tser·dütsh

Nouns in the dictionary, and adjectives affected by gender, have their gender indicated by ⓕ, ⓜ or ⓝ. If it's a plural noun, you'll also see pl. Where a word that could be either a noun or a verb has no gender indicated, it's a verb.

A

(to be) able *können* ker·nen
aboard *an Bord* an bort
abortion *Abtreibung* ⓕ ap·trai·bung
about *über* ü·ber
above *über* ü·ber
abroad *im Ausland* im ows·lant
accident *Unfall* ⓜ un·fal
accommodation *Unterkunft* ⓕ un·ter·kunft
accountant *Buchhalter(in)* ⓜ/ⓕ bookh·hal·ter/bookh·hal·te·rin
across (from) *gegenüber* gay·gen·ü·ber
across (to) *hinüber* hi·nü·ber
activist *Aktivist(in)* ⓜ/ⓕ ak·ti·vist/ak·ti·vis·tin
actor *Schauspieler(in)* ⓜ/ⓕ show·shpee·ler/show·shpee·le·rin
acupuncture *Akupunktur* ⓕ a·ku·pungk·toor
adaptor *Adapter* ⓜ a·dap·ter
addicted *abhängig* ap·heng·ikh
address *Adresse* ⓕ a·dre·se
administration *Verwaltung* ⓕ fer·val·tung
admire *bewundern* be·vun·dern
admission price *Eintrittspreis* ⓜ ain·trits·prais
admit (allow to enter) *einlassen* ain·la·sen
admit (accept as true) *zugeben* tsoo·gay·ben
adult *Erwachsene* ⓜ&ⓕ er·vak·se·ne
advertisement *Anzeige* ⓕ an·tsai·ge
advice *Rat* ⓜ raht
advise *raten* rah·ten
aerobics *Aerobics* pl e·ro·biks
aerogram *Aerogramm* ⓝ air·ro·gram
aeroplane *Flugzeug* ⓝ flook·tsoyk
(to be) afraid *Angst (haben)* angkst (hah·ben)
Africa *Afrika* ⓝ a·fri·kah

after *nach* nahkh
(this) afternoon *(heute) Nachmittag* ⓜ (hoy·te) nahkh·mi·tahk
aftershave *Aftershave* ⓝ ahf·ter·shayf
again *wieder* vee·der
against *gegen* gay·gen
age *Alter* ⓝ al·ter
(three days) ago *vor (drei Tagen)* fawr (drai tah·gen)
agree *zustimmen* tsoo·shti·men
agriculture *Landwirtschaft* ⓕ lant·virt·shaft
ahead *vor uns* fawr uns
AIDS *AIDS* ⓝ aydz
air *Luft* ⓕ luft
airmail *Luftpost* ⓕ luft·post
air pollution *Luftverschmutzung* ⓕ luft·fer·shmu·tsung
air-conditioned *mit Klimaanlage* ⓕ mit klee·ma·an·lah·ge
airline *Fluglinie* ⓕ flook·lee·ni·e
airplane *Flugzeug* ⓝ flook·tsoyk
airport *Flughafen* ⓜ flook·hah·fen
airport tax *Flughafengebühr* ⓕ flook·hah·fen·ge·bür
airsickness *Luftkrankheit* ⓕ luft·krangk·hait
aisle *Gang* ⓜ gang
aisle seat *Platz am Gang* ⓜ plats am gang
alarm clock *Wecker* ⓜ ve·ker
alcohol *Alkohol* ⓜ al·ko·hawl
alcoholic *Alkoholiker(in)* ⓜ/ⓕ al·ko·haw·li·ker/al·ko·haw·li·ke·rin
alcoholic *alkoholisch* al·ko·haw·lish
all *alle* a·le
allergy *Allergie* ⓕ a·lair·gee
allow *erlauben* er·low·ben
almond *Mandel* ⓕ man·del
almost *fast* fast
alone *allein* a·lain
already *schon* shawn
also *auch* owkh

altar *Altar* ⓜ al·tahr
altitude *Höhe* ⓕ her·e
always *immer* i·mer
amateur *Amateur(in)* ⓜ/ⓕ
a·ma·ter/a·ma·ter·rin
amazing *erstaunlich* er·shtown·likh
ambassador *Botschafter(in)* ⓜ/ⓕ
bawt·shaf·ter/bawt·shaf·te·rin
ambulance *Krankenwagen* ⓜ
krang·ken·vah·gen
among *unter* un·ter
amount *Betrag* ⓜ be·trahk
anaesthetic *Betäubung* ⓕ be·toy·bung
anarchist *Anarchist(in)* ⓜ/ⓕ
a·nar·khist/a·nar·khis·tin
ancient *alt* alt
and *und* unt
angry *wütend* vü·tent
animal *Tier* ⓝ teer
ankle *Knöchel* ⓜ kner·khel
answer *Antwort* ⓕ ant·vort
answer *antworten* ant·vor·ten
ant *Ameise* ⓕ ah·mai·ze
antibiotics *Antibiotika* ⓝ pl
an·ti·bi·aw·ti·ka
antinuclear *Anti-Atom-* an·ti·a·tawm·
antique *Antiquität* ⓕ an·ti·kvi·tayt
antiseptic *Antiseptikum* ⓝ
an·ti·zep·ti·kum
any *irgendein* ir·gent·ain
anything *(irgend)etwas* (ir·gent·)et·vas
anywhere *irgendwo* ir·gent·vaw
apart from (besides) *außer* ow·ser
apartment *Wohnung* ⓕ vaw·nung
appendix *Blinddarm* ⓜ blint·darm
apple *Apfel* ⓜ ap·fel
appointment *Termin* ⓜ ter·meen
apprentice *Auszubildende* ⓜ&ⓕ
ows·tsu·bil·den·de
approximately *ungefähr* un·ge·fair
apricot *Aprikose* ⓕ a·pri·kaw·ze
archaeological *archäologisch*
ar·khe·o·law·gish
architecture *Architektur* ⓕ
ar·khi·tek·toor
area code *Vorwahl* ⓕ fawr·vahl
argue *streiten* shtrai·ten
arm *Arm* ⓜ arm
arrest *Verhaftung* ⓕ fer·haf·tung

arrivals *Ankunft* ⓕ an·kunft
arrive *ankommen* an·ko·men
art *Kunst* ⓕ kunst
art collection *Kunstsammlung* ⓕ
kunst·zam·lung
art gallery *Kunstgalerie* ⓕ
kunst·ga·le·ree
artist *Künstler(in)* ⓜ/ⓕ
künst·ler/künst·le·rin
arts & crafts *Kunstgewerbe* ⓝ
kunst·ge·ver·be
as far as *bis zu* bis tsoo
ashtray *Aschenbecher* ⓜ
a·shen·be·kher
Asia *Asien* ⓝ ah·zi·en
ask a question *eine Frage stellen*
ai·ne frah·ge shte·len
ask (for something) *um etwas bitten*
um et·vas bi·ten
asleep *schlafen* shlah·fen
asparagus *Spargel* ⓜ shpar·gel
aspirin *Kopfschmerztablette* ⓕ
kopf·shmerts·ta·ble·te
asthma *Asthma* ⓝ ast·ma
asylum seeker *Asylant(in)* ⓜ/ⓕ
a·zü·lant/a·zü·lan·tin
at *in • an • auf • bei • zu*
in • an • owf • bai • tsoo
athletics *Leichtathletik* ⓕ
laikht·at·lay·tik
atmosphere *Atmosphäre* ⓕ
at·mos·fair·re
attic *Dachboden* ⓜ dakh·baw·den
aubergine *Aubergine* ⓕ
aw·ber·zhee·ne
aunt *Tante* ⓕ tan·te
Australia *Australien* ⓝ ows·trah·li·en
Austria *Österreich* ⓝ ers·ter·raikh
author *Autor(in)* ⓜ/ⓕ
ow·tor/ow·taw·rin
automatic *automatisch* ow·to·mah·tish
automatic teller machine (ATM)
Geldautomat ⓜ gelt·ow·to·maht
autumn *Herbst* ⓜ herpst
avalanche *Lawine* ⓕ la·vee·ne
avenue *Allee* ⓕ a·lay
avocado *Avokado* ⓝ a·vo·kah·do
axe *Axt* ⓕ akst

baby *Baby* ⑩ *bay*·bi
baby food *Babynahrung* ①
 bay·bi·nah·rung
baby powder *Babypuder* ⑩
 bay·bi·poo·der
babysitter *Babysitter* ⑩ *bay*·bi·si·ter
back (body) *Rücken* ⑩ *rü*·ken
back (return) *zurück* tsu·*rük*
backpack *Rucksack* ⑩ *ruk*·zak
bacon *Frühstücksspeck* ⑩
 frü·shtüks·shpek
bad *schlecht* shlekht
badger *Dachs* ⑩ daks
bag *Tasche* ① *ta*·she
baggage *Gepäck* ⑩ ge·*pek*
baggage allowance *Freigepäck* ⑩
 frai·ge·pek
baggage claim *Gepäckausgabe* ①
 ge·*pek*·ows·gah·be
bait *Köder* ⑩ *ker*·der
bakery *Bäckerei* ① be·ke·*rai*
balance (account) *Kontostand* ⑩
 kon·to·shtant
balcony *Balkon* ⑩ bal·*kawn*
ball *Ball* ⑩ bal
ballet *Ballett* ⑩ ba·*let*
banana *Banane* ① ba·*nah*·ne
band (music) *Band* ① bent
bandage *Verband* ⑩ fer·*bant*
Band-aids *Pflaster* ⑩ *pflas*·ter
bank *Bank* ① bangk
bank account *Bankkonto* ⑩
 bangk·kon·to
bankdraft *Bankauszug* ⑩
 bangk·ows·tsook
banknote *Geldschein* ⑩ *gelt*·shain
baptism *Taufe* ① *tow*·fe
bar *Lokal* ⑩ lo·*kahl*
baseball *Baseball* ⑩ *bays*·bawl
basket *Korb* ⑩ korp
bath *Bad* ⑩ baht
bath towel *Badetuch* ⑩ *bah*·de·lookh
bathing suit *Badeanzug* ⑩
 bah·de·an·tsook
bathroom *Badezimmer* ⑩
 bah·de·tsi·mer

battery *Batterie* ① ba·te·*ree*
bay *Bucht* ① bukht
be *sein* zain
beach *Strand* ⑩ shtrant
bean *Bohne* ① *baw*·ne
bear *Bär* ⑩ bair
beautiful *schön* shern
beauty salon *Schönheitssalon* ⑩
 shern·haits·za·long
because *weil* vail
because of *wegen* *vay*·gen
bed *Bett* ⑩ bet
bed & breakfast *Pension* ①
 pahng·*zyawn*
bedding *Bettzeug* ⑩ *bet*·tsoyk
bedroom *Schlafzimmer* ⑩
 shlahf·tsi·mer
bee *Biene* ① *bee*·ne
beef *Rindfleisch* ⑩ *rint*·flaish
beer *Bier* ⑩ beer
beetroot *rote Bete* ① *raw*·te *bay*·te
before *vor* fawr
beggar *Bettler(in)* ⑩/① *bet*·ler/*bet*·le·rin
begin *beginnen* be·*gi*·nen
behind *hinter* *hin*·ter
below *unter* *un*·ter
belt *Gürtel* ⑩ *gür*·tel
beside *neben* *nay*·ben
best *beste* *bes*·te
bet *Wette* ① *ve*·te
better *besser* *be*·ser
between *zwischen* *tsvi*·shen
bible *Bibel* ① *bee*·bel
bicycle *Fahrrad* ⑩ *fahr*·raht
big *groß* graws
bike *Fahrrad* ⑩ *fahr*·raht
bike chain *Fahrradkette* ①
 fahr·raht·ke·te
bike path *Radweg* ⑩ *raht*·vayk
bill (account) *Rechnung* ① *rekh*·nung
bin (rubbish) *Mülleimer* ⑩ *mül*·ai·mer
binoculars *Fernglas* ⑩ *fern*·glahs
bird *Vogel* ⑩ *faw*·gel
birth certificate *Geburtsurkunde* ①
 ge·*burts*·oor·kun·de
birthday *Geburtstag* ⑩ ge·*burts*·tahk
biscuit *Keks* ⑩ kayks
bite (dog) *Biss* ⑩ bis
bite (insect) *Stich* ⑩ shtikh

bitter *bitter* bi·ter
black *schwarz* shvarts
B&W (film) *schwarzweiß* shvarts·vais
blanket *Decke* ① de·ke
bless *segnen* zayg·nen
blind *blind* blint
blister *Blase* ① blah·ze
blocked *blockiert* blo·keert
blood *Blut* ① bloot
blood group *Blutgruppe* ①
 bloot·gru·pe
blood pressure *Blutdruck* ⑩ bloot·druk
blood test *Bluttest* ⑩ bloot·test
blue *blau* blow
boar *Wildschwein* ⑩ vilt·shvain
board *Brett* ⑩ bret
board (plane, ship) *besteigen*
 be·shtai·gen
boarding house *Pension* ①
 pahng·zyawn
boarding pass *Bordkarte* ① bort·kar·te
boat *Boot* ⑩ bawt
body *Körper* ⑩ ker·per
bone *Knochen* ⑩ kno·khen
book *Buch* ① bookh
book (reserve) *buchen* boo·khen
booked out *ausgebucht* ows·ge·bookht
bookshop *Buchhandlung* ①
 bookh·hand·lung
boot (trunk) *Kofferraum* ⑩ ko·fer·rowm
boot (footwear) *Stiefel* ⑩ shtee·fel
border *Grenze* ① gren·tse
bored *gelangweilt* ge·lang·vailt
boring *langweilig* lang·vai·likh
borrow *(aus)leihen* (ows·)lai·en
boss *Chef(in)* ⑩/① shef/she·fin
botanic garden *Botanischer Garten* ⑩
 bo·tah·ni·sher gar·ten
both *beide* bai·de
bottle *Flasche* ① fla·she
bottle opener *Flaschenöffner* ⑩
 fla·shen·erf·ner
at the bottom *unten* un·ten
bouncer (doorman) *Türsteher* ⑩
 tür·shtay·er
bowl *Schüssel* ① shü·sel
box *Karton* ⑩ kar·tong
boxer shorts *Shorts* pl shorts
boxing *Boxen* ⑩ bok·sen

boy *Junge* ⑩ yung·e
boyfriend *Freund* ⑩ froynt
bra *BH* ⑩ bay·hah
Braille *Blindenschrift* ① blin·den·shrift
brake fluid *Bremsflüssigkeit* ①
 brems·flü·sikh·kait
brakes *Bremsen* ① pl brem·zen
brandy *Weinbrand* ⑩ vain·brant
brave *mutig* moo·tikh
bread *Brot* ⑩ brawt
bread roll *Brötchen* ⑩ brert·khen
break *(zer)brechen* (tser·)bre·khen
break down *eine Panne haben* ai·ne
 pa·ne hah·ben
breakdown service *Abschleppdienst* ⑩
 ap·shlep·deenst
breakfast *Frühstück* ⑩ frü·shtük
breast *Brust* ① brust
breathe *atmen* aht·men
bribe *bestechen* be·shte·khen
bricklayer *Maurer(in)* ⑩/①
 mow·rer/mow·re·rin
bridge *Brücke* ① brü·ke
bridle path *Reitweg* ⑩ rait·vayk
briefcase *Aktentasche* ① ak·ten·ta·she
brilliant *brillant* bril·yant
bring *bringen* bring·en
broccoli *Brokkoli* ⑩ pl bro·ko·li
brochure *Broschüre* ① bro·shü·re
broken *kaputt* ka·put
bronchitis *Bronchitis* ① bron·khee·tis
brother *Bruder* ⑩ broo·der
brown *braun* brown
bruise *Schramme* ① shra·me
Brussels sprouts *Rosenkohl* ⑩
 raw·zen·kawl
bucket *Eimer* ⑩ ai·mer
Buddhist *Buddhist(in)* ⑩/①
 bu·dist/bu·dis·tin
buffet *Buffet* ⑩ bü·fay
bug (animal) *Insekt* ⑩ in·zekt
build *bauen* bow·en
building *Gebäude* ⑩ ge·boy·de
bumbag *Hüfttasche* ① hüft·ta·she
burn *(ver)brennen* (fer·)bre·nen
bus (city) *Bus* ⑩ bus
bus (intercity) *Fernbus* ⑩ fern·bus
bus station *Busbahnhof* ⑩
 bus·bahn·hawf
bus stop *Bushaltestelle* ①
 bus·hal·te·shte·le

business *Geschäft* ⑩ ge·*sheft*
business class *Business Class* ①
  bi·zi·nes klahs
business person *Geschäftsmann/*
  Geschäftsfrau ⑩/①
  ge·*shefts*·man/ge·*shefts*·frow
business trip *Geschäftsreise* ①
  ge·*shefts*·rai·ze
busker *Straßenmusiker(in)* ⑩/①
  shtrah·sen·moo·zi·ker/
  shtrah·sen·moo·zi·ke·rin
busy (person) *beschäftigt* be·*shef*·tikht
busy (phone) *besetzt* be·*zetst*
but *aber* ah·ber
butcher's shop *Metzgerei* ①
  mets·ge·*rai*
butter *Butter* ① *bu*·ter
butterfly *Schmetterling* ⑩ *shme*·ter·ling
button *Knopf* ⑩ knopf
buy *kaufen* kow·ten

C

cabbage *Kohl* ⑩ kawl
cable *Kabel* ⑩ *kah*·bel
cable car *Seilbahn* ① *zail*·bahn
cafe *Café* ⑩ ka·*fay*
cake *Kuchen* ⑩ *koo*·khen
cake shop *Konditorei* ① kon·dee·to·*rai*
calculator *Taschenrechner* ⑩
  ta·shen·rekh·ner
calendar *Kalender* ⑩ ka·*len*·der
camera *Kamera* ① *ka*·me·ra
camp *zelten* *tsel*·ten
camping ground *Campingplatz* ⑩
  kem·ping·plats
camping stove *Kocher* ⑩ *ko*·kher
camp site *Zeltplatz* ⑩ *tselt*·plats
can (be able) *können* *ker*·nen
can (have permission) *können* *ker*·nen
can (tin) *Dose* ① *daw*·ze
can opener *Dosenöffner* ⑩
  daw·zen·erf·ner
Canada *Kanada* ⑩ *ka*·na·dah
canary *Kanarienvogel* ⑩
  ka·*nah*·ri·en·faw·gel
cancel *stornieren* shtor·*nee*·ren
cancer *Krebs* ⑩ krayps
candle *Kerze* ① *ker*·tse

candy *Bonbon* ⑩ bong·*bong*
cantaloupe *Beutelmelone* ①
  boy·tel·me·law·ne
canteen *Kantine* ① kan·*tee*·ne
cape (offshore) *Kap* ⑩ kap
capitalism *Kapitalismus* ⑩
  ka·pi·ta·*lis*·mus
capsicum *Paprika* ① *pap*·ri·kah
car *Auto* ⑩ *ow*·to
car hire *Autoverleih* ⑩ *ow*·to·fer·lai
car owner's title (document)
  Fahrzeugpapiere ⑪ pl
  fahr·tsoyk·pa·pee·re
car registration *(PKW-)Zulassung* ①
  (pay·kah·vay·)tsoo·la·sung
caravan *Wohnwagen* ⑩ *vawn*·vah·gen
carburettor *Vergaser* ⑩ fer·*gah*·zer
cards *Karten* ① pl *kar*·ten
care (for someone) *sich kümmern um*
  zikh *kü*·mern um
careful *vorsichtig* fawr·zikh·tikh
caring *liebevoll* *lee*·be·fol
carpark *Parkplatz* ⑩ *park*·plats
carpenter *Schreiner(in)* ⑩/①
  shrai·ner/*shrai*·ne·rin
carriage (train) *Wagen* ⑩ *vah*·gen
carrot *Mohrrübe* ① *mawr*·rü·be
carry *tragen* *trah*·gen
carton *Karton* ⑩ kar·*tong*
carton (milk) *Tüte* ① *tü*·te
cash *Bargeld* ⑩ *bahr*·gelt
cash (a cheque) *(einen Scheck)*
  einlösen (ai·nen shek) *ain*·ler·zen
cash register *Kasse* ① *ka*·se
cashew *Cashewnuss* ① *kesh*·yoo·nus
cashier *Kassierer(in)* ⑩/① ka·*see*·rer/
  ka·*see*·re·rin
casino *Kasino* ⑩ ka·*zee*·no
cassette *Kassette* ① ka·*se*·te
castle *Burg* ① burk
casual work *Gelegenheitsarbeit* ①
  ge·*lay*·gen·haits·ar·bait
cat *Katze* ① *ka*·tse
cathedral *Dom* ⑩ dawm
Catholic *Katholik(in)* ⑩/①
  ka·to·*leek*/ka·to·*lee*·kin
cauliflower *Blumenkohl* ⑩
  bloo·men·kawl
cave *Höhle* ① *her*·le

caviar *Kaviar* ⓜ kah·vi·ahr
CD *CD* ① tsay·day
celebration *Feier* ① fai·er
cellar *Keller* ⓜ ke·ler
cemetery *Friedhof* ⓜ freet·hawf
centigrade *Celsius* ⓜ tsel·zi·us
centimetre *Zentimeter* ⓜ
  tsen·ti·may·ter
central heating *Zentralheizung* ①
  tsen·*trahl*·hai·tsung
centre *Zentrum* ⓝ tsen·trum
ceramic *Keramik* ① ke·*rah*·mik
cereal *Frühstücksflocke* ①
  frü·shtüks·flo·ke
certificate *Zertifikat* ⓝ tser·ti·fi·*kaht*
chain *Kette* ① ke·te
chair *Stuhl* ⓜ shtool
chairlift (skiing) *Sessellift* ⓜ ze·se·lift
championships *Meisterschaften* ① pl
  mais·ter·shaf·ten
chance *Zufall* ⓜ *tsoo*·fal
change (coins) *Wechselgeld* ⓝ
  vek·sel·gelt
change (money) *wechseln* vek·seln
change (trains) *umsteigen* um·shtai·gen
changing room *Umkleideraum* ⓜ
  um·klai·de·rowm
chapel *Kapelle* ① ka·pe·le
charming *charmant* shar·mant
chat up *anbaggern* an·ba·gern
cheap *billig* bi·likh
cheat *Betrüger(in)* ⓜ/①
  be·trü·ger/be·trü·ge·rin
check (banking) *Scheck* ⓜ shek
check (bill) *Rechnung* ① rekh·nung
check *prüfen* prü·fen
check-in (desk) *Abfertigungsschalter* ⓜ
  ap·fer·ti·gungks·shal·ter
checkpoint *Kontrollstelle* ①
  kon·trol·shte·le
cheese *Käse* ⓜ kay·ze
chef *Koch/Köchin* ⓜ/① kokh/ker·khin
chemist *Apotheke* ① a·po·tay·ke
cheque (banking) *Scheck* ⓜ shek
chess *Schach* ⓝ shakh
chest *Brustkorb* ⓜ brust·korp
chewing gum *Kaugummi* ⓝ kow·gu·mi
chicken *Huhn* ⓝ hoon
chicken breast *Hühnerbrust* ①
  hü·ner·brust

chicken drumstick *Hähnchenschenkel* ⓜ
  hayn·khen·sheng·kel
chickpea *Kichererbse* ① ki·kher·erp·se
child *Kind* ⓝ kint
child seat *Kindersitz* ⓜ kin·der·zits
childminding *Kinderbetreuung* ①
  kin·der·be·troy·ung
children *Kinder* ⓝ pl kin·der
chilli *Chili* ① chi·li
chocolate *Schokolade* ① sho·ko·*lah*·de
choose *(aus)wählen* (ows)*vay·len
christening *Taufe* ① tow·fe
Christian *Christ(in)* ⓜ/① krist/*kris*·tin
Christian name *Vorname* ⓜ
  fawr·nah·me
Christmas *Weihnachten* ⓝ
  vai·nakh·ten
Christmas Day *(erster)*
  Weihnachtsfeiertag ⓜ (ers·ter)
  vai·nakhts·fai·er·tahk
Christmas Eve *Heiligabend* ⓜ
  hai·likh·*ah*·bent
Christmas tree *Weihnachtsbaum* ⓜ
  vai·nakhts·bowm
church *Kirche* ① kir·khe
cider *Apfelmost* ⓜ ap·fel·most
cigar *Zigarre* ① tsi·ga·re
cigarette *Zigarette* ① tsi·ga·re·te
cigarette lighter *Feuerzeug* ⓝ
  foy·er·tsoyk
cinema *Kino* ⓝ kee·no
circus *Zirkus* ⓜ tsir·kus
citizenship *Staatsbürgerschaft* ①
  shtahts·bür·ger·shaft
city *Stadt* ① shtat
city centre *Innenstadt* ① i·nen·shtat
civil rights *Bürgerrechte* ⓝ pl
  bür·ger·rekh·te
civil servant *Beamte/Beamtin* ⓜ/①
  be·am·te/be·am·tin
class *Klasse* ① kla·se
classical *klassisch* kla·sish
clean *sauber* zow·ber
cleaning *Reinigung* ① rai·ni·gung
client *Kunde/Kundin* ⓜ/①
  kun·de/kun·din
cliff *Klippe* ① kli·pe
climate *Klima* ⓝ klee·ma
climb *klettern* kle·tern

cloak *Mantel* ⓜ man·tel
cloakroom *Garderobe* ⓕ gar·draw·be
clock *Uhr* ⓕ oor
close (shut) *schließen* shlee·sen
close (nearby) *nahe* nah·e
closed *geschlossen* ge·shlo·sen
clothesline *Wäscheleine* ⓕ
ve·she·lai·ne
clothing *Kleidung* ⓕ klai·dung
clothing store *Bekleidungsgeschäft* ⓝ
be·klai·dungks·ge·sheft
cloud *Wolke* ⓕ vol·ke
cloudy *wolkig* vol·kikh
clove (spice) *Gewürznelke* ⓕ
ge·vürts·nel·ke
clove (of garlic) *Zehe* ⓕ tsay·e
clutch (car) *Kupplung* ⓕ kup·lung
coach (bus) *Bus* ⓜ bus
coach (sport) *Trainer(in)* ⓜ/ⓕ
tray·ner/tray·ne·rin
coast *Küste* ⓕ küs·te
coat *Mantel* ⓜ man·tel
cocaine *Kokain* ⓝ ko·ka·een
cockroach *Kakerlake* ⓕ kah·ker·lah·ke
cocoa *Kakao* ⓝ ka·kow
coffee *Kaffee* ⓜ ka·fay
coins *Münzen* ⓕ pl mün·tsen
cold *kalt* kalt
have a cold *erkältet sein* er·kel·tet zain
colleague *Kollege/Kollegin* ⓜ/ⓕ
ko·lay·ge/ko·lay·gin
collect call *R-Gespräch* ⓝ
air·ge·shpraykh
college *College* ⓝ ko·lidzh
colour *Farbe* ⓕ far·be
comb *Kamm* ⓜ kam
come *kommen* ko·men
comedy *Komödie* ⓕ ko·mer·di·e
comfortable *bequem* be·kvaym
communion *Kommunion* ⓕ
ko·mun·yawn
companion *Begleiter(in)* ⓜ/ⓕ
be·glai·ter/be·glai·te·rin
company *Firma* ⓕ fir·ma
compass *Kompass* ⓜ kom·pas
complain *sich beschweren* zikh
be·shvair·ren
computer *Computer* ⓜ kom·pyoo·ter
computer game *Computerspiel* ⓝ
kom·pyoo·ter·shpeel

concert *Konzert* ⓝ kon·tsert
concert hall *Konzerthalle* ⓕ
kon·tsert·ha·le
conditioner *Spülung* ⓕ shpü·lung
condom *Kondom* ⓝ kon·dawm
conductor *Schaffner(in)* ⓜ/ⓕ
shaf·ner/shaf·ne·rin
confession (religious) *Beichte* ⓕ
baikh·te
confirm (a booking) *bestätigen*
be·shtay·ti·gen
connection *Verbindung* ⓕ fer·bin·dung
conservative *konservativ*
kon·zer·va·teef
constipation *Verstopfung* ⓕ
fer·shtop·fung
consulate *Konsulat* ⓝ kon·zu·laht
contact lenses *Kontaktlinsen* ⓕ pl
kon·takt lin·zen
contraceptives *Verhütungsmittel* ⓝ
fer·hü·tungks·mit·tel
contract *Vertrag* ⓜ fer·trahk
convenience store *Kiosk* ⓜ kee·osk
convent *Kloster* ⓝ klaws·ter
cook *Koch/Köchin* ⓜ/ⓕ kokh/ker·khin
cook *kochen* ko·khen
cookie *Keks* ⓜ kayks
corner *Ecke* ⓕ e·ke
cornflakes *Cornflakes* pl korn·flayks
corrupt *korrupt* ko·rupt
cost *kosten* kos·ten
cottage cheese *Hüttenkäse* ⓜ
hü·ten·kay·ze
cotton *Baumwolle* ⓕ bowm·vo·le
cotton balls *Watte-Pads* pl va·te·pedz
cough *husten* hoos·ten
cough medicine *Hustensaft* ⓜ
hoos·ten·zaft
count *zählen* tsay·len
counter (at bar) *Theke* ⓕ tay·ke
country *Land* ⓝ lant
countryside *Land* ⓝ lant
coupon *Coupon* ⓜ ku·pong
courgette *Zucchini* ⓕ tsu·kee·ni
court (legal) *Gericht* ⓝ ge·rikht
court (tennis) *Platz* ⓜ plats
couscous *Couscous* ⓜ kus·kus
cousin *Cousin(e)* ⓜ/ⓕ ku·zén/ku·zee·ne

cover charge *Eintrittsgeld* ⁿ
ain·trits·gelt
cow *Kuh* ① koo
cracker *Cracker* ⋒ kre·ker
crafts *Handwerk* ⁿ hant·verk
cramp *Krampf* ⋒ krampf
crash *Zusammenstoß* ⋒
tsu·za·men·staws
crazy *verrückt* fe·rükt
cream *Sahne* ① zah·ne
cream cheese *Frischkäse* ⋒ frish·kay·ze
creche *Kinderkrippe* ① kin·der·kri·pe
credit card *Kreditkarte* ①
kre·deet·kar·te
cricket *Cricket* ⁿ kri·ket
crop *Feldfrucht* ① felt·frukht
cross (religious) *Kreuz* ⁿ kroyts
cross (angry) *wütend* vü·tent
crowded *überfüllt* ü·ber·fült
cuckoo clock *Kuckucksuhr* ①
ku·kuks·oor
cucumber *Gurke* ① gur·ke
cup *Tasse* ① ta·se
cupboard *Schrank* ⋒ shrangk
currency *Währung* ① vair·rung
currency exchange *Geldwechsel* ⋒
gelt·vek·sel
current (electricity) *Strom* ⋒ shtrawm
current affairs *Aktuelles* ⁿ ak·tu·e·les
curry (powder) *Curry(pulver)* ⋒
ker·ri(·pul·ver)
customs *Zoll* ⋒ tsol
cut *schneiden* shnai·den
cutlery *Besteck* ⁿ be·shtek
CV *Lebenslauf* ⋒ lay·bens·lowf
cycle *radfahren* raht·fah·ren
cycling *Radsport* ⋒ raht·shport
cyclist *Radfahrer(in)* ⋒/①
raht·fah·rer/raht·fah·re·rin
cystitis *Blasenentzündung* ①
blah·zen·en·tsün·dung

D

dad *Papa* ⋒ pa·pa
daily *täglich* tayk·likh
dairy products *Milchprodukte* ⁿ pl
milkh·pro·duk·te
damp *feucht* foykht

dance *tanzen* tan·tsen
dangerous *gefährlich* ge·fair·likh
dark *dunkel* dung·kel
date (a person)
mit jemandem ausgehen
mit yay·man·dem ows·gay·en
date (appointment) *Verabredung* ①
fer·ap·ray·dung
date (day) *Datum* ⁿ dah·tum
date of birth *Geburtsdatum* ⁿ
ge·burts·dah·tum
daughter *Tochter* ① tokh·ter
daughter-in-law *Schwiegertochter* ①
shvee·ger·tokh·ter
dawn *Dämmerung* ① de·me·rung
day *Tag* ⋒ tahk
day after tomorrow *übermorgen*
ü·ber·mor·gen
day before yesterday *vorgestern*
fawr·ges·tern
dead *tot* tawt
deaf *taub* towp
deal (cards) *austeilen* ows·tai·len
decide *entscheiden* ent·shai·den
deep *tief* teef
deforestation *Abholzung* ①
ap·hol·tsung
degree *Grad* ⋒ graht
delay *Verspätung* ① fer·shpay·tung
delicatessen *Feinkostgeschäft* ⁿ
fain·kost·ge·sheft
delicious *köstlich* kerst·likh
deliver *(aus)liefern* (ows·)lee·fern
demand *Forderung* ① for·de·rung
democracy *Demokratie* ①
de·mo·kra·tee
demonstration *Demonstration* ①
de·mons·tra·tsyawn
dental floss *Zahnseide* ① tsahn·zai·de
dentist *Zahnarzt/Zahnärztin* ⋒/①
tsahn·artst/tsahn·erts·tin
deodorant *Deo* ⁿ day·o
depart (leave) *abfahren* ap·fah·ren
department store *Warenhaus* ⁿ
vah·ren·hows
departure *Abfahrt* ① ap·fahrt
deposit *Anzahlung* ① an·tsah·lung
descendant *Nachkomme* ⋒
nahkh·ko·me

desert *Wüste* ① vüs·te
design *entwerfen* ent·ver·fen
destination *(Reise)Ziel* ① (rai·ze·)tseel
detail *Detail* ① de·tai
diabetes *Diabetis* ① di·a·bay·tis
dial tone *Wählton* ① vayl·tawn
diaper *Windel* ① vin·del
diaphragm (body) *Zwerchfell* ①
    tsverkh·fel
diarrhoea *Durchfall* ① durkh·fal
diary (for appointments)
    Terminkalender ①
    ter·meen·ka·len·der
diary (record of events) *Tagebuch* ①
    tah·ge·bookh
dice (die) *Würfel* ① vür·fel
dictionary *Wörterbuch* ① ver·ter bookh
die *sterben* shter·ben
diet *Diät* ① di·ayt
different *andere* an·de·re
difficult *schwierig* shvee·rikh
dining car *Spelsewagen* ①
    shpai·ze·vah·gen
dinner *Abendessen* ① ah·bent·e·sen
direct *direkt* di·rekt
direct-dial *Durchwahl* ① durkh·vahl
director *Regisseur(in)* ①/① re·zhi·ser/
    re·zhi·ser·rin
directory enquiries *Telefonauskunft* ①
    te·le·fawn·ows·kunft
dirty *schmutzig* shmu·tsikh
disabled *behindert* be·hin·dert
disco *Disko(thek)* ① dis·ko(·tayk)
discount *Rabatt* ① ra·bat
discrimination *Diskriminierung* ①
    dis·kri·mi·nee·rung
disease *Krankheit* ① krangk·hait
disk (computer) *Diskette* ① dis·ke·te
diving *Tauchen* ① tow·khen
dizzy *schwindelig* shvin·de·likh
do *tun* toon
doctor (medical) *Arzt/Ärztin* ①/①
    artst/erts·tin
doctor (title) *Doktor(in)* ①/①
    dok·tor/dok·taw·rin
documentary *Dokumentation* ①
    do·ku·men·ta·tsyawn
dog *Hund* ① hunt

dole (unemployment benefit)
    Arbeitslosengeld ①
    ar·baits·law·zen·gelt
doll *Puppe* ① pu·pe
dollar *Dollar* ① do·lahr
door *Tür* ① tür
dope (drugs) *Dope* ① dawp/dohp
double *doppelt* do·pelt
double bed *Doppelbett* ① do·pel·bet
down (nach) unten (nahkh) un·ten
downhill *abwärts* ap·verts
dozen *Dutzend* ① du·tsent
drama *Schauspiel* ① show·shpeel
dream *träumen* troy·men
dress *Kleid* ① klait
dried fruit *Trockenobst* ①
    tro·ken·awpst
drink *Getränk* ① ge·trengk
drink *trinken* tring·ken
drive *fahren* fah·ren
driving licence *Führerschein* ①
    fü·rer·shain
drug *Droge* ① draw·ge
drug addiction *Drogenabhängigkeit* ①
    draw·gen·ap·heng·ikh·kait
drug dealer *Drogenhändler* ①
    draw·gen·hen·dler
drunk *betrunken* be·trung·ken
dry (clothes) *trocknen* trok·nen
dry (wine) *trocken* tro·ken
dry-cleaner *chemische Reinigung* ①
    khay·mi·she rai·ni·gung
duck *Ente* ① en·te
dummy (pacifier) *Schnuller* ① shnu·ler
during *während* vair·rent
dusk *Dämmerung* ① de·me·rung

E

each *jeder/jede/jedes* ①/①/①
    yay·der/yay·de/yay·des
ear *Ohr* ① awr
early *früh* frü
earn *verdienen* fer·dee·nen
earplugs *Ohrenstöpsel* ①
    aw·ren·shterp·sel
earrings *Ohrringe* ① pl awr·ring·e
Earth *Erde* ① er·de

earthquake *Erdbeben* ⓝ ert·bay·ben
east *Osten* ⓜ os·ten
Easter *Ostern* ⓝ aws·tern
easy *leicht* laikht
eat *essen* e·sen
economy class *Touristenklasse* ⓕ tu·ris·ten·kla·se
eczema *Ekzem* ⓝ ek·tsaym
editor *Herausgeber(in)* ⓜ/ⓕ he·rows·gay·ber/he·rows·gay·be·rin
education *Erziehung* ⓕ er·tsee·ung
egg *Ei* ⓝ ai
eggplant *Aubergine* ⓕ aw·ber·zhee·ne
elections *Wahlen* ⓕ pl vah·len
electrical store *Elektrogeschäft* ⓝ e·lek·tro·ge·sheft
electrician *Elektriker(in)* ⓜ/ⓕ e·lek·tri·ker/e·lek·tri·ke·rin
electricity *Elektrizität* ⓕ e·lek·tri·tsi·tayt
elevator *Lift* ⓜ lift
embarrassed *verlegen* fer·lay·gen
embassy *Botschaft* ⓕ bawt·shaft
embroidery *Stickerei* ⓕ shti·ke·rai
emergency *Notfall* ⓜ nawt·fal
emotional *emotional* e·mo·tsyo·nahl
employee *Angestellte* ⓜ&ⓕ an·ge·shtel·te
employer *Arbeitgeber* ⓜ ar·bait·gay·ber
empty *leer* lair
end *Ende* ⓝ en·de
end *beenden* be·en·den
endangered (species) *bedrohte (Art)* ⓕ be·draw·te art
energy *Energie* ⓕ e·ner·gee
engagement (marriage) *Verlobung* ⓕ fer·law·bung
engine *Motor* ⓜ maw·tor/mo·tawr
engineer *Ingenieur(in)* ⓜ/ⓕ in·zhe·nyer/in·zhe·nyer·rin
engineering *Ingenieurwesen* ⓝ in·zhe·nyer·vay·zen
England *England* ⓝ eng·lant
English *Englisch* ⓝ eng·lish
enjoy (oneself) *sich amüsieren* zikh a·mü·zee·ren
enough *genug* ge·nook
enter *eintreten* ain·tray·ten

entertainment guide *Veranstaltungskalender* ⓜ fer·an·shtal·tungks·ka·len·der
envelope *Briefumschlag* ⓜ breef·um·shlahk
environment *Umwelt* ⓕ um·velt
epilepsy *Epilepsie* ⓕ e·pi·lep·see
equal opportunity *Chancengleichheit* ⓕ shahng·sen·glaikh·hait
equality *Gleichheit* ⓕ glaikh·hait
equipment *Ausrüstung* ⓕ ows·rüs·tung
escalator *Rolltreppe* ⓕ rol·tre·pe
euro *Euro* ⓜ oy·ro
Europe *Europa* ⓝ oy·raw·pa
euthanasia *Euthanasie* ⓕ oy·ta·na·zee
evening *Abend* ⓜ ah·bent
every *jeder/jede/jedes* ⓜ/ⓕ/ⓝ yay·der/yay·de/yay·des
every day *alltäglich* al·tayk·likh
everyone *jeder* yay·der
everything *alles* a·les
example *Beispiel* ⓝ bai·shpeel
for example *zum Beispiel* tsum bai·shpeel
excellent *ausgezeichnet* ows·ge·tsaikh·net
excess baggage *Übergepäck* ⓝ ü·ber·ge·pek
exchange *Umtausch* ⓜ um·towsh
exchange *wechseln* vek·seln
exchange rate *Wechselkurs* ⓜ vek·sel·kurs
excluded *ausgeschlossen* ows·ge·shlo·sen
exhaust (car) *Auspuff* ⓜ ows·puf
exhibition *Ausstellung* ⓕ ows·shte·lung
exit *Ausgang* ⓜ ows·gang
expensive *teuer* toy·er
experience *Erfahrung* ⓕ er·fah·rung
exploitation *Ausbeutung* ⓕ ows·boy·tung
express *Express-* eks·pres·
express mail *Expresspost* ⓕ eks·pres·post
extension (visa) *Verlängerung* ⓕ fer·leng·e·rung
eye *Auge* ⓝ ow·ge
eye drops *Augentropfen* ⓜ pl ow·gen·trop·fen

200

F

fabric *Gewebe* ⓝ ge·vay·be
face *Gesicht* ⓝ ge·zikht
face cloth *Waschlappen* ⓜ vash·la·pen
factory *Fabrik* ⓕ fa·breek
factory worker *Fabrik-
arbeiter(in)* ⓜ/ⓕ
fa·breek·ar·bai·ter/fa·breek·ar·bai·te·rin
fair (trade) *Messe* ⓕ me·se
fall (autumn) *Herbst* ⓜ herpst
false *falsch* falsh
family *Familie* ⓕ fa·mee·li·e
family name *Familienname* ⓜ
fa·mee·li·en·nah·me
famous *berühmt* be·rümt
fan (sports) *Fan* ⓜ fen
fan (machine) *Ventilator* ⓜ
ven·ti·lah·tor
fanbelt *Keilriemen* ⓜ kail·ree·men
far *weit* vait
farm *Bauernhof* ⓝ bow·ern·hawf
farmer *Bauer/Bäuerin* ⓜ/ⓕ
bow·er/boy·e·rin
fast *schnell* shnel
fat *dick* dik
father *Vater* ⓜ fah·ter
father-in-law *Schwiegervater* ⓜ
shvee·ger·fah·ter
faucet *Wasserhahn* ⓜ va·ser·hahn
fault (someone's) *Schuld* ⓕ shult
faulty *fehlerhaft* fay·ler·haft
fax *Fax* ⓝ faks
feed *füttern* fü·tern
feel *fühlen* fü·len
feelings *Gefühle* ⓝ pl ge·fü·le
fence *Zaun* ⓜ tsown
fencing (sport) *Fechten* ⓝ fekh·ten
festival *Fest* ⓝ fest
fever *Fieber* ⓝ fee·ber
few *wenige* vay·ni·ge
a few *ein paar* ain pahr
fiancé/fiancée *Verlobte* ⓜ&ⓕ
fer·lawp·te
fiction *Prosa* ⓕ praw·za
field *Feld* ⓝ felt
fig *Feige* ⓕ fai·ge
fight *Kampf* ⓜ kampf
fill *füllen* fü·len

fillet *Filet* ⓝ fi·lay
film (cinema & camera) *Film* ⓜ film
film (for camera) *Film* ⓜ film
film speed *Empfindlichkeit* ⓕ
emp·fint·likh·kait
filtered *gefiltert* ge·fil·tert
find *finden* fin·den
fine (payment) *Geldbuße* ⓕ gelt·boo·se
finger *Finger* ⓜ fing·er
finish *beenden* be·en·den
fire *Feuer* ⓝ foy·er
firewood *Brennholz* ⓝ bren·holts
first *erste* ers·te
first class *erste Klasse* ⓕ ers·te kla·se
first-aid kit *Verbandskasten* ⓜ
fer·bants·kas·ten
fish *Fisch* ⓜ fish
fish shop *Fischgeschäft* ⓝ fish·ge·sheft
fishing *Fischen* ⓝ fi·shen
fishing rod *Angel* ⓕ ang·el
flag *Flagge* ⓕ fla·ge
flash *Blitz* ⓜ blits
flashlight *Taschenlampe* ⓕ
ta·shen·lam·pe
flat *flach* flakh
flea *Floh* ⓜ flaw
flea-market *Flohmarkt* ⓜ flaw·markt
flight *Flug* ⓜ flook
flooding *Überschwemmung* ⓕ
ü·ber·shve·mung
floor *Boden* ⓜ baw·den
floor (storey) *Stock* ⓜ shtok
florist *Blumenhändler* ⓜ
bloo·men·hen·dler
flour *Mehl* ⓝ mayl
flower *Blume* ⓕ bloo·me
fly *Fliege* ⓕ flee·ge
fly *fliegen* flee·gen
foggy *neblig* nay·blikh
follow *folgen* fol·gen
food *Essen* ⓝ e·sen
food poisoning *Lebensmittelvergiftung* ⓕ
lay·bens·mi·tel·fer·gif·tung
foot *Fuß* ⓜ foos
football (soccer) *Fußball* ⓜ foos·bal
American football *American Football* ⓜ
e·me·ri·ken fut·bawl
Australian Rules football *Australian
Rules Football* ⓝ aws·tray·li·en roolz
fut·bawl

english–german

footpath *Gehweg* ⓜ *gay*·vayk
for *für* für
foreign *ausländisch* ows·len·dish
forest *Wald* ⓜ valt
forever *immer* i·mer
forget *vergessen* fer·ge·sen
forgive *verzeihen* fer·tsai·en
fork *Gabel* ⓕ *gah*·bel
formal *formell* for·mel
fortnight *vierzehn Tage* ⓝ pl
  feer·tsayn *tah*·ge
foul *Foul* ⓝ fowl
fountain *Brunnen* ⓜ bru·nen
foyer *Foyer* ⓝ fo·a·yay
fragile *zerbrechlich* tser·brekh·likh
frame *Rahmen* ⓜ *rah*·men
France *Frankreich* ⓝ *frangk*·raikh
free (gratis) *gratis* *grah*·tis
free (not bound) *frei* frai
freeze *gefrieren* ge·*free*·ren
fresh (not stale) *frisch* frish
Friday *Freitag* ⓜ *frai*·lahk
friend *Freund(in)* ⓜ/ⓕ froynt/*froyn*·din
friendly *freundlich* froynt·likh
frog *Frosch* ⓜ frosh
from *aus* • *von* ows • fon
in front of *vor* fawr
frost *Frost* ⓜ frost
fruit *Frucht* ⓕ frukht
fruit picking *Obsternte* ⓕ *awpst*·ern·te
fry *braten* brah·ten
frying pan *Bratpfanne* ⓕ *braht*·pfa·ne
fuel *Brennstoff* ⓜ *bren*·shtof
full *voll* fol
full-time *Vollzeit* ⓕ *fol*·tsait
fun *Spaß* ⓜ shpahs
funeral *Begräbnis* ⓝ be·*grayp*·nis
funny *lustig* lus·tikh
furniture *Möbel* ⓝ pl *mer*·bel
fuse *Sicherung* ⓕ *zi*·khe·rung
future *Zukunft* ⓕ *tsoo*·kunft

G

game (sport) *Spiel* ⓝ shpeel
garage (car repair) *Werkstatt* ⓕ
  verk·shtat
garage (car shelter) *Garage* ⓕ
  ga·*rah*·zhe

garbage *Abfall* ⓜ *ap*·fal
garden *Garten* ⓜ *gar*·ten
garlic *Knoblauch* ⓜ *knawp*·lowkh
gas (for cooking) *Gas* ⓝ gahs
gas (petrol) *Benzin* ⓝ ben·*tseen*
gas cartridge *Gaskartusche* ⓕ
  gahs·kar·tu·she
gas cylinder *Gasflasche* ⓕ *gahs*·fla·she
gastroenteritis *Magen-Darm-Katarrh* ⓜ
  mah·gen·darm·ka·tar
gate *Tor* ⓝ tawr
gay *schwul* shvool
gears *Gänge* ⓝ pl geng·e
general *allgemein* al·ge·*main*
German *Deutsch* doytsh
Germany *Deutschland* ⓝ *doytsh*·lant
gift *Geschenk* ⓝ ge·shengk
gig *Auftritt* ⓜ *owf*·trit
gin *Gin* ⓜ dzhin
ginger *Ingwer* ⓜ *ing*·ver
girl *Mädchen* ⓝ *mayt*·khen
girlfriend *Freundin* ⓕ *froyn*·din
give *geben* gay·ben
glacier *Gletscher* ⓜ *glet*·sher
glandular fever *Drüsenfieber* ⓝ
  drü·zen·fee·ber
glass *Glas* ⓝ glahs
glasses (spectacles) *Brille* ⓕ *bri*·le
glove *Handschuh* ⓜ *hant*·shoo
go (on foot) *gehen* gay·en
go (by vehicle) *fahren* fah·ren
go out with *ausgehen mit*
  ows·gay·en mit
go shopping *einkaufen gehen*
  ain·kow·fen gay·en
goal *Tor* ⓝ tawr
goalkeeper *Torwart/Torhüterin* ⓜ/ⓕ
  tawr·vart/*tawr*·hü·te·rin
goat *Ziege* ⓕ *tsee*·ge
god *Gott* ⓜ got
goggles (skiing) *Skibrille* ⓕ *shee*·bri·le
gold *Gold* ⓝ golt
golf ball *Golfball* ⓜ *golf*·bal
golf course *Golfplatz* ⓜ *golf*·plats
good *gut* goot
gorge *Schlucht* ⓕ shlukht
government *Regierung* ⓕ re·*gee*·rung
gram *Gramm* ⓜ gram
grandchild *Enkelkind* ⓝ *eng*·kel·kint

grandfather *Großvater • Opa* ⓜ
  graws·fah·ter • aw·pa
grandmother *Großmutter • Oma* ⓕ
  graws·mu·ter • aw·ma
grandparents *Großeltern* ⓝ pl
  graws·el·tern
grapefruit *Pampelmuse* ⓕ
  pam·pel·moo·ze
grapes *Weintrauben* ⓕ pl vain·trow·ben
graphic art *grafische Kunst* ⓕ
  grah·fi·she kunst
grass *Gras* ⓝ grahs
grave *Grab* ⓝ grahp
gray *grau* grow
great *groß* graws
green *grün* grün
greengrocer *Lebensmittelhändler* ⓜ
  lay·bens·mi·tel·hen·dler
grey *grau* grow
grocery store *Lebensmittelladen* ⓜ
  lay·bens·mi·tel·lah·den
groundnut *Erdnuss* ⓕ ert·nus
grow *wachsen* vak·sen
guess *raten* rah·ten
guide (audio) *Führer* ⓜ fü·rer
guide (person) *Führer* ⓜ fü·rer
guide dog *Blindenhund* ⓜ
  blin·den·hunt
guidebook *Reiseführer* ⓜ rai·ze·fü·rer
guided tour *Führung* ⓕ fü·rung
guilty *schuldig* shul·dikh
guitar *Gitarre* ⓕ gi·ta·re
gum (mouth) *Zahnfleisch* ⓝ
  tsahn·flaish
gym *Fitness-Studio* ⓝ fit·nes·shtoo·di·o
gymnastics *Gymnastik* ⓕ güm·nas·tik
gynaecologist
  Gynäkologe/Gynäkologin ⓜ/ⓕ
  gü·ne·ko·law·ge/gü·ne·ko·law·gin

H

hair *Haar* ⓝ hahr
hairbrush *Haarbürste* ⓕ hahr·bürs·te
hairdresser *Friseur(in)* ⓜ/ⓕ tri·zer/
  fri·zer·rin
Halal *Halal* ha·lal
half *Hälfte* ⓕ helf·te
half a litre *ein halber Liter* ⓜ ain
  hal·ber lee·ter

hallucinate *halluzinieren*
  ha·lu·tsi·nee·ren
ham *Schinken* ⓝ shing·ken
hammer *Hammer* ⓜ ha·mer
hammock *Hängematte* ⓕ heng·e·ma·te
hamster *Hamster* ⓜ hams·ter
hand *Hand* ⓕ hant
handbag *Handtasche* ⓕ hant·ta·she
handicrafts *Kunsthandwerk* ⓝ
  kunst·hant·verk
handlebar *Lenker* ⓜ leng·ker
handmade *handgemacht*
  hant·ge·makht
handsome *gutaussehend*
  goot·ows·zay·ent
hang-gliding *Drachenfliegen* ⓝ
  dra·khen·flee·gen
happy *glücklich* glük·likh
harassment *Belästigung* ⓕ
  be·les·ti·gung
harbour *Hafen* ⓜ hah·fen
hard (difficult) *schwer* shvair
hard (not soft) *hart* hart
hardware store *Eisenwarengeschäft* ⓝ
  ai·zen·vah·ren·ge·sheft
hash *Haschee* ⓝ ha·shay
hat *Hut* ⓜ hoot
hate *hassen* ha·sen
have *haben* hah·ben
hay fever *Heuschnupfen* ⓜ
  hoy·shnup·fen
he *er* air
head *Kopf* ⓜ kopf
headache *Kopfschmerzen* ⓜ pl
  kopf·shmer·tsen
headlights *Scheinwerfer* ⓜ pl
  shain·ver·fer
health *Gesundheit* ⓕ ge·zunt·hait
hear *hören* her·ren
hearing aid *Hörgerät* ⓝ her·ge·rayt
heart *Herz* ⓝ herts
heart condition *Herzleiden* ⓝ
  herts·lai·den
heat *Hitze* ⓕ hi·tse
heater *Heizgerät* ⓝ haits·ge·rayt
heavy *schwer* shvair
hello *hallo* ha·lo
helmet *Helm* ⓜ helm

help *helfen* hel·fen
hepatitis *Hepatitis* ① he·pa·tee·tis
her *ihr* eer
herbalist *Naturheilkundige* ⓜ&① na·*toor*·hail·kun·di·ge
herbs *Kräuter* ⓝ pl kroy·ter
here *hier* heer
heroin *Heroin* ⓝ he·ro·*een*
herring *Hering* ⓜ hay·ring
high *hoch* hawkh
high school *Sekundarschule* ① ze·kun·*dahr*·shoo·le
hike *wandern* van·dern
hiking *Wandern* ⓝ van·dern
hiking boots *Wanderstiefel* ⓜ pl van·der·shtee·fel
hiking route *Wanderweg* ⓜ van·der·vayk
hill *Hügel* ⓜ hü·gel
Hindu *Hindu* ⓜ&① hin·du
hire *mieten* mee·ten
his *sein* zain
historical *historisch* his·taw·rish
hitchhike *trampen* trem·pen
HIV positive *HIV-positiv* hah·ee·fow·paw·zi·teef
hockey *Hockey* ⓝ ho·ki
holiday *Urlaub* ⓜ oor·lowp
holidays *Ferien* pl fair·ri·en
holy *heilig* hai·likh
Holy Week *Karwoche* ① kahr·vo·khe
home *Heim* ⓝ haim
(at) home *zu Hause* tsoo how·ze
(go) home *nach Hause* nahkh how·ze
homeless *obdachlos* op·dakh·laws
homemaker *Hausmann/Hausfrau* ⓜ/① hows·man/hows·frow
to be homesick *Heimweh haben* haim·vay hah·ben
homeopathic medicine *homöopathisches Mittel* ⓝ haw·mer·o·pah·ti·shes mi·tel
homosexual *homosexuell* haw·mo·zek·su·el
honest *ehrlich* air·likh
honey *Honig* ⓜ haw·nikh
honeymoon *Flitterwochen* ① pl fli·ter·vo·khen

horoscope *Horoskop* ⓝ ho·ros·kawp
horse *Pferd* ⓝ pfert
horse riding *Reiten* ⓝ rai·ten
horseradish *Meerrettich* ⓜ mair·re·tikh
hospital *Krankenhaus* ⓝ krang·ken·hows
hospitality *Gastfreundschaft* ① gast·froynt·shaft
hot *heiß* hais
hot water *warmes Wasser* ⓝ var·mes va·ser
hotel *Hotel* ⓝ ho·tel
house *Haus* ⓝ hows
housework *Hausarbeit* ① hows·ar·bait
how *wie* vee
hug *umarmen* um·ar·men
huge *riesig* ree·zikh
human *menschlich* mensh·likh
human rights *Menschenrechte* ⓝ pl men·shen·rekh·te
humanities *Geisteswissenschaften* ① pl gais·tes·vi·sen·shaf·ten
hundred *hundert* hun·dert
hungry *hungrig* hung·rikh
hunting *Jagd* ① yahkt
in a hurry *in Eile* in ai·le
hurt *verletzen* fer·le·tsen
hurt (yourself) *sich weh tun* zikh vay toon
husband *Ehemann* ⓜ ay·e·man
hut *Hütte* ① hü·te

I

I *ich* ikh
ice *Eis* ⓝ ais
ice axe *Eispickel* ⓜ ais·pi·kel
ice cream *Eiscreme* ① ais·kraym
ice cream parlour *Eisdiele* ① ais·dee·le
ice hockey *Eishockey* ⓝ ais·ho·ki
ice skating *Eislaufen* ⓝ ais·low·fen
idea *Idee* ① i·day
identification *Ausweis* ⓜ ows·vais
identification card *Personalausweis* ⓜ per·zo·nahl·ows·vais
idiot *Idiot* ⓜ i·di·awt
if *wenn* ven
ignition *Zündung* ① tsün·dung

ill *krank* krangk
illegal *illegal* i·le·gahl
imagination *Phantasie* ① fan·ta·zee
immediately *sofort* zo·fort
immigration *Immigration* ①
i·mi·gra·tsyawn
important *wichtig* vikh·tikh
impossible *unmöglich* un·*merk*·likh
in *in* in
in front of *vor* fawr
included *inbegriffen* in·be·gri·fen
income tax *Einkommensteuer* ①
ain·ko·men·shtoy·er
India *Indien* ⑩ in·di·en
indicator *Blinker* ⑩ bling·ker
indigestion *Magenverstimmung* ①
mah·gen·fer·shti·mung
industry *Industrie* ① in·dus·tree
inequality *Ungleichheit* ①
un·glaikh·hait
infection *Entzündung* ① en·tsün·dung
inflammation *Entzündung* ①
en·tsün·dung
influenza *Grippe* ① gri·pe
information *Auskunft* ① ows·kunft
ingredient *Zutat* ① tsoo·taht
inject *injizieren* in·yi·tsee·ren
injection (car) *Einspritzung* ①
ain·shpri·tsung
injection (medical) *Injektion* ①
in·yek·tsyawn
injury *Verletzung* ① fer·le·tsung
in-line skating *Rollschuhfahren* ⑩
rol·shoo·fah·ren
innocent *unschuldig* un·shul·dikh
insect repellent *Insektenschutzmittel* ⑩
in·zek·ten·shuts·mi·tel
inside *innen* i·nen
instead of *(an)statt (an-)shtatt*
instructor *Lehrer(in)* ⑩/①
lair·rer/lair·re·rin
insurance *Versicherung* ①
fer·zi·khe·rung
interesting *interessant* in·tre·sant
intermission *Pause* ① pow·ze
international *international*
in·ter·na·tsyo·nahl
Internet *Internet* ⑩ in·ter·net

Internet cafe *Internetcafé* ⑩
in·ter·net·ka·fay
interpreter *Dolmetscher(in)* ⑩/①
dol·met·sher/dol·met·she·rin
interview *Interview* ⑩ in·ter·vyoo
invite *einladen* ain·lah·den
Ireland *Irland* ⑩ ir·lant
iron (clothes) *bügeln* bü·geln
island *Insel* ① in·zel
IT *Informationstechnologie* ①
in·for·ma·tsyawns·tekh·no·lo·gee
itch *Juckreiz* ⑩ yuk·raits
itemized *einzeln aufgeführt*
ain·tseln owf·ge·fürt
itinerary *Reiseroute* ① rai·ze·roo·te
IUD *Intrauterinpessar* ⑩
in·tra·u·te·reen·pe·sahr

J

jacket *Jacke* ① ya·ke
jail *Gefängnis* ⑩ ge·feng·nis
jam *Marmelade* ① mar·me·lah·de
Japan *Japan* ⑩ yah·pahn
jar *Glas* ⑩ glahs
jaw *Kiefer* ⑩ kee·fer
jealous *eifersüchtig* ai·fer·zükh·tikh
jeans *Jeans* ① pl dzheens
jeep *Jeep* ⑩ dzheep
jet lag *Jetlag* ⑩ dzhet·leg
jewellery *Schmuck* ⑩ shmuk
Jewish *jüdisch* yü·dish
job *Arbeitsstelle* ① ar·baits·shte·le
jockey *Jockey* ⑩ dzho·ki
jogging *Joggen* ⑩ dzho·gen
joke *Witz* ⑩ vits
journalist *Journalist(in)* ⑩/①
zhur·na·list/zhur·na·lis·tin
journey *Reise* ① rai·ze
judge *Richter(in)* ⑩/① rikh·ter/
rikh·te·rin
juice *Saft* ⑩ zaft
jump *springen* shpring·en
jumper (sweater) *Pullover* ⑩
pu·law·ver
jumper leads *Überbrückungskabel* ⑩
ü·ber·brü·kungks·kah·bel
justice *Gerechtigkeit* ①
ge·rekh·tikh·kait

K

ketchup *Ketchup* ⓝ ket·chap
kettle *Kessel* ⓜ ke·sel
key *Schlüssel* ⓜ shlü·sel
keyboard *Tastatur* ⓕ tas·ta·*toor*
kick *treten* tray·ten
kill *töten* ter·ten
kilogram *Kilogramm* ⓝ kee·lo·gram
kilometre *Kilometer* ⓜ ki·lo·*may*·ter
kind *nett* net
kindergarten *Kindergarten* ⓜ
  kin·der·gar·ten
king *König* ⓜ ker·nikh
kiss *Kuss* ⓜ kus
kiss *küssen* kü·sen
kitchen *Küche* ⓕ kü·khe
kitten *Kätzchen* ⓝ kets·khen
kiwifruit *Kiwifrucht* ⓕ kee·vi·frukht
knapsack *Rucksack* ⓜ ruk·zak
knee *Knie* ⓝ knee
knife *Messer* ⓝ me·ser
know (a person) *kennen* ke·nen
know (something) *wissen* vi·sen
kosher *koscher* kaw·sher

L

labourer *Arbeiter(in)* ⓜ/ⓕ
  ar·bai·ter/ar·bai·te·rin
lace *Spitze* ⓕ shpi·tse
lager *Lager* ⓝ lah·ger
lake *See* ⓜ zay
lamb *Lamm* ⓝ lam
land *Land* ⓝ lant
landlady *Vermieterin* ⓕ fer·mee·te·rin
landlord *Vermieter* ⓜ fer·mee·ter
language *Sprache* ⓕ shprah·khe
laptop *Laptop* ⓜ lep·top
lard *Schmalz* ⓝ shmalts
large *groß* graws
last (week) *letzte (Woche)*
  lets·te (vo·khe)
late *spät* shpayt
laugh *lachen* la·khen
laundrette *Wäscherei* ⓕ ve·she·*rai*
laundry (room) *Waschküche* ⓕ
  vash·kü·khe

law (subject) *Jura* ⓝ yoo·ra
law (rules) *Gesetz* ⓝ ge·zets
lawyer *Rechtsanwalt/
  Rechtsanwältin* ⓜ/ⓕ
  rekhts·an·valt/rekhts·an·vel·tin
laxatives *Abführmittel* ⓝ ap·für·mi·tel
lazy *faul* fowl
leader *Anführer* ⓜ an·fü·rer
leaf *Blatt* ⓝ blat
learn *lernen* ler·nen
lease *Mietvertrag* ⓜ meet·fer·trahk
leather *Leder* ⓝ lay·der
leave (depart) *abfahren* ap·fah·ren
lecturer *Dozent(in)* ⓜ/ⓕ
  do·*tsent*/do·*tsen*·tin
leek *Lauch* ⓜ lowkh
left (direction) *links* lingks
left luggage *Gepäckaufbewahrung* ⓕ
  ge·pek·owf·be·vah·rung
left-wing *links(gerichtet)*
  lingks(·ge·rikh·tet)
leg (body) *Bein* ⓝ bain
legal *legal* le·gahl
legislation *Gesetzgebung* ⓕ
  ge·zets·gay·bung
legume *Hülsenfrucht* ⓕ hül·zen·frukht
lemon *Zitrone* ⓕ tsi·traw·ne
lemonade *Limonade* ⓕ li·mo·*nah*·de
lens (camera) *Objektiv* ⓝ op·yek·*teef*
Lent *Fastenzeit* ⓕ fas·ten·tsait
lentil *Linse* ⓕ lin·ze
lesbian *Lesbierin* ⓕ les·bi·e·rin
less *weniger* vay·ni·ger
letter *Brief* ⓜ breef
lettuce *Kopfsalat* ⓜ kopf·za·laht
liar *Lügner(in)* ⓜ/ⓕ lüg·ner/lüg·ne·rin
library *Bibliothek* ⓕ bi·bli·o·*tayk*
lice *Läuse* ⓕ pl loy·ze
license plate number *Autokennzeichen* ⓝ ow·to·ken·tsai·khen
lie (not stand) *liegen* lee·gen
life *Leben* ⓝ lay·ben
lifejacket *Schwimmweste* ⓕ
  shvim·ves·te
lift (elevator) *Lift* ⓜ lift
light *Licht* ⓝ likht
light *hell* hel
light bulb *Glühbirne* ⓕ glü·bir·ne
light meter *Belichtungsmesser* ⓜ
  be·likh·tungks·me·ser

lighter (cigarette) *Feuerzeug* ⓝ
foy·er·tsoyk

lightning *Blitz* ⓜ blits

lights (on car) *Scheinwerfer* ⓜ pl
shain·ver·fer

like *mögen* mer·gen

lime *Limone* ⓕ li·maw·ne

line *Linie* ⓕ lee·ni·e

linen (bed) *Bettwäsche* ⓕ bet·ve·she

linen (fabric) *Leinen* ⓝ lai·nen

lip balm *Lippenbalsam* ⓜ
li·pen·bal·zahm

lips *Lippen* ⓝ pl li·pen

lipstick *Lippenstift* ⓜ li·pen·shtift

liquor store *Getränkehandel* ⓝ
ge·treng·ke·han·del

listen *hören* her·ren

little *klein* klain

little (not much) *wenig* vay·nikh

a little *ein bisschen* ain bis·khen

live *leben* lay·ben

live (reside) *wohnen* vaw·nen

liver *Leber* ⓕ lay·ber

lizard *Echse* ⓕ ek·se

local *örtlich* ert·likh

lock *Schloss* ⓝ shlos

locked *abgeschlossen* ap·ge·shlo·sen

lollies *Süßigkeiten* ⓕ pl zü·sikh·kai·ten

lonely *einsam* ain·zahm

long *lang* lang

long-sleeved *langärmelig*
lang·er·me·likh

look *(an)sehen* (an·)zay·en

look after *sich kümmern um* zikh
kü·mern um

look for *suchen nach* zoo·khen nahkh

lookout *Aussichtspunkt* ⓜ
ows·zikhts·pungkt

loose change *Kleingeld* ⓝ klain·gelt

lose *verlieren* fer·lee·ren

lost *verloren* fer·law·ren

lost property office *Fundbüro* ⓝ
funt·bü·raw

a lot (of) *viel* feel

loud *laut* lowt

love *lieben* lee·ben

lover *Liebhaber(in)* ⓜ/ⓕ
leep·hah·ber/leep·hah·be·rin

low *niedrig* nee·drikh

lubricant *Schmiermittel* ⓝ
shmeer·mi·tel

luck *Glück* ⓝ glük

lucky *glücklich* glük·likh

luggage *Gepäck* ⓝ ge·pek

luggage lockers *Schließfächer* ⓝ pl
shlees·fe·kher

luggage tag *Adressanhänger* ⓜ
a·dres·an·heng·er

lump (health) *Knoten* ⓜ knaw·ten

lunch *Mittagessen* ⓝ mi·tahk·e·sen

lungs *Lungen* ⓕ pl lung·en

luxury *luxuriös* luk·su·ri·ers

M

machine *Maschine* ⓕ ma·shee·ne

made of (cotton) *aus (Baumwolle)*
ows (bowm·vo·le)

magazine *Zeitschrift* ⓕ tsait·shrift

magician *Zauberer(in)* ⓜ/ⓕ
tsow·be·rer/tsow·be·re·rin

mail *Post* ⓕ post

mailbox *Briefkasten* ⓜ breef·kas·ten

main *Haupt-* howpt·

main square *Hauptplatz* ⓜ howpt·plats

make *machen* ma·khen

make-up *Schminke* ⓕ shming·ke

mammogram *Mammogramm* ⓝ
ma·mo·gram

man *Mann* ⓜ man

man (human being) *Mensch* ⓜ mensh

manager *Manager(in)* ⓜ/ⓕ
me·ne·dzher/me·ne·dzhe·rin

mandarin *Mandarine* ⓕ man·da·ree·ne

mango *Mango* ⓝ mang·go

manual worker *Arbeiter(in)* ⓜ/ⓕ
ar·bai·ter/ar·bai·te·rin

many *viele* fee·le

map *Karte* ⓕ kar·te

margarine *Margarine* ⓕ mar·ga·ree·ne

marijuana *Marihuana* ⓝ ma·ri·hu·ah·na

marital status *Familienstand* ⓜ
fa·mee·li·en·shtant

market *Markt* ⓜ markt

market square *Marktplatz* ⓜ
markt·plats

marmalade *Orangenmarmelade* ⓕ
o·rahng·zhen·mar·me·lah·de

marriage *Ehe* ⓕ ay·e

marry *heiraten* hai·rah·ten

martial arts *Kampfsport* ⓜ
kampf·shport
mass (Catholic) *Messe* ⓕ me·se
massage *Massage* ⓕ ma·sah·zhe
masseur *Masseur* ⓜ ma·ser
masseuse *Masseurin* ⓕ ma·ser·rin
mat *Matte* ⓕ ma·te
match (sport) *Spiel* ⓝ shpeel
matches *Streichhölzer* ⓝ pl
shtraikh·herl·tser
material *Material* ⓝ ma·te·ri·ahl
mattress *Matratze* ⓕ ma·tra·tse
maybe *vielleicht* fi·laikht
mayonnaise *Majonnaise* ⓕ
ma·yo·nay·ze
mayor *Bürgermeister(in)* ⓜ/ⓕ
bür·ger·mais·ter/bür·ger·mais·te·rin
measles *Masern* pl mah·zern
meat *Fleisch* ⓝ flaish
mechanic *Mechaniker(in)* ⓜ/ⓕ
me·khah·ni·ker/me·khah·ni·ke·rin
media *Medien* pl may·di·en
medicine *Medizin* ⓕ me·di·tseen
meditation *Meditation* ⓕ
me·di·ta·tsyawn
meet *treffen* tre·fen
melon *Melone* ⓕ me·law·ne
member *Mitglied* ⓝ mit·gleet
member of parliament *Abgeordnete* ⓜ&ⓕ ap·ge·ord·ne·te
menstruation *Menstruation* ⓕ
mens·tru·a·tsyawn
menu *Speisekarte* ⓕ shpai·ze·kar·te
message *Mitteilung* ⓕ mi·tai·lung
metal *Metall* ⓝ me·tal
metre *Meter* ⓜ may·ter
metro station *U-Bahnhof* ⓜ
oo·bahn·hawf
microwave *Mikrowelle* ⓕ mee·kro·ve·le
Middle East *Nahe Osten* ⓜ nah·e os·ten
midnight *Mitternacht* ⓕ mi·ter·nakht
migraine *Migräne* ⓕ mi·gray·ne
military *Militär* ⓝ mi·li·tair
military service *Wehrdienst* ⓜ
vair·deenst
milk *Milch* ⓕ milkh
millimetre *Millimeter* ⓜ mi·li·may·ter
million *Million* ⓕ mi·lyawn
mince *Gehacktes* ⓝ ge·hak·tes

mind (look after) *aufpassen* owf·pa·sen
mineral water *Mineralwasser* ⓝ
mi·ne·rahl·va·ser
mints *Pfefferminzbonbons* ⓝ pl
pfe·fer·mints·bong·bongs
minute *Minute* ⓕ mi·noo·te
mirror *Spiegel* ⓜ shpee·gel
miscarriage *Fehlgeburt* ⓕ fayl·ge·burt
miss (feel absence of) *vermissen*
fer·mi·sen
miss (the bus) *verpassen* fer·pa·sen
mistake *Fehler* ⓜ fay·ler
mix *mischen* mi·shen
mobile phone *Handy* ⓝ hen·di
modem *Modem* ⓝ maw·dem
moisturiser *Feuchtigkeitscreme* ⓕ
foykh·tikh·kaits·kraym
monastery *Kloster* ⓝ klaws·ter
Monday *Montag* ⓜ mawn·tahk
money *Geld* ⓝ gelt
month *Monat* ⓜ maw·nat
monument *Denkmal* ⓝ dengk·mahl
(full) moon *(Voll) Mond* ⓜ
(fol·)mawnt
more *mehr* mair
morning (6am–10am) *Morgen* ⓜ
mor·gen
morning (10am–12pm) *Vormittag* ⓜ
fawr·mi·tahk
morning sickness
(Schwangerschafts-)Erbrechen ⓝ
(shvang·er·shafts·)er·bre·khen
mosque *Moschee* ⓕ mo·shay
mosquito *Stechmücke* ⓕ shtekh·mü·ke
mosquito coil *Moskitospirale* ⓕ
mos·kee·to·shpi·rah·le
mother *Mutter* ⓕ mu·ter
mother-in-law *Schwiegermutter* ⓕ
shvee·ger·mu·ter
motorboat *Motorboot* ⓝ
maw·tor·bawt
motorcycle *Motorrad* ⓝ maw·tor·raht
motorway (tollway) *Autobahn* ⓕ
ow·to·bahn
mountain *Berg* ⓜ berk
mountain bike *Mountainbike* ⓝ
mown·ten·baik
mountain hut *Berghütte* ⓕ berk·hü·te

mountain path *Bergweg* ⓜ berk·vayk
mountain range *Gebirgszug* ⓜ
   ge·*birks*·tsook
mountaineering *Bergsteigen* ⓝ
   berk·*shtai*·gen
mouse *Maus* ⓕ mows
mouth *Mund* ⓜ munt
movie *Film* ⓜ film
mud *Schlamm* ⓜ shlam
muesli *Müsli* ⓝ *müs*·li
muggy *schwül* shvül
mum *Mama* ⓕ *ma*·ma
muscle *Muskel* ⓜ *mus*·kel
museum *Museum* ⓝ mu·*zay*·um
mushroom *Pilz* ⓜ pilts
music *Musik* ⓕ mu·*zeek*
musician *Musiker(in)* ⓜ/ⓕ
   moo·*zi*·ker/moo·*zi*·ke·rin
Muslim *Moslem/Moslime* ⓜ/ⓕ
   mos·lem/*mos*·lee·me
mussel *Muschel* ⓕ *mu*·shel
mustard *Senf* ⓜ zenf
mute *stumm* shtum
my *mein/meine/mein* ⓜ/ⓕ/ⓝ
   main/*mai*·ne/main

N

nail clippers *Nagelknipser* ⓜ pl
   nah·gel·knip·ser
name *Name* ⓜ *nah*·me
napkin *Serviette* ⓕ zer·*vye*·te
nappy *Windel* ⓕ *vin*·del
nappy rash *Windeldermatitis* ⓕ
   vin·del·der·ma·tee·tis
national park *Nationalpark* ⓜ
   na·*tsyo*·nahl·park
nationality *Staatsangehörigkeit* ⓕ
   shtahts·an·ge·her·rikh·kait
nature *Natur* ⓕ na·*toor*
nature reserve *Naturreservat* ⓝ
   na·*toor*·re·zer·vaht
naturopathy *Naturheilkunde* ⓕ
   na·*toor*·hail·kun·de
nausea *Übelkeit* ⓕ *ü*·bel·kait
near *nahe* *nah*·e
nearby *in der Nähe* in dair *nay*·e
nearest *nächste* *naykhs*·te
necessary *notwendig* *nawt*·ven·dikh

necklace *Halskette* ⓕ *hals*·ke·te
need *brauchen* *brow*·khen
needle (sewing) *Nadel* ⓕ *nah*·del
needle (syringe) *Nadel* ⓕ *nah*·del
neither *auch nicht* owkh nikht
nephew *Neffe* ⓜ *ne*·fe
net *Netz* ⓝ nets
Netherlands *Niederlande* pl
   nee·der·lan·de
never *nie* nee
new *neu* noy
New Year's Day *Neujahrstag* ⓜ
   noy·yahrs·tahk
New Year's Eve *Silvester* ⓝ zil·*ves*·ter
New Zealand *Neuseeland* ⓝ
   noy·zay·lant
news *Nachrichten* ⓕ pl *nahkh*·rikh·ten
newsagency *Zeitungshändler* ⓜ
   tsai·tungks·hen·dler
newspaper *Zeitung* ⓕ *tsai*·tung
newsstand *Zeitungskiosk* ⓜ
   tsai·tungks·kee·osk
next *nächste* *naykhs*·te
next to *neben* *nay*·ben
nice *nett* net
nickname *Spitzname* ⓜ *shpits*·nah·me
niece *Nichte* ⓕ *nikh*·te
night *Nacht* ⓕ nakht
no *nein* nain
noisy *laut* lowt
none *keine* *kai*·ne
non-smoking *Nichtraucher-*
   nikht·row·kher
noodles *Nudeln* ⓕ pl *noo*·deln
noon *Mittag* ⓜ *mi*·tahk
north *Norden* ⓜ *nor*·den
nose *Nase* ⓕ *nah*·ze
not *nicht* nikht
notebook *Notizbuch* ⓝ no·*teets*·bookh
nothing *nichts* nikhts
now *jetzt* yetst
nuclear energy *Atomenergie* ⓕ
   a·*lawm*·e·ner·gee
nuclear testing *Atomtest* ⓜ
   a·*tawm*·test
nuclear waste *Atommüll* ⓜ
   a·*tawm*·mül
number (numeral) *Zahl* ⓕ tsahl
number (telephone) *Nummer* ⓕ *nu*·mer

nun *Nonne* ① no·ne
nurse *Krankenpfleger/*
Krankenschwester ⑩/①
krang·ken·pflay·ger/
krang·ken·shves·ter
nut *Nuss* ① nus

O

O

oats *Hafer(flocken)* ⑩ pl
hah·fer(·flo·ken)
obvious *offensichtlich* o·fen·*zihkt*·likh
occupation *Beruf* ⑩ be·*roof*
ocean *Ozean* ⑩ aw·tse·*ahn*
off (food) *schlecht* shlekht
office *Büro* ⑪ bü·*raw*
office worker *Büroangestellte* ⑩&①
bü·*raw*·an·ge·shtel·te
offside *abseits* ap·zaits
often *oft* oft
oil *Öl* ⑪ erl
OK *okay* o·*kay*
old *alt* alt
olive *Olive* ① o·*lee*·ve
olive oil *Olivenöl* ⑪ o·*lee*·ven·erl
Olympic Games *Olympische*
Spiele ⑪ pl o·*lüm*·pi·she *shpee*·le
on *auf* owf
once *einmal* *ain*·mahl
one *ein(s)* ain(s)
onion *Zwiebel* ① *tsvee*·bel
only *nur* noor
open *offen* o·fen
open (unlock) *öffnen* erf·nen
opening hours *Öffnungszeiten* ① pl
erf·nungks·tsai·ten
opera *Oper* ① *aw*·per
opera house *Opernhaus* ⑪
aw·pern·hows
operation *Operation* ① o·pe·ra·*tsyawn*
operator *Vermittlung* ① fer·*mit*·lung
opinion *Meinung* ① *mai*·nung
opposite *gegenüber* gay·gen·*ü*·ber
optician *Optiker(in)* ⑩/①
op·ti·ker/op·ti·ke·rin
or *oder* *aw*·der
orange (fruit) *Orange* ① o·*rahng*·zhe
orange (colour) *orange* o·*rahngzh*
orange juice *Orangensaft* ⑩
o·*rahng*·zhen·zaft

orchestra *Orchester* ⑪ or·*kes*·ter
order (restaurant) *Bestellung* ①
be·*shte*·lung
order *bestellen* be·*shte*·len
ordinary *normal* nor·*mahl*
organ (church) *Orgel* ① *or*·gel
organise *organisieren* or·ga·ni·*zee*·ren
orgasm *Orgasmus* ⑩ or·*gas*·mus
original (not copied) *Original-*
o·ri·gi·*nahl*
other *andere* *an*·de·re
our *unser* *un*·zer
out *aus* ows
outside *draußen* *drow*·sen
ovarian cyst *Eierstockzyste* ①
ai·er·shtok·tsüs·te
oven *Ofen* ⑩ *aw*·fen
over *über* *ü*·ber
overcoat *Mantel* ⑩ *man*·tel
overdose *Überdosis* ① *ü*·ber·daw·zis
overnight *über Nacht* ü·ber nakht
owe *schulden* *shul*·den
owner *Besitzer(in)* ⑩/①
be·*zi*·tser/be·zi·tse·rin
oxygen *Sauerstoff* ⑩ *zow*·er·shtof
oyster *Auster* ① *ows*·ter
ozone layer *Ozonschicht* ①
o·*tsawn*·shikht

P

pacemaker (heart) *Herzschrittmacher* ⑩
herts·shrit·ma·kher
pacifier (dummy) *Schnuller* ⑩ *shnu*·ler
package *Paket* ⑪ pa·*kayt*
packet (general) *Packung* ① *pa*·kung
padlock *Vorhängeschloss* ⑪
fawr·heng·e·shlos
page *Seite* ① *zai*·te
pain *Schmerz* ⑩ shmerts
painful *schmerzhaft* shmerts·haft
painkillers *Schmerzmittel* ⑪
shmerts·mi·tel
painter *Maler(in)* ⑩/①
mah·ler/mah·le·rin
painting (the art) *Malerei* ① mah·le·*rai*
paints *Farben* ① pl *far*·ben
pair (couple) *Paar* ⑪ pahr
palace *Schloss* ⑪ shlos
pan *Pfanne* ① *pfa*·ne

pants (trousers) *Hose* ① haw·ze
panty liner *Slipeinlage* ①
  slip·ain·lah·ge
pantyhose *Strumpfhose* ①
  shtrumpf·haw·ze
pap smear *Abstrich* ⓜ ap·shtrikh
paper *Papier* ⓝ pa·peer
paperback *Taschenbuch* ⓝ
  ta·shen·bookh
paperwork *Schreibarbeit* ①
  shraip·ar·bait
parachuting *Fallschirmspringen* ⓝ
  fal·shirm·shpring·en
paragliding *Gleitschirmfliegen* ⓝ
  glait·shirm·flee·gen
paraplegic *Querschnittsgelähmte* ⓜ&①
  kvair·shnits·ge·laym·te
parcel *Paket* ⓝ pa·kayt
parents *Eltern* ⓝ pl el·tern
park *Park* ⓜ park
park (car) *Parkplatz* ⓜ park·plats
parliament *Parlament* ⓝ par·la·ment
parrot *Papagei* ⓜ pa·pa·gai
parsley *Petersilie* ① pay·tor·zee·li·e
part *Teil* ⓝ tail
participate *sich beteiligen* zikh
  be·tai·li·gen
part-time *Teilzeit-* ① tail·tsait
party (fiesta/ball) *Fest* ⓝ fest
party (politics) *Partei* ① par·tai
pass *Pass* ⓜ pas
passenger (bus/taxi) *Fahrgast* ⓜ
  fahr·gast
passenger (plane) *Fluggast* ⓜ
  flook·gast
passenger (train) *Reisende(r)* ⓜ/①
  rai·zen·de
passport *(Reise)Pass* ⓜ (rai·ze·)pas
passport number *Passnummer* ①
  pas·nu·mer
past *Vergangenheit* ① fer·gang·en·hait
pasta *Nudeln* ① pl noo·deln
path *Pfad* ⓜ pfaht
patio *Terrasse* ① ter·ra·se
pay *bezahlen* be·tsah·len
pay phone *Münztelefon* ⓝ
  münts·te·le·fawn
payment *Zahlung* ① tsah·lung
pea *Erbse* ① erp·se

peace *Frieden* ⓜ free·den
peach *Pfirsich* ⓜ pfir·zikh
peak *Gipfel* ⓜ gip·fel
peanuts *Erdnüsse* ① pl ert·nü·se
pear *Birne* ① bir·ne
pedal *Pedal* ⓝ pe·dahl
pedestrian *Fußgänger(in)* ⓜ/①
  foos·geng·er/foos·geng·e·rin
pen (ballpoint) *Kugelschreiber* ⓜ
  koo·gel·shrai·ber
pencil *Bleistift* ⓜ blai·shtift
penis *Penis* ⓜ pay·nis
penknife *Taschenmesser* ⓝ
  ta·shen·me·ser
pensioner *Rentner(in)* ⓜ/①
  rent·ner/rent·ne·rin
people *Menschen* ⓜ pl men·shen
pepper *Pfeffer* ⓜ pfe·fer
pepper (bell) *Paprika* ① pap·ri·kah
per *pro* praw
percent *Prozent* ⓝ pro·tsent
performance *Aufführung* ①
  owf·fü·rung
perfume *Parfüm* ⓝ par·füm
period pain
  Menstruationsbeschwerden ⓨ pl
  mens·tru·a·tsyawns·be·shver·den
permission *Erlaubnis* ① er·lowp·nis
permit *Genehmigung* ①
  ge·nay·mi·gung
person *Person* ① per·zawn
personal *persönlich* per·zern·likh
petition *Petition* ① pe·ti·tsyawn
petrol *Benzin* ⓝ ben·tseen
petrol can *Benzinkanister* ⓜ
  ben·tseen·ka·nis·ter
pharmacy *Apotheke* ① a·po·tay·ke
phone book *Telefonbuch* ⓝ
  te·le·fawn·bookh
phone box *Telefonzelle* ①
  te·le·fawn·tse·le
phonecard *Telefonkarte* ①
  te·le·fawn·kar·te
photo *Foto* ⓝ faw·to
photograph *Fotografie* ① fo·to·gra·fee
photograph *fotografieren*
  fo·to·gra·fee·ren
photographer *Fotograf(in)* ⓜ/①
  fo·to·grahf/fo·to·grah·fin

photography *Fotografie* ①
fo·to·gra·fee

phrasebook *Sprachführer* ⑩
shprahkh·fü·rer

physics *Physik* ① fü·zeek

piano *Klavier* ⑩ kla·veer

pick *pflücken* pflü·ken

pick up *aufheben* owf·hay·ben

pickaxe *Spitzhacke* ① shpits·ha·ke

picnic *Picknick* ⑩ pik·nik

pie *Pastete* ① pas·tay·te

piece *Stück* ⑩ shtük

pig *Schwein* ⑩ shvain

pilgrimage *Pilgerfahrt* ① pil·ger·fahrt

pill *Pille* ① pi·le

the Pill *die Pille* ① dee pi·le

pillow *Kissen* ⑩ ki·sen

pillowcase *Kissenbezug* ⑩
ki·sen·be·tsook

pineapple *Ananas* ① a·na·nas

pink *rosa* raw·za

pipe *Pfeife* ① pfai·fe

pistachio *Pistazie* ① pis·tah·tsi·e

place *Platz* ⑩ plats

place of birth *Geburtsort* ⑩
ge·burts·ort

plain *Ebene* ① ay·be·ne

plane *Flugzeug* ⑩ flook·tsoyk

planet *Planet* ⑩ pla·nayt

plant *Pflanze* ① pflan·tse

plastic *Plastik* ⑩ plas·tik

plate *Teller* ⑩ te·ler

plateau *Hochebene* ① hawkh·ay·be·ne

platform *Bahnsteig* ⑩ bahn·shtaik

play (theatre) *Schauspiel* ⑩
show·shpeel

play (game) *spielen* shpee·len

play (instrument) *spielen* shpee·len

please *bitte* bi·te

plenty *viel* feel

plug (bath) *Stöpsel* ⑩ shterp·sel

plug (electricity) *Stecker* ⑩ shte·ker

plum *Pflaume* ① pflow·me

plumber *Installateur(in)* ⑩/①
in·sta·la·ter/in·sta·la·ter(·rin)

pocket *Tasche* ① ta·she

poetry *Dichtung* ① dikh·tung

point *Punkt* ⑩ pungkt

point *zeigen* tsai·gen

poisonous *giftig* gif·tikh

poker (game) *Poker* ⑩ paw·ker

police *Polizei* ① po·li·tsai

police station *Polizeirevier* ⑩
po·li·tsai·re·veer

policy *Politik* ① po·li·teek

politician *Politiker(in)* ⑩/①
po·lee·ti·ker/po·lee·ti·ke·rin

politics *Politik* ① po·li·teek

pollen *Pollen* ⑩ po·len

polls *Umfrage* ① um·frah·ge

pollution *Umweltverschmutzung* ①
um·velt·fer·shmu·tsung

pony *Pony* ⑩ po·ni

pool (game) *Billard* ⑩ bil·yart

pool (swimming, indoors) *Hallenbad* ⑩
ha·len·baht

pool (swimming, outdoors) *Freibad* ⑩
frai·baht

poor *arm* arm

popular *beliebt* be·leept

pork *Schweinefleisch* ⑩ shvai·ne·flaish

port *Hafen* ⑩ hah·fen

possible *möglich* merk·likh

post office *Postamt* ⑩ post·amt

postage *Porto* ⑩ por·to

postcard *Postkarte* ① post·kar·te

postcode *Postleitzahl* ① post·lai·tsahl

poste restante *postlagernd*
post·lah·gernt

poster *Plakat* ⑩ pla·kaht

pot (ceramics) *Topf* ⑩ topf

pot (dope) *Gras* ⑩ grahs

potato *Kartoffel* ① kar·to·fel

pottery *Töpferwaren* ① pl
terp·fer·vah·ren

pound (money & weight) *Pfund* ⑩
pfunt

poverty *Armut* ① ar·moot

power *Kraft* ① kraft

practical *praktisch* prak·tish

prawn *Garnele* ① gar·nay·le

prayer *Gebet* ⑩ ge·bayt

prefer *vorziehen* fawr·tsee·en

pregnancy test kit
Schwangerschaftstest ⑩
shvang·er·shafts·test

pregnant *schwanger* shvang·er

premenstrual tension
prämenstruelle Störung ①
pray·mens·tru·e·le shter·rung

prepare *vorbereiten* fawr·be·rai·ten
present (gift) *Geschenk* ⑩ ge·shengk
present (time) *Gegenwart* ①
  gay·gen·vart
president *Präsident(in)* ⑩/①
  pre·zi·dent/pre·zi·den·tin
pressure *Druck* ⑩ druk
pretty *hübsch* hüpsh
prevent *verhindern* fer·hin·dern
price *Preis* ⑩ prais
priest *Priester* ⑩ prees·ter
prime minister
  Premierminister(in) ⑩/①
  prem·yay·mi·nis·ter/
  prem·yay·mi·nis·te·rin
prime minister (in Germany &
  Austria) *Bundeskanzler(in)* ⑩/①
  bun·des·kants·ler/bun·des·kants·le·rin
print (artwork) *Druck* ⑩ druk
print (photography) *Abzug* ⑩ ap·tsook
prison *Gefängnis* ⑩ ge·feng·nis
prisoner *Gefangene* ⑩&① ge·fang·e·ne
private *privat* pri·vaht
produce *produzieren* pro·du·tsee·ren
profession *Beruf* ⑩ be·roof
profit *Gewinn* ⑩ ge·vin
program *Programm* ⑩ pro·gram
projector *Projektor* ⑩ pro·yek·tor
promise *versprechen* fer·shpre·khen
proposal *Vorschlag* ⑩ fawr·shlahk
prostitute *Prostituierte* ①
  pros·ti·tu·eer·te
protect *beschützen* be·shü·tsen
protected *geschützte* ge·shüts·te
protest *Protest* ⑩ pro·test
protest *protestieren* pro·tes·tee·ren
provisions *Verpflegung* ①
  fer·pflay·gung
prune *Backpflaume* ① bak·pflow·me
psychology *Psychologie* ①
  psü·kho·lo·gee
pub *Kneipe* ① knai·pe
public telephone *öffentliches Telefon* ⑩
  er·fent·li·khes te·le·fawn
public toilet *öffentliche Toilette* ①
  er·fent·li·khe to·a·le·te
pull *ziehen* tsee·en
pump *(Luft)Pumpe* ① (luft·)pum·pe
pumpkin *Kürbis* ⑩ kür·bis
puncture *Reifenpanne* ① rai·fen·pa·ne

punish *bestrafen* be·shtrah·fen
pure *rein* rain
purple *lila* lee·la
push *schieben* shee·ben
put (horizontal) *legen* lay·gen
put (vertical) *stellen* shte·len

Q

qualifications *Qualifikationen* ① pl
  kva·li·fi·ka·tsyaw·nen
quality *Qualität* ① kva·li·tayt
quarantine *Quarantäne* ①
  ka·ran·tay·ne
quarrel *Streit* ⑩ shtrait
quarter *Viertel* ⑩ feer·tel
queen *Königin* ① ker·ni·gin
question *Frage* ① frah·ge
queue *Schlange* ① shlang·e
quick *schnell* shnel
quiet *ruhig* roo·ikh
quit (job) *kündigen* kün·di·gen

R

rabbit *Kaninchen* ⑩ ka·neen·khen
race (sport) *Rennen* ⑩ re·nen
racetrack *Rennbahn* ① ren·bahn
racing bike *Rennrad* ⑩ ren·raht
racism *Rassismus* ⑩ ra·sis·mus
racquet *Schläger* ⑩ shlay·ger
radiator *Kühler* ⑩ kü·ler
radio *Radio* ⑩ rah·di·o
radish *Rettich* ⑩ re·tikh
railway station *Bahnhof* ⑩ bahn·hawf
rain *Regen* ⑩ ray·gen
raincoat *Regenmantel* ⑩
  ray·gen·man·tel
raisin *Rosine* ① ro·zee·ne
rally *Rallye* ① re·li
rape *vergewaltigen* fer·ge·val·ti·gen
rapids *Stromschnellen* ① pl
  shtrawm·shne·len
rare *selten* zel·ten
rash *Ausschlag* ⑩ ows·shlahk
raspberry *Himbeere* ① him·bair·re
rat *Ratte* ① ra·te
rate of pay *Lohn(satz)* ⑩ lawn(·zats)
raw *roh* raw

Q

razor *Rasierer* ⓜ ra·zee·rer
razor blades *Rasierklingen* ① pl
  ra·zeer·kling·en
read *lesen* lay·zen
reading *Lesung* ① lay·zung
ready *fertig* fer·tikh
real estate agent *Makler(in)* ⓜ/①
  mahk·ler/mahk·le·rin
realistic *realistisch* re·a·lis·tish
reason *Grund* ⓜ grunt
receipt *Quittung* ① kvi·tung
receive *erhalten* er·hal·ten
recently *vor kurzem* fawr kur·tsem
recharge *aufladen* owf·lah·den
recommend *empfehlen* emp·fay·len
recording *Aufnahme* ① owf·nah·me
recyclable *wiederverwertbar*
  vee·der·fer·vert·bahr
recycle *recyceln* ri·sai·keln
red *rot* rawt
referee *Schiedsrichter(in)* ⓜ/①
  sheets·rikh·ter/sheets·rikh·te·rin
reference (work) *Zeugnis* ⓝ tsoyk·nis
referendum *Volksentscheid* ⓜ
  folks·ent·shait
refrigerator *Kühlschrank* ⓜ kül·shrangk
refugee *Flüchtling* ⓜ flükht·ling
refund *Rückzahlung* ① rük·tsah·lung
refuse *ablehnen* ap·lay·nen
region *Region* ① re·gyawn
registered mail *Einschreiben* ⓝ
  ain·shrai·ben
regulation *Vorschrift* ① fawr·shrift
relation (family) *Verwandte* ⓜ&①
  fer·van·te
relationship *Beziehung* ① be·tsee·ung
relax *sich entspannen* zikh ent·shpa·nen
relic (religious) *Reliquie* ① re·lee·kvi·e
religion *Religion* ① re·li·gyawn
religious *religiös* re·li·gyers
remote *abgelegen* ap·ge·lay·gen
remote control *Fernbedienung* ①
  fern·be·dee·nung
rent *mieten* mee·ten
repair *reparieren* re·pa·ree·ren
repeat *wiederholen* vee·der·haw·len
republic *Republik* ① re·pu·bleek
reservation *Reservierung* ①
  re·zer·vee·rung

reserve *reservieren* re·zer·vee·ren
rest *eine Pause machen*
  ai·ne pow·ze ma·khen
restaurant *Restaurant* ⓝ res·to·rahng
resume (CV) *Lebenslauf* ⓜ
  lay·bens·lowf
retired *pensioniert* pahng·zyo·neert
return *zurückkommen* tsu·rük·ko·men
return (ticket) *Rückfahrkarte* ①
  rük·fahr·kar·te
review (arts) *Kritik* ① kri·teek
rhythm *Rhythmus* ⓜ rüt·mus
rice *Reis* ⓜ rais
rich (wealthy) *reich* raikh
ride *Ritt* ⓜ rit
ride (horse) *reiten* rai·ten
riding school *Reitschule* ① rait·shoo·le
right (correct) *richtig* rikh·tikh
right (direction) *rechts* rekhts
right there *gleich dort* glaikh dort
right-wing *rechts(gerichtet)*
  rekhts(·ge·rikh·tet)
ring (on finger) *Ring* ⓜ ring
ring (of phone) *klingeln* kling·eln
rip-off *Abzockerei* ① ap·tso·ke·rai
risk *Risiko* ⓝ ree·zi·ko
river *Fluss* ⓜ flus
road *Straße* ① shtrah·se
road map *Straßenkarte* ①
  shtrah·sen·kar·te
rob *berauben* be·row·ben
robbery *Raub* ⓜ rowp
rock *Fels* ⓜ fels
rock (music) *Rockmusik* ①
  rok·mu·zeek
rock climbing *Klettern* ⓝ kle·tern
rock group *Rockgruppe* ① rok·gru·pe
roll (bread) *Brötchen* ⓝ brert·khen
romantic *romantisch* ro·man·tish
roof *Dach* ⓝ dakh
room *Zimmer* ⓝ tsi·mer
rope *Seil* ⓝ zail
round *rund* runt
roundabout *Kreisverkehr* ⓜ
  krais·fer·kair
route *Route* ① roo·te
rowing *Rudern* ⓝ roo·dern
rubbish *Müll* ⓜ mül
rug *Teppich* ⓜ te·pikh

rugby *Rugby* ⑩ rag·bi
ruins *Ruinen* ① pl ru·ee·nen
rules *Regeln* ① pl ray·geln
rum *Rum* ⑩ rum
run *laufen* low·fen
run out of *ausgehen* ows·gay·en

S

Sabbath *Sabbat* ⑩ za·bat
sad *traurig* trow·rikh
saddle *Sattel* ⑩ za·tel
safe *Safe* ⑩ sayf
safe *sicher* zi·kher
safe sex *Safe Sex* ⑩ sayf seks
safety *Sicherheit* ① zi·kher·hait
sailing *Segeln* ⑪ zay·geln
saint *Heilige* ⑩&① hai·li·ge
salad *Salat* ⑩ za·laht
salami *Salami* ① za·lah·mi
salary *Gehalt* ⑪ ge·halt
sale *(Sonder)Angebot* ⑪
  (zon·der·)an·ge·bawt
sales tax *Umsatzsteuer* ①
  um·zats·shtoy·er
salmon *Lachs* ⑩ laks
salt *Salz* ⑪ zalts
same *gleiche* glai·khe
sand *Sand* ⑩ zant
sandals *Sandalen* ⑪ pl zan·dah·len
sanitary napkins *Damenbinden* ① pl
  dah·men·bin·den
sardine *Sardine* ① zar·dee·ne
Saturday *Samstag* ⑩ zams·tahk
sauce *Sauce/Soße* ① zaw·se
sauna *Sauna* ① zow·na
sausage *Wurst* ① vurst
save (money) *sparen* shpah·ren
save (someone) *retten* re·ten
say *sagen* zah·gen
scarf *Schal* ⑩ shahl
scenery *Landschaft* ① lant·shaft
school *Schule* ① shoo·le
science *Wissenschaft* ⑪ vi·sen·shaft
scientist *Wissenschaftler(in)* ⑩/①
  vi·sen·shaft·ler/vi·sen·shaft·le·rin
scissors *Schere* ① shair·re
score *ein Tor schießen* ain tawr shee·sen
scoreboard *Anzeigetafel* ①
  an·tsai·ge·tah·fel

Scotland *Schottland* ⑪ shot·lant
screen (TV/computer) *Bildschirm* ⑩
  bilt·shirm
screwdriver *Schraubenzieher* ⑩
  shrow·ben·tsee·er
script *Drehbuch* ⑪ dray·bookh
sculpture *Skulptur* ① skulp·toor
sea *Meer* ⑪ mair
seagull *Möwe* ① mer·ve
seasick *seekrank* zay·krangk
seaside *Meeresküste* ① mair·res·küs·te
season *Jahreszeit* ① yah·res·tsait
seat (car) *Sitz* ⑩ zits
seat (train/cinema) *Platz* ⑩ plats
seatbelt *Sicherheitsgurt* ⑩
  zi·kher·haits·gurt
second *Sekunde* ① ze·kun·de
second *zweite* tsvai·te
second-hand *gebraucht* ge·browkht
second-hand shop
  Secondhandgeschäft ⑪
  se·kend·hend·ge·sheft
secret *Geheimnis* ⑪ ge·haim·nis
secretary *Sekretär(in)* ⑩/①
  ze·kre·tair(·rin)
see *sehen* zay·en
self-employed *selbstständig*
  zelpst·shten·dikh
selfish *egoistisch* e·go·is·tish
self-service *Selbstbedienung* ①
  zelpst·be·dee·nung
sell *verkaufen* fer·kow·fen
send *senden* zen·den
sensible *vernünftig* fer·nünf·tikh
sensual *sinnlich* zin·likh
separate *getrennt* ge·trent
serial *Serien-* zair·ri·en·
series *Serie* ① zair·ri·e
serious *ernst* ernst
service charge *Bedienungszuschlag* ⑩
  be·dee·nungks·tsoo·shlahk
service station *Tankstelle* ①
  tangk·shte·le
several *einige* ai·ni·ge
sew *nähen* nay·en
sex *Sex* ⑩ seks
sexism *Sexismus* ⑩ sek·sis·mus
sexy *sexy* sek·si
shade *Schatten* ⑩ sha·ten

shadow *Schatten* ⓝ sha·ten
shampoo *Shampoo* ⓝ sham·poo
shape *Form* ⓕ form
share (with) *teilen (mit)* tai·len (mit)
shave *rasieren* ra·zee·ren
shaving cream *Rasiercreme* ⓕ
ra·zeer·kraym
she *sie* zee
sheep *Schaf* ⓝ shahf
sheet (bed) *Bettlaken* ⓝ bet·lah·ken
shelf *Regal* ⓝ re·gahl
ship *Schiff* ⓝ shif
shirt *Hemd* ⓝ hemt
shoe shop *Schuhgeschäft* ⓝ
shoo·ge·sheft
shoes *Schuhe* ⓜ pl shoo·e
shoot (gun) *schießen* shee·sen
shop *Geschäft* ⓝ ge·sheft
shopping centre *Einkaufszentrum* ⓝ
ain·kowfs·tsen·trum
short *kurz* kurts
short (height) *klein* klain
shortage *Knappheit* ⓕ knap·hait
shortcut *Abkürzung* ⓕ ap·kür·tsung
shorts *Shorts* pl shorts
short-sleeved *kurzärmelig*
kurts·er·me·likh
shoulder *Schulter* ⓕ shul·ter
shout *schreien* shrai·en
show *Show* ⓕ shoh
show *zeigen* tsai·gen
shower *Dusche* ⓕ doo·she
shrine *Schrein* ⓜ shrain
shut (closed) *geschlossen* ge·shlo·sen
shut (close) *schließen* shlee·sen
shy *schüchtern* shükh·tern
sick *krank* krangk
side *Seite* ⓕ zai·te
sign *Schild* ⓝ shilt
signature *Unterschrift* ⓕ un·ter·shrift
signpost *Wegweiser* ⓜ vayk·vai·zer
silk *Seide* ⓕ zai·de
silver *silbern* zil·bern
similar *ähnlich* ayn·likh
simple *einfach* ain·fakh
since (May) *seit (Mai)* zait (mai)
sing *singen* zing·en
Singapore *Singapur* ⓝ zing·a·poor
singer *Sänger(in)* ⓜ/ⓕ
zeng·er/zeng·e·rin

single (person) *Single* ⓜ singl
single (unmarried) *ledig* lay·dikh
single room *Einzelzimmer* ⓝ
ain·tsel·tsi·mer
singlet *Unterhemd* ⓝ un·ter·hemt
sister *Schwester* ⓕ shves·ter
sit *sitzen* zi·tsen
situation *Lage* ⓕ lah·ge
size *Größe* ⓕ grer·se
skate *eislaufen* ais·low·fen
skateboarding *Skateboarden* ⓝ
skayt·bor·den
ski *skifahren* shee·fah·ren
skiing *Skifahren* ⓝ shee·fah·ren
skimmed milk *fettarme Milch* ⓕ
fet·ar·me milkh
skin *Haut* ⓕ howt
skirt *Rock* ⓜ rok
sky *Himmel* ⓜ hi·mel
sleep *schlafen* shlah·fen
sleeping bag *Schlafsack* ⓜ shlahf·zak
sleeping car *Schlafwagen* ⓜ
shlahf·vah·gen
sleeping pills *Schlaftabletten* ⓕ pl
shlahf·ta·ble·ten
sleepy *schläfrig* shlayf·rikh
slide (film) *Dia* ⓝ dee·a
slippery *glatt* glat
slope *Hang* ⓜ hang
slow *langsam* lang·zahm
slowly *langsam* lang·zahm
small *klein* klain
smell *Geruch* ⓜ ge·rookh
smile *lächeln* le·kheln
smoke *rauchen* row·khen
snack *Snack* ⓜ snek
snail *Schnecke* ⓕ shne·ke
snake *Schlange* ⓕ shlang·e
snorkelling *Schnorcheln* ⓝ shnor·kheln
snow *Schnee* ⓜ shnay
snow pea *Zuckererbse* ⓕ tsu·ker·erp·se
snowboarding *Snowboarden* ⓝ
snoh·bor·den
snowfield *Schneefeld* ⓝ shnay·felt
soap *Seife* ⓕ zai·fe
soap opera *Seifenoper* ⓕ
zai·fen·aw·per
soccer *Fußball* ⓜ foos·bal
social welfare *Wohlfahrt* ⓕ vawl·fahrt

socialist *sozialistisch* zo·tsya·*lis*·tish

socks *Socken* ① pl *zo*·ken

soft drink *alkoholfreies Getränk* ⑩ al·ko·*hawl*·frai·es ge·*trengk*

sold out *ausverkauft* ows·fer·kowft

solid *fest* fest

some *einige* *ai*·ni·ge

someone *jemand* *yay*·mant

something *etwas* *et*·vas

sometimes *manchmal* *mankh*·mahl

son *Sohn* ⑩ zawn

song *Lied* ⑩ leet

son-in-law *Schwiegersohn* ⑩ *shvee*·ger·zawn

soon *bald* balt

sore *schmerzhaft* *shmerts*·haft

sore throat *Halsschmerzen* ⑩ pl *hals*·shmer·tsen

soup *Suppe* ① *zu*·pe

sour cream *Schmand* ⑩ shmant

south *Süden* ⑩ *zü*·den

souvenir *Souvenir* ⑩ zu·ve·*neer*

souvenir shop *Souvenirladen* ⑩ zu·ve·*neer*·lah·den

soy milk *Sojamilch* ① *zaw*·ya·milkh

soy sauce *Sojasauce* ① *zaw*·ya·zaw·se

space *Raum* ⑩ rowm

spade *Spaten* ⑩ *shpah*·ten

Spain *Spanien* ⑩ *shpah*·ni·en

spare tyre *Reservereifen* ⑩ re·*zer*·ve·rai·fen

speak *sprechen* *shpre*·khen

special *speziell* shpe·*tsyel*

specialist *Spezialist(in)* ⑩/① shpe·tsya·*list*/shpe·tsya·*lis*·tin

speed *Geschwindigkeit* ① ge·*shvin*·dikh·kait

speed limit *Geschwindigkeits-begrenzung* ① ge·*shvin*·dikh·kaits·be·gren·tsung

spicy *würzig* *vür*·tsikh

spider *Spinne* ① *shpi*·ne

spinach *Spinat* ⑩ shpi·*naht*

spokes *Speichen* ① pl *shpai*·khen

spoon *Löffel* ⑩ *ler*·fel

sport *Sport* ⑩ shport

sportsperson *Sportler(in)* ⑩/① *shport*·ler/*shport*·le·rin

sprain *Muskelzerrung* ① *mus*·kel·tser·rung

spring (coil) *Feder* ① *fay*·der

spring (season) *Frühling* ⑩ *frü*·ling

square (town) *Platz* ⑩ plats

stadium *Stadion* ⑩ *shtah*·di·on

stage *Stadium* ⑩ *shtah*·di·um

stage (theatre) *Bühne* ① *bü*·ne

stairway *Treppe* ① *tre*·pe

stamp *Briefmarke* ① *breef*·mar·ke

standby ticket *Standby-Ticket* ⑩ *stend*·bai·ti·ket

standing room *Stehplatz* ⑩ *shtay*·plats

star sign *Sternzeichen* ⑩ *shtern*·tsai·khen

star *Stern* ⑩ shtern

(four-)star *(Vier-)Sterne-* (feer·)*shter*·ne·

start *Beginn* ⑩ be·*gin*

start (sport) *Start* ⑩ shtart

start *anfangen* *an*·fang·en

state *Staat* ⑩ shtaht

station *Bahnhof* ⑩ *bahn*·hawf

stationer *Schreibwarenhandlung* ① *shraip*·vah·ren·han·dlung

statue *Statue* ① *shtah*·tu·e

stay (at a hotel) *übernachten* ü·ber·*nakh*·ten

stay (not leave) *bleiben* *blai*·ben

steak (beef) *Steak* ⑩ stayk

steal *stehlen* *shtay*·len

steep *steil* shtail

step (stairs) *Stufe* ① *shtoo*·fe

stereo *Stereoanlage* ① *shtai*·re·o·an·lah·ge

stingy *geizig* *gai*·tsikh

stock *Vorrat* ⑩ *fawr*·raht

stockings *Strümpfe* ⑩ pl *shtrüm*·fe

stomach *Magen* ⑩ *mah*·gen

stomachache *Magenschmerzen* ⑩ pl *mah*·gen·shmer·tsen

stone *Stein* ⑩ shtain

stoned (drugged) *stoned* stohnd

stop *Halt* ⑩ halt

stop *anhalten* *an*·hal·ten

storm *Sturm* ⑩ shturm

story *Geschichte* ① ge·*shikh*·te

stove *Herd* ⑩ hert

straight *gerade* ge·*rah*·de

strange *fremd* fremt

stranger *Fremde* ⑩&① *frem*·de

strawberry *Erdbeere* ① *ert*·bair·re

stream *Bach* ⓜ bakh
street *Straße* ⓕ shtrah·se
street kids *Straßenkinder* ⓟ pl
  shtrah·sen·kin·der
on strike *streiken* shtrai·ken
string *Schnur* ⓕ shnoor
strong *stark* shtark
stubborn *stur* shtoor
student *Student(in)* ⓜ/ⓕ
  shtu·*dent*/shtu·*den*·tin
student card *Studentenausweis* ⓜ
  shtu·*den*·ten·ows·vais
studio *Studio* ⓝ shtoo·di·o
studio (art) *Atelier* ⓝ a·tel·*yay*
study *studieren* shtu·*dee*·ren
stupid *dumm* dum
style *Stil* ⓜ shteel
subtitles *Untertitel* ⓜ pl un·ter·tee·tel
suburb *Vorort* ⓜ fawr·ort
subway *U-Bahn* ⓕ oo·bahn
sugar *Zucker* ⓜ tsu·ker
suitcase *Koffer* ⓜ ko·fer
summer *Sommer* ⓜ zo·mer
sun *Sonne* ⓕ zo·ne
sunblock *Sonnencreme* ⓕ
  zo·nen·kraym
sunburn *Sonnenbrand* ⓜ zo·nen·brant
Sunday *Sonntag* ⓜ zon·tahk
sunglasses *Sonnenbrille* ⓕ
  zo·nen·bri·le
sunny *sonnig* zo·nikh
sunrise *Sonnenaufgang* ⓜ
  zo·nen·owf·gang
sunset *Sonnenuntergang* ⓜ
  zo·nen·un·ter·gang
supermarket *Supermarkt* ⓜ
  zoo·per·markt
superstition *Aberglaube* ⓜ
  ah·ber·glow·be
supporters *Anhänger* ⓜ pl an·heng·er
surf *surfen* ser·fen
surface mail *normale Post* ⓕ
  nor·*mah*·le post
surfboard *Surfbrett* ⓝ serf·bret
surname *Nachname* ⓜ nahkh·nah·me
surprise *Überraschung* ⓕ
  ü·ber·*ra*·shung
sweater *Pullover* ⓜ pu·*law*·ver
sweet *süß* züs

swim *schwimmen* shvi·men
swimming pool *Schwimmbad* ⓝ
  shvim·baht
swimsuit *Badeanzug* ⓜ
  bah·de·an·tsook
Switzerland *Schweiz* ⓕ shvaits
synagogue *Synagoge* ⓕ zü·na·*gaw*·ge
synthetic *synthetisch* zün·*tay*·tish
syringe *Spritze* ⓕ shpri·tse

T

table *Tisch* ⓜ tish
table tennis *Tischtennis* ⓝ tish·te·nis
tablecloth *Tischdecke* ⓕ tish·de·ke
tail *Schwanz* ⓜ shvants
tailor *Schneider(in)* ⓜ/ⓕ
  shnai·der/shnai·de·rin
take *nehmen* nay·men
take (to) *bringen* bring·en
take off *Abflug* ⓜ ap·flook
talk *sprechen* shpre·khen
tall *groß* graws
tampons *Tampons* ⓜ pl tam·pons
tanning lotion *Bräunungsmilch* ⓕ
  broy·nungks·milkh
tap *Wasserhahn* ⓜ va·ser·hahn
target *Ziel* ⓝ tseel
tasty *schmackhaft* shmak·haft
tax *Steuer* ⓕ shtoy·er
taxi *Taxi* ⓝ tak·si
taxi stand *Taxistand* ⓜ tak·si·shtant
tea *Tee* ⓜ tay
teacher *Lehrer(in)* ⓜ/ⓕ
  lair·rer/lair·re·rin
team *Mannschaft* ⓕ man·shaft
teaspoon *Teelöffel* ⓜ tay·ler·fel
technique *Technik* ⓕ tekh·nik
teeth *Zähne* ⓜ pl tsay·ne
telegram *Telegramm* ⓝ te·le·gram
telephone *Telefon* ⓝ te·le·*fawn*
telephone *telefonieren* te·le·fo·nee·ren
telephone book *Telefonbuch* ⓝ
  te·le·*fawn*·bookh
telephone centre *Telefonzentrale* ⓕ
  te·le·*fawn*·tsen·trah·le
telescope *Teleskop* ⓝ te·les·*kawp*
television *Fernseher* ⓜ fern·zay·er
tell *erzählen* er·*tsay*·len
temperature (fever) *Fieber* ⓝ fee·ber

temperature (weather) *Temperatur* ⓕ
tem·pe·ra·*toor*

temple *Tempel* ⓜ *tem*·pel

ten *zehn* tsayn

tennis *Tennis* ⓝ *te*·nis

tennis court *Tennisplatz* ⓜ *te*·nis·plats

tent *Zelt* ⓝ tselt

tent pegs *Heringe* ⓜ pl *hay*·ring·e

terminal (transport) *Endstation* ⓕ
ent·shta·tsyawn

terrible *schrecklich* *shrek*·likh

test *Test* ⓜ test

thank *danken* *dang*·ken

theatre *Theater* ⓝ te·*ah*·ter

their *ihr* eer

there *dort* dort

thermos *Thermosflasche* ⓕ
ter·mos·fla·she

they *sie* zee

thick *dick* dik

thief *Dieb* ⓜ deep

thin *dünn* dün

think *denken* *deng*·ken

third *dritte* *dri*·te

thirsty *durstig* *durs*·tikh

this (month) *diesen (Monat)*
dee·zen (*maw*·nat)

this (one) *dieser/diese/dieses* ⓜ/ⓕ/ⓝ
dee·zer/*dee*·ze/*dee*·zes

thousand *tausend* *tow*·zent

throat *Hals* ⓜ hals

through *durch* durkh

thrush (condition) *Mundfäule* ⓕ
munt·foy·le

thunder *Donner* ⓜ *do*·ner

Thursday *Donnerstag* ⓜ *do*·ners·tahk

ticket (bus/metro/train) *Fahrkarte* ⓕ
fahr·kar·te

ticket (cinema/museum) *Eintrittskarte* ⓕ *ain*·trits·kar·te

ticket (plane) *Flugticket* ⓝ *flook*·li·ket

ticket collector
Fahrkartenkontrolleur/in ⓜ/ⓕ
fahr·kar·ten·kon·tro·ler/
fahr·kar·ten·kon·tro·ler·rin

ticket machine *Fahrkartenautomat* ⓜ
fahr·kar·ten·ow·to·maht

ticket office *Fahrkartenverkauf* ⓜ
fahr·kar·ten·fer·kowf

ticket office (theatre) *Theaterkasse* ⓕ
te·*ah*·ter·ka·se

tides *Gezeiten* pl ge·*tsai*·ten

tight *eng* eng

time *Zeit* ⓕ tsait

time difference *Zeitunterschied* ⓜ
tsait·un·ter·sheet

timetable *Fahrplan* ⓜ *fahr*·plahn

tin (can) *Dose* ⓕ *daw*·ze

tin opener *Dosenöffner* ⓜ
daw·zen·erf·ner

tiny *winzig* *vin*·tsikh

tip (gratuity) *Trinkgeld* ⓝ *tringk*·gelt

tire *ermüden* er·*mü*·den

tired *müde* *mü*·de

tissues *Papiertaschentücher* ⓝ pl
pa·*peer*·ta·shen·tü·kher

toast *Toast* ⓜ tawst

toaster *Toaster* ⓜ *taws*·ter

tobacco *Tabak* ⓜ ta·*bak*

tobacconist *Tabakladen* ⓜ
la·bak·lah·den

tobogganing *Rodeln* ⓝ *raw*·deln

today *heute* *hoy*·te

toe *Zehe* ⓕ *tsay*·e

tofu *Tofu* ⓜ *taw*·fu

together *zusammen* tsu·*za*·men

toilet *Toilette* ⓕ to·a·*le*·te

toilet paper *Toilettenpapier* ⓝ
to·a·*le*·ten·pa·peer

tomato *Tomate* ⓕ to·*mah*·te

tomato sauce *Tomatensauce* ⓕ
to·*mah*·ten·zaw·se

tomb *Grab* ⓝ grahp

tomorrow *morgen* *mor*·gen

tomorrow morning *morgen früh*
mor·gen frü

tonight *heute Abend* *hoy*·te *ah*·bent

too (also) *auch* owkh

too (many) *zu (viele)* tsoo (*fee*·le)

tools *Werkzeug* ⓝ *verk*·tsoyk

tooth *Zahn* ⓜ tsahn

toothache *Zahnschmerzen* ⓜ pl
tsahn·shmer·tsen

toothbrush *Zahnbürste* ⓕ *tsahn*·bürs·te

toothpaste *Zahnpasta* ⓕ *tsahn*·pas·ta

toothpick *Zahnstocher* ⓜ
tsahn·shto·kher

torch (flashlight) *Taschenlampe* ⓕ
ta·shen·lam·pe

touch *berühren* be·rü·ren
tour *Tour* ① toor
tourist *Tourist/in* ⑩/① tu·rist/tu·ris·tin
tourist office *Fremdenverkehrsbüro* ⑩
  frem·den·fer·kairs·bü·raw
towards *auf ... zu* owf ... tsoo
towel *Handtuch* ⑩ hant·tookh
tower *Turm* ⑩ turm
town *Stadt* ① shtat
toxic waste *Giftmüll* ⑩ gift·mül
toy *Spielzeug* ⑩ shpeel·tsoyk
track (path) *Weg* ⑩ vayk
track (sports) *Bahn* ① bahn
trade *Handel* ⑩ han·del
traffic *Verkehr* ⑩ fer·kair
traffic lights *Ampel* ① am·pel
trail *Pfad* ⑩ pfaht
train *Zug* ⑩ tsook
train station *Bahnhof* ⑩ bahn·hawf
tram *Straßenbahn* ① shtrah·sen·bahn
transit lounge *Transitraum* ⑩
  tran·zeet·rowm
translate *übersetzen* ü·ber·ze·tsen
transport *Transport* ⑩ trans·port
travel *reisen* rai·zen
travel agency *Reisebüro* ⑩
  rai·ze·bü·raw
travel sickness *Reisekrankheit* ①
  rai·ze·krangk·hait
travellers cheque *Reisescheck* ⑩
  rai·ze·shek
tree *Baum* ⑩ bowm
trip *Reise* ① rai·ze
trousers *Hose* ① haw·ze
truck *Lastwagen* ⑩ last·vah·gen
true *wahr* vahr
trust *trauen* trow·en
try (attempt) *versuchen* fer·zoo·khen
T-shirt *T-Shirt* ⑩ tee·shert
tube (tyre) *Schlauch* ⑩ shlowkh
Tuesday *Dienstag* ⑩ deens·tahk
tuna *Thunfisch* ⑩ toon·fish
tune *Melodie* ① me·lo·dee
turkey *Truthahn* ⑩ troot·hahn
turn *abbiegen* ap·bee·gen
TV (set) *Fernseher* ⑩ fern·zay·er
TV series *Fernsehserie* ①
  fern·zay·zair·ri·e
tweezers *Pinzette* ① pin·tse·te

twice *zweimal* tsvai·mahl
twin beds *zwei Einzelbetten* ⑩ pl
  tsvai ain·tsel·be·ten
twins *Zwillinge* ⑩ pl tsvi·ling·e
type *Typ* ⑩ tüp
typical *typisch* tü·pish
tyre *Reifen* ⑩ rai·fen

U

ultrasound *Ultraschall* ⑩ ul·tra·shal
umbrella *Regenschirm* ⑩ ray·gen·shirm
uncle *Onkel* ⑩ ong·kel
uncomfortable *unbequem* un·be·kvaym
under *unter* un·ter
underground *U-Bahn* ① oo·bahn
understand *verstehen* fer·shtay·en
underwear *Unterwäsche* ①
  un·ter·ve·she
unemployed *arbeitslos* ar·baits·laws
unemployment *Arbeitslosigkeit* ①
  ar·baits·law·zikh·kait
unfair *unfair* un·fair
uniform *Uniform* ① u·ni·form
universe *Universum* ⑩ u·ni·vair·zum
university *Universität* ① u·ni·ver·zi·tayt
unleaded *bleifrei* blai·frai
unsafe *nicht sicher* nikht zi·kher
until (June) *bis (Juni)* bis (yoo·ni)
unusual *ungewöhnlich* un·ge·vern·likh
up *nach oben* nahkh aw·ben
uphill *aufwärts* owf·verts
upstairs *oben* aw·ben
urgent *dringend* dring·ent
USA *USA* ① pl oo·es·ah
useful *nützlich* nüts·likh

V

vacant *frei* frai
vacation *Ferien* pl fair·i·en
vaccination *Schutzimpfung* ①
  shuts·im·pfung
vagina *Vagina* ① va·gee·na
validate (ticket) *entwerten* ent·ver·ten
valley *Tal* ⑩ tahl
valuable *wertvoll* vert·fol
value (price) *Wert* ⑩ vert
van *Lieferwagen* ⑩ lee·fer·vah·gen

veal *Kalbfleisch* ⓝ *kalp*-flaish
vegetable *Gemüse* ⓝ *ge*-mü-ze
vegetarian *Vegetarier(in)* ⓜ/ⓕ
  ve-ge-*tah*-ri-er/ve-ge-*tah*-ri-e-rin
vein *Vene* ⓕ *vay*-ne
venereal disease *Geschlechts-*
  krankheit ⓕ ge-*shlekhts*-krangk-hait
venue *Veranstaltungsort* ⓜ
  fer-*an*-shtal-tungks-ort
very *sehr* zair
video tape *Videokassette* ⓕ
  vee-de-o-ka-*se*-te
view *Aussicht* ⓕ *ows*-zikht
village *Dorf* ⓝ dorf
vine *Rebe* ⓕ *ray*-be
vinegar *Essig* ⓜ *e*-sikh
vineyard *Weinberg* ⓜ *vain*-berk
virus *Virus* ⓜ *vee*-rus
visa *Visum* ⓝ *vee*-zum
visit *besuchen* be-*zoo*-khen
vitamins *Vitamine* ⓝ pl vi-ta-*mee*-ne
vodka *Wodka* ⓜ *vot*-ka
voice *Stimme* ⓕ *shti*-me
volume (amount) *Volumen* ⓝ
  vo-*loo*-men
volume (book) *Band* ⓜ bant
volume (loudness) *Lautstärke* ⓕ
  lowt-shter-ke
vomit *brechen* *bre*-khen
vote *wählen* *vay*-len

W

wage *Lohn* ⓜ lawn
wait *warten* *var*-ten
waiter *Kellner(in)* ⓜ/ⓕ
  kel-ner/*kel*-ne-rin
waiting room (doctor's)
  Wartezimmer ⓝ *var*-te-tsi-mer
waiting room (train station)
  Wartesaal ⓜ *var*-te-zahl
walk *gehen* *gay*-en
wall (outer) *Mauer* ⓕ *mow*-er
want *wollen* *vo*-len
war *Krieg* ⓜ kreek
wardrobe *Garderobe* ⓕ gar-*draw*-be
warm *warm* varm
warn *warnen* *var*-nen
wash (oneself) *sich waschen*
  zikh *va*-shen

wash (something) *waschen* *va*-shen
wash cloth (flannel) *Waschlappen* ⓜ
  vash-la-pen
washing machine *Waschmaschine* ⓕ
  vash-ma-shee-ne
washing powder *Waschpulver* ⓝ
  vash-pul-ver
wasp *Wespe* ⓕ *ves*-pe
watch *Uhr* ⓕ oor
watch *beobachten* be-*aw*-bakh-ten
watch (TV) *fernsehen* *fern*-zay-en
water *Wasser* ⓝ *va*-ser
  tap water *Leitungswasser* ⓝ
  lai-tungks-va-ser
water bottle *Wasserflasche* ⓕ
  va-ser fla-she
waterfall *Wasserfall* ⓜ *va*-ser-fal
watermelon *Wassermelone* ⓕ
  va-ser-me-law-ne
waterproof *wasserdicht* *va*-ser-dikht
waterskiing *Wasserskifahren* ⓝ
  va-ser-shee-fah-ren
wave *Welle* ⓕ *ve*-le
way *Weg* ⓜ vayk
we *wir* veer
weak *schwach* shvakh
wealthy *reich* raikh
weapon *Waffe* ⓕ *va*-fe
wear *tragen* *trah*-gen
weather *Wetter* ⓝ *ve*-ter
wedding *Hochzeit* ⓕ *hokh*-tsait
wedding cake *Hochzeitstorte* ⓕ
  hokh-tsaits-tor-te
wedding present *Hochzeitsgeschenk* ⓝ
  hokh-tsaits-ge-shengk
Wednesday *Mittwoch* ⓜ *mit*-vokh
(this) week *(diese) Woche* ⓕ
  (dee-ze) *vo*-khe
weekend *Wochenende* ⓝ
  vo-khen-en-de
weigh *wiegen* *vee*-gen
weight *Gewicht* ⓝ ge-*vikht*
welcome *willkommen* vil-*ko*-men
welfare *Sozialhilfe* ⓕ zo-*tsyahl*-hil-fe
welfare state *Sozialstaat* ⓜ
  zo-*tsyahl*-shtaht
well *gut* goot
west *Westen* ⓜ *ves*-ten
wet *nass* nas

what *was* vas
wheel *Rad* ⊙ raht
wheelchair *Rollstuhl* ⊙ rol·shtool
when (adverb) *wann* van
when (conjunction) *wenn* ven
whenever *wann immer* van i·mer
where *wo* vaw
whisky *Whisky* ⊙ vis·ki
white *weiß* vais
who *wer* vair
whole *ganz* gants
why *warum* va·*rum*
wide *breit* brait
wife *Ehefrau* ① ay·e·frow
wild *wild* vilt
win *gewinnen* ge·vi·nen
wind *Wind* ⊙ vint
window *Fenster* ⊙ fens·ter
windscreen *Windschutzscheibe* ①
    vint·shuts·shai·be
windsurfing *Windsurfen* ⊙ vint·ser·fen
windy *windig* vin·dikh
wine *Wein* ⊙ vain
    red wine *Rotwein* ⊙ rawt·vain
    sparkling wine *Schaumwein* ⊙
       showm·vain
    white wine *Weißwein* ⊙ vais·vain
wings *Flügel* ⊙ pl flü·gel
winner *Sieger(in)* ⊙/①
    zee·ger/zee·ge·rin
winter *Winter* ⊙ vin·ter
wire *Draht* ⊙ draht
wish *wünschen* vün·shen
with *mit* mit
within (an hour)
    innerhalb (einer Stunde)
    i·ner·halp (ai·ner shtun·de)
without *ohne* aw·ne
woman *Frau* ① frow
wonderful *wunderbar* vun·der·bahr
wood *Holz* ⊙ holts
wool *Wolle* ① vo·le
word *Wort* ⊙ vort
work *Arbeit* ① ar·bait
work *arbeiten* ar·bai·ten

work permit *Arbeitserlaubnis* ①
    ar·baits·er·lowp·nis
workout *Training* ⊙ tray·ning
workshop *Werkstatt* ① verk·shtat
world *Welt* ① velt
World Cup *Weltmeisterschaft* ①
    velt·mais·ter·shaft
worms *Würmer* ⊙ pl vür·mer
worried *besorgt* be·zorkt
worse *schlechter* shlekh·ter
worship *einen Gottesdienst besuchen*
    ai·nen go·tes·deenst be·zoo·khen
write *schreiben* shrai·ben
writer *Schriftsteller(in)* ⊙/①
    shrift·shte·ler/shrift·shte·le·rin
wrong *falsch* falsh

(this) year *(dieses) Jahr* ⊙
    (dee·zes) yahr
yellow *gelb* gelp
yes *ja* yah
yesterday *gestern* ges·tern
yet *schon* shawn
not yet *noch nicht* nokh nikht
yoga *Joga* ⊙ yaw·ga
yogurt *Joghurt* ⊙ yaw·gurt
you sg inf *du* doo
you sg&pl pol *Sie* zee
young *jung* yung
your sg inf *dein* dain
your sg&pl pol *Ihr* eer
youth hostel *Jugendherberge* ①
    yoo·gent·her·ber·ge

zero *null* nul
zipper *Reißverschluss* ⊙ rais·fer·shlus
zodiac *Sternzeichen* ⊙ shtern·tsai·khen
zoo *Zoo* ⊙ tsaw
zucchini *Zucchini* ① tsu·kee·ni

Nouns in the dictionary, and adjectives affected by gender, have their gender indicated by ⓕ, ⓜ or ⓝ. If it's a plural noun, you'll also see pl. Where a word that could be either a noun or a verb has no gender indicated, it's a verb.

A

A

abbiegen *ap*·bee·gen *turn*
Abend ⓜ *ah*·bent *evening*
Abendessen ⓝ *ah*·bent·e·sen *dinner*
aber *ah*·ber *but*
Aberglaube ⓜ *ah*·ber·glow·be *superstition*
abfahren *ap*·fah·ren *leave (depart)*
Abfahrt ⓕ *ap*·fahrt *departure*
Abfall ⓜ *ap*·fal *garbage*
Abfertigungsschalter ⓜ *ap*·fer·ti·gungks·shal·ter *check in (desk)*
Abflug ⓜ *ap*·flook *take off*
Abführmittel ⓝ *ap*·für·mi·tel *laxatives*
abgelegen *ap*·ge·lay·gen *remote*
Abgeordnete ⓕ&ⓜ *ap*·ge·ordne·te *member of parliament*
abgeschlossen *ap*·ge·shlo·sen *locked*
abhängig *ap*·heng·ikh *addicted*
Abholzung ⓕ *ap*·hol·tsung *deforestation*
Abkürzung ⓕ *ap*·kür·tsung *shortcut*
ablehnen *ap*·lay·nen *refuse*
Abschleppdienst ⓜ *ap*·shlep·deenst *breakdown service*
abseits *ap*·zaits *offside*
Abstrich ⓜ *ap*·shtrikh *pap smear*
Abtreibung ⓕ *ap*·trai·bung *abortion*
abwärts *ap*·verts *downhill*
Abzockerei ⓕ *ap*·tso·ke·rai *rip-off*
Abzug ⓜ *ap*·tsook *print (photography)*
Adapter ⓜ *a*·dap·ter *adaptor*
Adressanhänger ⓜ *a*·dres·an·heng·er *luggage tag*
Adresse ⓕ *a*·dre·se *address*
Aerobics pl e·ro·biks *aerobics*
Aerogramm ⓝ *air*·ro·gram *aerogram*
Afrika ⓝ *a*·fri·kah *Africa*
Aftershave ⓝ *ahf*·ter·shayf *aftershave*
ähnlich *ayn*·likh *similar*
AIDS ⓝ *aydz* *AIDS*

Aktentasche ⓕ *ak*·ten·ta·she *briefcase*
Aktivist(in) ⓜ/ⓕ ak·ti·*vist*/ak·ti·*vis*·tin *activist*
Aktuelles ⓝ ak·tu·e·les *current affairs*
Akupunktur ⓕ a·ku·pungk·*toor* *acupuncture*
Alkohol ⓜ *al*·ko·hawl *alcohol*
alkoholfreies Getränk ⓝ al·ko·hawl·frai·es ge·*trengk* *soft drink*
Alkoholiker(in) ⓜ/ⓕ al·ko·*haw*·li·ker/al·ko·*haw*·li·ke·rin *alcoholic*
alkoholisch al·ko·*haw*·lish *alcoholic*
alle *a*·le *all*
Allee ⓕ a·*lay* *avenue*
allein a·*lain* *alone*
Allergie ⓕ a·ler·*gee* *allergy*
alles *a*·les *everything*
allgemein al·ge·*main* *general*
alltäglich al·*tayk*·likh *every day*
alt alt *old • ancient*
Altar ⓜ al·*tahr* *altar*
Alter ⓝ *al*·ter *age*
Amateur(in) ⓜ/ⓕ a·ma·*ter*(·rin) *amateur*
Ameise ⓕ *ah*·mai·ze *ant*
Ampel ⓕ *am*·pel *traffic lights*
sich amüsieren zikh a·mü·*zee*·ren *enjoy (oneself)*
an an *at • to*
Anarchist(in) ⓜ/ⓕ a·nar·*khist*/a·nar·*khis*·tin *anarchist*
anbaggern *an*·ba·gern *chat up*
andere *an*·de·re *other • different*
anfangen *an*·fang·en *start*
Anführer ⓜ *an*·fü·rer *leader*
Angel ⓕ *ang*·el *fishing rod*
Angestellte ⓜ&ⓕ *an*·ge·shtel·te *employee*
Angst (haben) angkst (*hah*·ben) *(to be) afraid*
anhalten *an*·hal·ten *stop*

Anhänger ⓜ pl *an·heng·er* supporters
ankommen *an·ko·men* arrive
Ankunft ⓕ *an·kunft* arrivals
ansehen *an·zay·en* look at
(an)statt *an·shtat* instead of
Anti-Atom- *an·ti·a·tawm·* antinuclear
Antibiotika ⓝ pl *an·ti·bi·aw·ti·ka* antibiotics
Antiquariat ⓝ *an·ti·kva·ri·aht* second-hand bookshop
Antiquität ⓕ *an·ti·kvi·tayt* antique
Antiseptikum ⓝ *an·ti·zep·ti·kum* antiseptic
Antwort ⓕ *ant·vort* answer
antworten *ant·vor·ten* answer
Anzahlung ⓕ *an·tsah·lung* deposit
Anzeige ⓕ *an·tsai·ge* advertisement
Anzeigetafel ⓕ *an·tsai·ge·tah·fel* scoreboard
Apfel ⓜ *ap·fel* apple
Apfelmost ⓜ *ap·fel·most* cider
Apotheke ⓕ *a·po·tay·ke* chemist • pharmacy
Aprikose ⓕ *a·pri·kaw·ze* apricot
Arbeit ⓕ *ar·bait* work
arbeiten *ar·bai·ten* work
Arbeiter(in) ⓜ/ⓕ *ar·bai·ter/ar·bai·te·rin* worker • labourer
Arbeitgeber ⓜ *ar·bait·gay·ber* employer
Arbeitserlaubnis ⓕ *ar·baits·er·lowp·nis* work permit
arbeitslos *ar·baits·laws* unemployed
Arbeitslosengeld ⓝ *ar·baits·law·zen·gelt* dole • unemployment benefit
Arbeitslosigkeit ⓕ *ar·baits·law·zikh·kait* unemployment
Arbeitsstelle ⓕ *ar·baits·shte·le* job
archäologisch *ar·khe·o·law·gish* archaeological
Architektur ⓕ *ar·khi·tek·toor* architecture
Arm ⓜ *arm* arm
arm *arm* poor
Armut ⓕ *ar·moot* poverty
Arzt ⓜ *artst* doctor (medical)
Ärztin ⓕ *erts·tin* doctor (medical)
Aschenbecher ⓜ *a·shen·be·kher* ashtray
Asien ⓝ *ah·zi·en* Asia
Asthma ⓝ *ast·ma* asthma

Asylant(in) ⓜ/ⓕ *a·zü·lant/a·zü·lan·tin* asylum seeker
Atelier ⓝ *a·tel·yay* studio (art)
atmen *aht·men* breathe
Atmosphäre ⓕ *at·mos·fair·re* atmosphere
Atomenergie ⓕ *a·tawm·e·ner·gee* nuclear energy
Atommüll ⓜ *a·tawm·mül* nuclear waste
Aubergine ⓕ *aw·ber·zhee·ne* eggplant • aubergine
auch *owkh* too • also
auch nicht *owkh nikht* neither
auf *owf* on • at
auf … zu *owf … tsoo* towards
Aufführung ⓕ *owf·fü·rung* performance
aufheben *owf·hay·ben* pick up (object)
Aufnahme ⓕ *owf·nah·me* recording
aufpassen *owf·pa·sen* mind (object) • pay attention
Auftritt ⓜ *owf·trit* gig
aufwärts *owf·verts* uphill
Auge ⓝ *ow·ge* eye
Augenblick ⓜ *ow·gen·blik* moment
Augentropfen ⓜ pl *ow·gen·trop·fen* eye drops
aus *ows* from • out
aus (Baumwolle) *ows (bawm·vo·le)* made of (cotton)
Ausbeutung ⓕ *ows·boy·tung* exploitation
Ausgang ⓜ *ows·gang* exit
ausgebucht *ows·ge·bookht* booked out
ausgehen *ows·gay·en* go out • run out of
mit jemandem ausgehen mit *yay·man·dem ows·gay·en* date someone
ausgeschlossen *ows·ge·shlo·sen* excluded
ausgezeichnet *ows·ge·tsaikh·net* excellent
Auskunft ⓕ *ows·kunft* information
im Ausland im *ows·lant* abroad
ausländisch *ows·len·dish* foreign
Auspuff ⓜ *ows·puf* exhaust (car)
Ausrüstung ⓕ *ows·rüs·tung* equipment
Ausschlag ⓜ *ows·shlahk* rash

außer ow·ser *apart from • besides*
Aussicht ① ows·zikht *view*
Aussichtspunkt ⑩ ows·zikhts·pungkt *lookout*
Ausstellung ① ows·shte·lung *exhibition*
austeilen ows·tai·len *deal (cards)*
Auster ① ows·ter *oyster*
Australien ⑩ ows·trah·li·en *Australia*
ausverkauft ows·fer·kowft *sold out*
Ausweis ⑩ ows·vais *identification*
Auto ⑩ ow·to *car*
Autobahn ① ow·to·bahn *motorway (tollway)*
Autokennzeichen ⑪ ow·to·ken·tsai·khen *licence plate number*
automatisch ow·to·mah·tish *automatic*
Autor(in) ⑩/① ow·tor/ow·taw·rin *author*
Autoverleih ⑩ ow·to·fer·lai *car hire*
Avokado ① a·vo·kah·do *avocado*
Axt ① akst *axe*

B

Baby ⑩ bay·bi *baby*
Babynahrung ① bay·bi·nah·rung *baby food*
Babypuder ⑩ bay·bi·poo·der *baby powder*
Babysitter ⑩ bay·bi·si·ter *babysitter*
Bach ⑩ bakh *stream*
Bäckerei ① be·ke·rai *bakery*
Backpflaume ① bak·pflow·me *prune*
Bad ⑪ baht *bath*
Badeanzug ⑩ bah·de·an·tsook *swimsuit*
Badetuch ⑪ bah·de·tookh *bath towel*
Badezimmer ⑪ bah·de·tsi·mer *bathroom*
Bahn ① bahn *track (sports) • railway*
Bahnhof ⑩ bahn·hawf *railway station*
Bahnsteig ⑩ bahn·shtaik *platform*
bald balt *soon*
Balkon ⑩ bal·kawn *balcony*
Ball ⑩ bal *ball*
Ballett ⑪ ba·let *ballet*
Banane ① ba·nah·ne *banana*
Band ① bent *band (music)*
Band ⑩ bant *volume (book)*

Bank ① bangk *bank*
Bankauszug ⑩ bangk·ows·tsook *bankdraft*
Bankkonto ⑪ bangk·kon·to *bank account*
Bär ⑩ bair *bear*
Bargeld ⑪ bahr·gelt *cash*
Batterie ① ba·te·ree *battery*
bauen bow·en *build*
Bauer ⑩ bow·er *farmer*
Bäuerin ① boy·e·rin *farmer*
Bauernhof ⑩ bow·ern·hawf *farm*
Baum ⑩ bowm *tree*
Baumwolle ① bowm·vo·le *cotton*
Bedienungszuschlag ⑩ be·dee·nungks·tsoo·shlahk *service·charge*
bedrohte be·draw·te *endangered*
beenden be·en·den *finish*
Beginn ⑩ be·gin *beginning*
beginnen be·gi·nen *begin*
Begleiter(in) ⑩/① be·glai·ter/be·glai·te·rin *companion*
Begräbnis ⑪ be·grayp·nis *funeral*
behindert be·hin·dert *disabled*
bei bai *at*
Beichte ① baikh·te *confession (religious)*
beide bai·de *both*
Bein ⑪ bain *leg (body)*
Beispiel ⑪ bai·shpeel *example*
Bekleidungsgeschäft ⑪ be·klai·dungks·ge·sheft *clothing store*
Belästigung ① be·les·ti·gung *harassment*
Belichtungsmesser ⑩ be·likh·tungks·me·ser *light meter*
beliebt be·leept *popular*
Benzin ⑪ ben·tseen *gas/petrol*
Benzinkanister ⑩ ben·tseen·ka·nis·ter *petrol can*
beobachten be·aw·bakh·ten *watch*
bequem be·kvaym *comfortable*
berauben be·row·ben *rob*
Berg ⑩ berk *mountain*
Berghütte ① berk·hü·te *mountain hut*
Bergsteigen ⑪ berk·shtai·gen *mountaineering*
Bergweg ⑩ berk·vayk *mountain path*

Beruf ⓜ be·*roof*
  occupation • profession
berühmt be·*rümt famous*
berühren be·*rü·ren touch*
beschäftigt be·*shef·*tikht *busy (person)*
beschützen be·*shü·*tsen *protect*
sich beschweren zikh be·*shvair·*ren
  complain
besetzt be·*zetst busy (phone)*
Besitzer(in) ⓜ/ⓕ be·*zi·*tser/be·*zi·*tse·rin
  owner
besorgt be·*zorkt worried*
besser be·*ser better*
bestätigen be·*shtay·*ti·gen
  confirm (reservation)
beste *bes·*te *best*
bestechen be·*shte·*khen *bribe*
Besteck ⓝ be·*shtek cutlery*
besteigen be·*shtai·*gen
  board (plane, ship)
bestellen be·*shte·*len *order*
Bestellung ⓕ be·*shte·*lung
  order (restaurant)
bestrafen be·*shtrah·*fen *punish*
besuchen be·*zoo·*khen *visit*
Betäubung ⓕ be·*toy·*bung *anaesthetic*
sich beteiligen zikh be·*tai·*li·gen
  participate
Betrag ⓜ be·*trahk amount*
Betrüger(in) ⓜ/ⓕ be·*trü·*ger/
  be·*trü·*ge·rin *cheat*
betrunken be·*trung·*ken *drunk*
Bett ⓝ bet *bed*
Bettlaken ⓝ bet·*lah·*ken *sheet (bed)*
Bettler(in) ⓜ/ⓕ bet·*ler/bet·*le·rin *beggar*
Bettwäsche ⓕ bet·*ve·*she *linen (bed)*
Bettzeug ⓝ bet·*tsoyk bedding*
Beutelmelone ⓕ boy·*tel·*me·law·ne
  cantaloupe
bezahlen be·*tsah·*len *pay*
Beziehung ⓕ be·*tsee·*ung *relationship*
BH ⓜ bay·*hah bra*
Bibel ⓕ bee·*bel bible*
Bibliothek ⓕ bi·bli·o·*tayk library*
Biene ⓕ bee·*ne bee*
Bier ⓝ beer *beer*
Bildschirm ⓜ bilt·*shirm screen (TV,*
  computer)
Billard ⓝ bil·*yart pool (game)*

billig bi·*likh cheap*
Birne ⓕ bir·*ne pear*
bis (Juni) bis (yoo·ni) *until (June)*
bis zu ... bis tsoo ... *as far as ...*
Biss ⓜ bis *bite (animal)*
ein bisschen ain bis·*khen a little*
bitte bi·*te please*
um etwas bitten um et·vas bi·*ten*
  ask for something
bitter bi·*ter bitter*
Blase ⓕ blah·*ze blister*
Blasenentzündung ⓕ
  blah·zen·en·*tsün·*dung *cystitis*
Blatt ⓝ blat *leaf*
blau blow *blue*
bleiben blai·*ben stay (remain)*
bleifrei blai·*frai unleaded*
Bleistift ⓜ blai·*shtift pencil*
blind blint *blind*
Blinddarm ⓜ blint·*darm appendix*
Blindenhund ⓜ blin·den·*hunt*
  guide dog
Blindenschrift ⓕ blin·den·*shrift Braille*
Blinker ⓜ bling·*ker indicator*
Blitz ⓜ blits *lightning • flash*
blockiert blo·*keert blocked*
Blume ⓕ bloo·*me flower*
Blumenhändler ⓜ bloo·men·*hen·*dler
  florist
Blumenkohl ⓜ bloo·men·*kawl*
  cauliflower
Blut ⓝ bloot *blood*
Blutdruck ⓜ bloot·*druk blood pressure*
Blutgruppe ⓕ bloot·*gru·*pe
  blood group
Bluttest ⓜ bloot·*test blood test*
Boden ⓜ baw·*den floor*
Bohne ⓕ baw·*ne bean*
Bonbon ⓝ bong·*bong candy*
Boot ⓝ bawt *boat*
an Bord an bort *aboard*
Bordkarte ⓕ bort·*kar·*te *boarding pass*
Botanischer Garten ⓜ bo·*tah·*ni·sher
  gar·ten botanic garden
Botschaft ⓕ bawt·*shaft embassy*
Botschafter(in) ⓜ/ⓕ bawt·*shaf·*ter/
  bawt·shaf·te·rin ambassador
Boxen ⓝ bok·*sen boxing*
braten brah·*ten fry*

Bratpfanne ① braht·pfa·ne *frying pan*

brauchen *brow·khen need*

braun brown *brown*

brechen bre·khen *vomit*

breit brait *wide*

Bremsen ① *brem·zen brakes*

Bremsflüssigkeit ① brems·flü·sikh·kait *brake fluid*

Brennholz ⑩ *bren·holts firewood*

Brennstoff ⑩ *bren·shtof fuel*

Brett ⑪ bret *board (plank)*

Brief ⑩ breef *letter*

Briefkasten ⑩ breef·kas·ten *mailbox*

Briefmarke ① breef·mar·ke *stamp*

Briefumschlag ⑩ breef·um·shlahk *envelope*

brillant bril·yant *brilliant*

Brille ① bri·le *glasses (spectacles)*

bringen bring·en *bring • take (something somewhere)*

Brokkoli ⑩ pl bro·ko·li *broccoli*

Bronchitis ① bron·khee·tis *bronchitis*

Broschüre ① bro·shü·re *brochure*

Brot ⑪ brawt *bread*

Brötchen ⑪ brœt·khen *broad roll*

Brücke ① brü·ke *bridge*

Bruder ⑩ broo·der *brother*

Brunnen ⑩ bru·nen *fountain*

Brust ① brust *breast*

Brustkorb ⑩ brust·korp *chest*

Buch ⑪ bookh *book*

buchen boo·khen *book (reserve)*

Buchhalter(in) ⑩/① bookh·hal·ter/ bookh·hal·te·rin *accountant*

Buchhandlung ① bookh·han·dlung *bookshop*

Buddhist(in) ⑩/① bu·dist/bu·dis·tin *Buddhist*

Buffet ⑪ bü·*fay buffet*

bügeln bü·geln *iron (clothes)*

Bühne ① bü·ne *stage (theatre)*

Bundeskanzler(in) ⑩/① bun·des·kants·ler/bun·des·kants·le·rin *prime minister (in Germany & Austria)*

Burg ① burk *castle*

Bürgermeister(in) ⑩/① bür·ger·mais·ter/bür·ger·mais·te·rin *mayor*

Bürgerrechte ① pl bür·ger·rekh·te *civil rights*

Büro ⑪ bü·*raw office*

Büroangestellte ⑩&① bü·raw·an·ge·shtel·te *office worker*

Bus ⑩ bus *bus (city)*

Busbahnhof ⑩ bus·bahn·hawf *bus station*

Bushaltestelle ① bus·hal·te·shte·le *bus stop*

Butter ① bu·ter *butter*

C

Café ⑪ ka·*fay cafe*

Campingplatz ⑩ kem·ping·plats *camping ground*

Cashewnuss ① kesh·yoo·nus *cashew*

CD ① tsay·day *CD*

Celsius ⑩ tsel·zi·us *centigrade*

Chancengleichheit ① shahng·sen·glaikh·hait *equal opportunity*

charmant shar·mant *charming*

Chef(in) ⑩/① shef/she·fin *boss*

chemische Reinigung ① khay·mi·she rai·ni·gung *dry-cleaner*

Chili(sauce) ① chi·li(·zaw·se) *chilli (sauce)*

Christ(in) ⑩/① krist/kris·tin *Christian*

Computerspiel ⑪ kom·pyoo·ter·shpeel *computer game*

Coupon ⑩ ku·pong *coupon*

Couscous ⑩ kus·kus *couscous*

Cousin(e) ⑩/① ku·zen/ku·zee·ne *cousin*

Cracker ⑩ kre·ker *cracker*

Cricket ⑪ kri·ket *cricket*

Curry(pulver) ⑩ ker·ri(·pul·ver) *curry (powder)*

D

Dach ⑪ dakh *roof*

Dachboden ⑩ dakh·baw·den *attic*

Dachs ⑩ daks *badger*

Damenbinden ① pl dah·men·bin·den *sanitary napkins*

Dämmerung ① de·me·rung *dawn • dusk*

danken dang·ken *thank*

Datum ⑪ dah·tum *date (day)*

Decke ① *de*·ke *blanket*
dein dain *your* sg inf
Demokratie ① *de*·mo·kra·*tee* *democracy*
Demonstration ① *de*·mon·stra·*tsyawn* *demonstration*
denken *deng*·ken *think*
Denkmal ⑩ *dengk*·mahl *monument*
Deo ⑩ *day*·o *deodorant*
Detail ⑩ *de*·*tai* *detail*
Deutsch ⑩ *doytsh* *German*
Deutschland ⑩ *doytsh*·lant *Germany*
Dia ⑩ *dee*·a *slide (film)*
Diabetis ① *di*·a·*bay*·tis *diabetes*
Diät ① *di*·*ayt* *diet*
Dichtung ① *dikh*·tung *poetry*
dick dik *thick • fat*
Dieb ⑩ *deep* *thief*
Dienstag ⑩ *deens*·tahk *Tuesday*
dieser ⑩ *dee*·zer *this (one)*
direkt di·*rekt* *direct*
Diskette ① *dis*·ke·te *disk (computer)*
Disko(thek) ① *dis*·ko(·*tayk*) *disco*
Diskriminierung ① *dis*·kri·mi·*nee*·rung *discrimination*
Doktor(in) ⑩/① *dok*·tor/dok·*taw*·rin *doctor (title)*
Dokumentation ① do·ku·men·ta·*tsyawn* *documentary*
Dollar ⑩ *do*·lahr *dollar*
Dolmetscher(in) ⑩/① *dol*·met·sher/ *dol*·met·she·rin *interpreter*
Dom ⑩ *dawm* *cathedral*
Donner ⑩ *do*·ner *thunder*
Donnerstag ⑩ *do*·ners·tahk *Thursday*
Dope ⑩ *dawp/dohp* *dope (drugs)*
Doppelbett ⑩ *do*·pel·bet *double bed*
doppelt *do*·pelt *double*
Doppelzimmer ⑩ *do*·pel·tsi·mer *double room*
Dorf ⑩ *dorf* *village*
dort dort *there*
Dose ① *daw*·ze *can (tin)*
Dosenöffner ⑩ *daw*·zen·erf·ner *can opener*
Dozent(in) ⑩/① do·*tsent*/do·*tsen*·tin *lecturer*
Drachenfliegen ⑩ *dra*·khen·flee·gen *hang-gliding*

Draht ⑩ *draht* *wire*
draußen *drow*·sen *outside*
dringend *dring*·ent *urgent*
dritte *dri*·te *third*
Droge ① *draw*·ge *drug*
Drogenabhängigkeit ① *draw*·gen·ap·heng·ikh·kait *drug addiction*
Drogenhändler ⑩ *draw*·gen·hen·dler *drug dealer*
Druck ⑩ *druk* *pressure • print (artwork)*
Drüsenfieber ⑩ *drü*·zen·fee·ber *glandular fever*
du doo *you* sg inf
dumm dum *stupid*
dunkel *dung*·kel *dark*
dünn dün *thin*
durch durkh *through*
Durchfall ⑩ *durkh*·fal *diarrhoea*
Durchwahl ① *durkh*·vahl *direct-dial*
durstig *durs*·tikh *thirsty*
Dusche ① *doo*·she *shower*
Dutzend ⑩ *du*·tsent *dozen*

E

Ebene ① *ay*·be·ne *plain*
Echse ① *ek*·se *lizard*
Ecke ① *e*·ke *corner*
egoistisch e·go·*is*·tish *selfish*
Ehe ① *ay*·e *marriage*
Ehefrau ① *ay*·e·frow *wife*
Ehemann ⑩ *ay*·e·man *husband*
ehrlich *air*·likh *honest*
Ei ⑩ *ai* *egg*
Eierstockzyste ① *ai*·er·shtok·tsüs·te *ovarian cyst*
eifersüchtig *ai*·fer·zükh·tikh *jealous*
in Eile in *ai*·le *in a hurry*
Eimer ⑩ *ai*·mer *bucket*
ein(s) ain(s) *one*
einfach *ain*·fakh *simple*
einfache Fahrkarte ① *ain*·fa·khe *fahr*·kar·te *one-way ticket*
einige *ai*·ni·ge *some • several*
einkaufen gehen *ain*·kow·fen gay·en *go shopping*
Einkaufszentrum ⑩ *ain*·kowfs·tsen·trum *shopping centre*
Einkommensteuer ① *ain*·ko·men·shtoy·er *income tax*

einladen *ain*·lah·den *invite*
einlassen *ain*·la·sen *admit (allow to enter)*
einlösen *ain*·ler·zen *cash (a cheque)*
einmal *ain*·mahl *once*
Einschreiben ⓝ *ain*·shrai·ben *registered mail*
eintreten *ain*·tray·ten *enter*
Eintrittsgeld ⓝ *ain*·trits·gelt *cover charge*
Eintrittskarte ⓕ *ain*·trits·kar·te *(admission) ticket*
Eintrittspreis ⓜ *ain*·trits·prais *admission price*
einzeln aufgeführt *ain*·tseln owf·ge·fürt *itemised*
Einzelzimmer ⓝ *ain*·tsel·tsi·mer *single room*
Eis ⓝ *ais* *ice*
Eiscreme ⓕ *ais*·kraym *ice cream*
Eisdiele ⓕ *ais*·dee·le *ice cream parlour*
Eisenwarengeschäft ⓝ ai·zen·vah·ren·ge·sheft *hardware store*
Eishockey ⓝ *ais*·ho·ki *ice hockey*
eislaufen *ais*·low·fen *ice skating*
Eispickel ⓜ *ais*·pi·kel *ice axe*
Ekzem ⓝ ek·*tsaym* *eczema*
Elektrizität ⓕ e·lek·tri·tsi·*tayt* *electricity*
Elektrogeschäft ⓝ e·*lek*·tro·ge·sheft *electrical store*
Eltern ⓝ pl *el*·tern *parents*
emotional e·mo·tsyo·*nahl* *emotional*
empfehlen emp·*fay*·len *recommend*
Empfindlichkeit ⓕ emp·*fint*·likh·kait *film speed • sensitivity*
(am) Ende (am) *en*·de *(at the) end*
Endstation ⓕ *ent*·shta·tsyawn *terminal*
Energie ⓕ e·ner·*gee* *energy*
eng *eng* *tight*
Englisch ⓝ *eng*·lish *English*
Enkelkind ⓝ *eng*·kel·kint *grandchild*
Ente ⓕ *en*·te *duck*
entscheiden ent·*shai*·den *decide*
sich entspannen zikh ent·*shpa*·nen *relax*
entwerfen ent·*ver*·fen *design*
entwerten ent·*ver*·ten *validate (ticket)*
Entzündung ⓕ en·*tsün*·dung *infection • inflammation*
Epilepsie ⓕ e·pi·lep·*see* *epilepsy*

er *air* *he*
erbrechen er·*bre*·khen *vomit*
Erbse ⓕ *erp*·se *pea*
Erdbeben ⓝ ert·*bay*·ben *earthquake*
Erdbeere ⓕ ert·*bair*·re *strawberry*
Erde ⓕ *er*·de *Earth*
Erdnuss ⓕ *ert*·nus *peanut • ground nut*
Erfahrung ⓕ er·*fah*·rung *experience*
erhalten er·*hal*·ten *receive*
erkältet sein er·*kel*·tet zain *have a cold*
Erlaubnis ⓕ er·*lowp*·nis *permission*
ermüden er·*mü*·den *tire*
ernst *ernst* *serious*
erstaunlich er·*shtown*·likh *amazing*
erste *ers*·te *first*
Erwachsene ⓜ&ⓕ er·*vak*·se·ne *adult*
erzählen er·*tsay*·len *tell*
Erziehung ⓕ er·*tsee*·ung *education*
Essen ⓝ *e*·sen *food*
essen *e*·sen *eat*
Essig ⓜ *e*·sikh *vinegar*
etwas *et*·vas *something • anything*
Euro ⓜ *oy*·ro *euro*
Europa ⓝ oy·*raw*·pa *Europe*
Euthanasie ⓕ oy·ta·na·*zee* *euthanasia*
Express- *eks*·pres- *express*
Expresspost ⓕ eks·*pres*·post *express mail*

F

Fabrik ⓕ fa·*breek* *factory*
fahren *fah*·ren *travel by vehicle*
Fahrgast ⓜ *fahr*·gast *passenger (bus/taxi)*
Fahrkarte ⓕ *fahr*·kar·te *ticket*
Fahrkartenautomat ⓜ *fahr*·kar·ten·ow·to·maht *ticket machine*
Fahrkartenkontrolleur(in) ⓜ/ⓕ *fahr*·kar·ten·kon·tro·*ler*·(rin) *ticket collector*
Fahrkartenverkauf ⓜ *fahr*·kar·ten·fer·kowf *ticket office*
Fahrplan ⓜ *fahr*·plahn *timetable*
Fahrrad ⓝ *fahr*·raht *bicycle*
Fahrradkette ⓕ *fahr*·raht·ke·te *bicycle chain*
Fahrzeugpapiere ⓝ pl *fahr*·tsoyk·pa·pee·re *car owner's title (document)*
Fallschirmspringen ⓝ *fahl*·shirm·shpring·en *parachuting*

falsch falsh *false • wrong*
Familie ① fa·mee·li·e *family*
Familienname ⓜ fa·mee·li·en·nah·me *family name*
Familienstand ⓜ fa·mee·li·en·shtant *marital status*
Fan ⓜ fen *fan (sports)*
Farbe ① far·be *colour*
Farben ① pl far·ben *paints*
fast fast *almost*
Fastenzeit ① fas·ten·tsait *Lent*
faul fowl *lazy*
Fax ⓝ faks *fax*
Fechten ⓝ fekh·ten *fencing (sports)*
Feder ① fay·der *spring (coil)*
Fehler ⓜ fay·ler *mistake*
fehlerhaft fay·ler·haft *faulty*
Fehlgeburt ① fayl·ge·burt *miscarriage*
Feier ① fai·er *celebration*
Feige ① fai·ge *fig*
Feinkostgeschäft ⓝ fain·kost·ge·sheft *delicatessen*
Feld ⓝ felt *field*
Feldfrucht ① felt·frukht *crop*
Fels ⓜ fels *rock*
Fenster ⓝ fens·ter *window*
Ferien pl fair·ri·en *holidays/vacation*
Fern- fern- *long-distance*
Fernbedienung ① fern·be·dee·nung *remote control*
Fernbus ⓜ fern·bus *bus (intercity)*
Fernglas ⓝ fern·glahs *binoculars*
fernsehen fern·zay·en *watch TV*
Fernseher ⓜ fern·zay·er *TV set*
Fernsehserie ① fern·zay·zair·ri·e *TV series*
fertig fer·tikh *ready • finished*
Fest ⓝ fest *festival • party*
fest fest *solid*
fettarme Milch ① fet·ar·me milkh *skimmed milk*
feucht foykht *damp*
Feuchtigkeitscreme ① foykh·tikh·kaits·kraym *moisturiser*
Feuer ⓝ foy·er *fire*
Feuerzeug ⓝ foy·er·tsoyk *cigarette lighter*
Fieber ⓝ fee·ber *fever*
Filet ⓝ fi·lay *fillet*

Film ⓜ film *movie (cinema) • film (for camera)*
finden fin·den *find*
Finger ⓜ fing·er *finger*
Firma ① fir·ma *company*
Fisch ⓜ fish *fish*
Fischen ⓝ fi·shen *fishing*
Fitness-Studio ⓝ fit·nes·shtoo·di·o *gym*
flach flakh *flat*
Flagge ① fla·ge *flag*
Flasche ① fla·she *bottle*
Flaschenöffner ⓜ fla·shen·erf·ner *bottle opener*
Fleisch ⓝ flaish *meat*
Fliege ① flee·ge *fly*
fliegen flee·gen *fly*
Flitterwochen pl fli·ter·vo·khen *honeymoon*
Floh ⓜ flaw *flea*
Flohmarkt ⓜ flaw·markt *flea-market*
Flüchtling ⓜ flükht·ling *refugee*
Flug ⓜ flook *flight*
Flügel ⓜ pl flü·gel *wings*
Fluggast ⓜ flook·gast *passenger (plane)*
Flughafen ⓜ flook·hah·fen *airport*
Flughafengebühr ① flook·hah·fen·ge·bür *airport tax*
Fluglinie ① flook·lee·ni·e *airline*
Flugticket ⓝ flook·ti·ket *plane ticket*
Flugzeug ⓝ flook·tsoyk *aeroplane*
Fluss ⓜ flus *river*
folgen fol·gen *follow*
Forderung ① for·de·rung *demand*
Form ① form *shape*
formell for·mel *formal*
Foto ⓝ faw·to *photo*
Fotogeschäft ⓝ faw·to·ge·sheft *camera shop*
Fotograf(in) ⓜ/① fo·to·grahf/fo·to·grah·fin *photographer*
Fotografie ① fo·to·gra·fee *photograph • photography*
fotografieren fo·to·gra·fee·ren *take a photograph*
Foul ⓝ fowl *foul*
Foyer ⓝ fo·a·yay *foyer*
Frage ① frah·ge *question*
eine Frage stellen ai·ne frah·ge shte·len *ask a question*

Frankreich ⓝ frangk·raikh France

Frau ① frow woman

frei frai free (not bound) • vacant

Freibad ⓝ frai·baht (outdoor) swimming pool

Freigepäck ⓝ frai·ge·pek baggage allowance

Freitag ⓜ frai·tahk Friday

fremd fremt strange

Fremde ⓜ&① frem·de stranger

Fremdenverkehrsbüro ⓝ frem·den·fer·kairs·bü·raw tourist office

Freund ⓜ froynt male friend • boyfriend

Freundin ① froyn·din female friend • girlfriend

freundlich froynt·likh friendly

Frieden ⓜ free·den peace

Friedhof ⓜ treet·hawf cemetery

frisch frish fresh (not stale)

Frischkäse ⓜ frish·kay·ze cream cheese

Friseur(in) ⓜ/① fri·zer/fri·zer·nn hairdresser

Frosch ⓜ frosh frog

Frost ⓜ frost frost

Frucht ① frukht fruit

früh frü early

Frühling ⓜ frü·ling spring (season)

Frühstück ⓝ frü·shtük breakfast

Frühstücksflocke ① frü·shtüks·flo·ke breakfast cereal

Frühstücksspeck ⓜ frü·shtüks·shpek bacon

fühlen fü·len feel

Führer ⓜ fü·rer (tour) guide • guidebook

Führerschein ⓜ fü·rer·shain driving licence

Führung ① fü·rung guided tour

füllen fü·len fill

Fundbüro ⓝ funt·bü·raw lost property office

für für for

Fuß ⓜ foos foot

Fußball ⓜ foos·bal football • soccer

Fußgänger(in) ⓜ/① foos·geng·er/foos·geng·e·rin pedestrian

füttern fü·tern feed

G

Gabel ① gah·bel fork

Gang ⓜ gang aisle

Gänge ⓜ pl geng·e gears

ganz gants whole

Garage ① ga·rah·zhe garage (car shelter)

Garderobe ① gar·draw·be wardrobe • cloakroom

Garnele ① gar·nay·le prawn

Garten ⓜ gar·ten garden

Gas ⓝ gahs gas (for cooking)

Gasflasche ① gahs·fla·she gas cylinder

Gaskartusche ① gahs·kar·tu·she gas cartridge

Gastfreundschaft ① gast·froynt·shaft hospitality

Gebäude ⓝ ge·boy·de building

geben gay·ben give

Gebet ⓝ ge·bayt prayer

Gebirgszug ⓜ ge·birks·tsook mountain range

gebraucht ge·browkht second-hand

Geburtsdatum ⓝ ge·burts·dah·tum date of birth

Geburtsort ⓜ ge·burts·ort place of birth

Geburtstag ⓜ ge·burts·tahk birthday

Geburtsurkunde ① ge·burts·oor·kun·de birth certificate

gefährlich ge·fair·likh dangerous

Gefangene ⓜ&① ge·fang·e·ne prisoner

Gefängnis ⓝ ge·feng·nis prison

gefiltert ge·fil·tert filtered

getrieren ge·free·ren freeze

Gefühle ⓝ pl ge·fü·le feelings

gegen gay·gen against

gegenüber gay·gen·ü·ber opposite

Gegenwart ① gay·gen·vart present (time)

Gehacktes ⓝ ge·hāk·tes mince

Gehalt ⓝ ge·halt salary

Geheimnis ⓝ ge·haim·nis secret

gehen gay·en walk

Gehweg ⓜ gay·vayk footpath

Geisteswissenschaften ① pl gais·tes·vissen·shaf·ten humanities

geizig *gai*·tsikh *stingy*
gelangweilt ge·*lang*·vailt *bored*
gelb gelp *yellow*
Geld ⑩ gelt *money*
Geldautomat ⑩ *gelt*·ow·to·maht *automatic teller machine (ATM)*
Geldbuße ① gelt·*boo*·se *fine (payment)*
Geldschein ⑩ *gelt*·shain *banknote*
Geldwechsel ⑩ *gelt*·vek·sel *currency exchange*
Gelegenheitsarbeit ① ge·*lay*·gen·haits·ar·bait *casual work*
Gemüse ⑩ ge·*mü*·ze *vegetable*
Genehmigung ① ge·*nay*·mi·gung *permit*
genug ge·*nook* *enough*
Gepäck ⑩ ge·*pek* *luggage*
Gepäckaufbewahrung ① ge·*pek*·owf·be·vah·rung *left luggage*
Gepäckausgabe ① ge·*pek*·ows·gah·be *luggage claim*
gerade ge·*rah*·de *straight (direction)*
Gerechtigkeit ① ge·*rekh*·tikh·kait *justice*
Gericht ⑩ ge·*rikht* *court (legal)*
Geruch ⑩ ge·*rookh* *smell*
Geschäft ⑩ ge·*sheft* *shop • business*
Geschäftsfrau ① ge·*shefts*·frow *businesswoman*
Geschäftsmann ⑩ ge·*shefts*·man *businessman*
Geschäftsreise ① ge·*shefts*·rai·ze *business trip*
Geschenk ⑩ ge·*shengk* *present (gift)*
Geschichte ① ge·*shikh*·te *story*
Geschlechtskrankheit ① ge·*shlekhts*·krangk·hait *venereal disease*
geschlossen ge·*shlo*·sen *closed*
geschützte (Tierarten) ① pl ge·*shüts*·te (*teer*·ar·ten) *protected (species)*
Geschwindigkeit ① ge·*shvin*·dikh·kait *speed*
Geschwindigkeitsbegrenzung ① ge·*shvin*·dikh·kaits·be·gren·tsung *speed limit*
Gesetz ⑩ ge·*zets* *law*
Gesetzgebung ① ge·*zets*·gay·bung *legislation*
Gesicht ⑩ ge·*zikht* *face*

gestern ges·*tern* *yesterday*
Gesundheit ① ge·*zunt*·hait *health*
Getränk ⑩ ge·*trengk* *drink*
Getränkehandel ⑩ ge·*treng*·ke·han·del *liquor store*
getrennt ge·*trent* *separate (distinct)*
Gewebe ⑩ ge·*vay*·be *fabric*
Gewicht ⑩ ge·*vikht* *weight*
Gewinn ⑩ ge·*vin* *profit*
gewinnen ge·*vi*·nen *win*
Gewürznelke ① ge·*vürts*·nel·ke *clove (spice)*
Gezeiten pl ge·*tsai*·ten *tides*
giftig gif·*tikh* *poisonous*
Giftmüll ⑩ gift·*mül* *toxic waste*
Gin ⑩ dzhin *gin*
Gipfel ⑩ gip·*fel* *peak*
Gitarre ① gi·*ta*·re *guitar*
Glas ⑩ glahs *glass • jar*
glatt glat *slippery*
gleich dort glaikh dort *right (exactly) there*
gleiche glai·*khe* *same*
Gleichheit ① glaikh·*hait* *equality*
Gleis ⑩ glais *platform*
Gleitschirmfliegen ⑩ glait·*shirm*·flee·gen *paragliding*
Gletscher ⑩ glet·*sher* *glacier*
Glück ⑩ glük *luck • happiness*
glücklich glük·*likh* *lucky • happy*
Glückwunsch ⑩ glük·*vunsh* *congratulations*
Glühbirne ① glü·*bir*·ne *light bulb*
Gold ⑩ golt *gold*
Golfplatz ⑩ golf·*plats* *golf course*
Gott ⑩ got *god (general)*
Gottesdienst ⑩ go·*tes*·deenst *church service*
Grab ⑩ grahp *grave • tomb*
Grad ⑩ graht *degree*
grafische Kunst ① grah·*fi*·she kunst *graphic art*
Gramm ⑩ gram *gram*
Gras ⑩ grahs *grass • pot (dope)*
gratis grah·*tis* *free (gratis)*
grau grow *grey*
Grenze ① gren·*tse* *border*
Grippe ① gri·*pe* *influenza*
groß graws *big • great • tall*

Größe ① *grer·se size (general)*
Großeltern pl *graws·el·tern grandparents*
Großmutter ① *graws·mu·ter grandmother*
Großvater ⓜ *graws·fah·ter grandfather*
grün grün *green*
Grund ⓜ grunt *reason*
Gurke ① *gur·ke cucumber*
Gürtel ⓜ *gür·tel belt*
gut goot *good • well*
gutaussehend *goot·ows·zay·ent handsome*
Gymnastik ① *güm·nas·tik gymnastics*
Gynäkologe ⓜ *gü·ne·ko·law·ge gynaecologist*
Gynäkologin ① *gü·ne·ko·law·gin gynaecologist*

H

Haar ⓝ hahr *hair*
Haarbürste ① *hahr·bürs·te hairbrush*
haben *hah·ben have*
Hafen ⓜ *hah·fen port • harbour*
Hafer(flocken) ⓜ pl *hah·fer(·flo·ken) oats*
Hähnchenschenkel ⓜ *hayn·khen·sheng·kel chicken drumstick*
Halal- ha·*lal halal*
Hälfte ① *helf·te half*
Hallenbad ⓝ *ha·len·baht (indoor) swimming pool*
hallo *ha·lo/ha·law hello*
halluzinieren *ha·lu·tsi·nee·ren hallucinate*
Hals ⓜ hals *throat*
Halskette ① *hals·ke·te necklace*
Halsschmerzen pl *hals·shmer·tsen sore throat*
Halt ⓜ halt *stop*
Hammer ⓜ *ha·mer hammer*
Hamster ⓜ *hams·ter hamster*
Hand ① hant *hand*
Handel ⓜ *han·del trade*
handgemacht *hant·ge·makht handmade*
Handschuh ⓜ *hant·shoo glove*
Handtasche ① *hant·ta·she handbag*
Handtuch ⓝ *han·tookh towel*

Handwerk ⓝ *hant·verk crafts*
Handy ⓝ *hen·di mobile phone*
Hang ⓜ hang *slope*
Hängematte ① *heng·e·ma·te hammock*
hart hart *hard (not soft)*
Haschee ⓝ *ha·shay hash*
Haupt- *howpt· main*
Hauptplatz ⓜ *howpt·plats main square*
Haus ⓝ hows *house*
Hausarbeit ① *hows·ar·bait housework*
nach Hause *nahkh how·ze (go) home*
Hausfrau ① *hows·frow homemaker*
Hausmann ⓜ *hows·man homemaker*
Haut ① howt *skin*
heilig *hai·likh holy*
Heiligabend ⓜ *hai·likh·ah·bent Christmas Eve*
Heilige ⓜ&① *hai·li·ge saint*
Helm ⓝ haim *home*
Helmweh haben *haim·vay hah·ben to be homesick*
heiraten *hai·rah·ten marry*
heiß hais *hot*
Heizgerät ⓝ *haits·ge·rayt heater*
helfen *hel·fen help*
hell hel *light (weight)*
Helm ⓜ helm *helmet*
Hemd ⓝ hemt *shirt*
Herausgeber(in) ⓜ/① *he·rows·gay·ber/ he·rows·gay·be·rin editor*
Herbst ⓜ *herpst autumn • fall*
Herd ⓜ hert *stove*
Hering ⓜ *hay·ring herring*
Heringe ⓜ pl *hay·ring·e tent pegs*
Heroin ⓝ *he·ro·een heroin*
Herz ⓝ herts *heart*
Herzleiden ⓝ *herts·lai·den heart condition*
Herzschrittmacher ⓜ *herts·shrit·ma·kher pacemaker (heart)*
Heuschnupfen ⓜ *hoy·shnup·fen hay fever*
heute *hoy·te today*
heute Abend *hoy·te ah·bent tonight*
hier heer *here*
Hilfe ① *hil·fe help*
Himbeere ① *him·bair·re raspberry*
Himmel ⓜ *hi·mel sky*
Hindu ⓜ&① *hin·du Hindu*

I

hinten *hin*·ten *at the back*
hinter *hin*·ter *behind*
hinüber hi·*nü*·ber *across (to)*
historisch his·*taw*·rish *historical*
Hitze ① *hi*·tse *heat*
HIV-positiv hah·ee·fow·*paw*·zi·teef *HIV positive*
hoch hawkh *high (up)*
Hochebene ① *hawkh*·ay·be·ne *plateau*
Hochzeit ① hokh·tsait *wedding*
Hochzeitsgeschenk ⓝ hokh·tsaits·ge·shengk *wedding present*
Hochzeitstorte ① hokh·tsaits·tor·te *wedding cake*
Hockey ⓝ *ho*·ki *hockey*
Höhe ① *her*·e *altitude*
Höhle ① *her*·le *cave*
Holz ⓝ holts *wood*
homöopathisches Mittel ⓝ haw·mer·o·*pah*·ti·shes *mi*·tel *homeopathic medicine*
homosexuell haw·mo·zek·su·*el* *homosexual*
Honig ⓜ *haw*·nikh *honey*
hören *her*·ren *hear • listen*
Hörgerät ⓝ *her*·ge·rayt *hearing aid*
Horoskop ⓝ ho·ros·*kawp* *horoscope*
Hose ① *haw*·ze *trousers/pants*
Hotel ⓝ ho·*tel* *hotel*
hübsch hüpsh *pretty*
Hüfttasche ① *hüft*·ta·she *bumbag*
Hügel ⓜ *hü*·gel *hill*
Huhn ⓝ hoon *chicken*
Hühnerbrust ① *hü*·ner·brust *chicken breast*
Hülsenfrucht ① *hül*·zen·frukht *legume*
Hund ⓜ hunt *dog*
hundert hun·*dert* *hundred*
hungrig hung·rikh *hungry*
husten hoos·ten *cough*
Hustensaft ⓜ hoos·ten·zaft *cough medicine*
Hut ⓜ hoot *hat*
Hütte ① *hü*·te *hut*
Hüttenkäse ⓜ *hü*·ten·kay·ze *cottage cheese*

I

ich ikh *I*
Idee ① i·*day* *idea*
Idiot ⓜ i·di·*awt* *idiot*

ihr eer *her • their*
Ihr eer *your (polite)*
illegal i·le·*gahl* *illegal*
immer *i*·mer *always • forever*
Immigration ① i·mi·gra·*tsyawn* *immigration*
in in *in • at*
inbegriffen *in*·be·gri·fen *included*
Indien ⓝ *in*·di·en *India*
Industrie ① in·dus·*tree* *industry*
Informationstechnologie ① in·for·ma·*tsyawns*·tekh·no·lo·gee *IT*
Ingenieuer(in) ⓜ/① in·zhe·*nyer*(·rin) *engineer*
Ingenieurwesen ⓝ in·zhe·*nyer*·vay·zen *engineering*
Ingwer ⓜ *ing*·ver *ginger*
Injektion ① in·yek·*tsyawn* *injection (medical)*
injizieren in·yi·*tsee*·ren *inject*
innen *i*·nen *inside*
Innenstadt ① *i*·nen·shtat *city centre*
innerhalb (einer Stunde) *i*·ner·halp (*ai*·ner *shtun*·de) *within (an hour)*
Insekt ⓝ in·*zekt* *insect*
Insektenschutzmittel ⓝ in·*zek*·ten·shuts·mi·tel *insect repellant*
Insel ① *in*·zel *island*
Installateur(in) ⓜ/① in·sta·la·*ter*/in·sta·la·*ter*·rin *plumber*
interessant in·tre·*sant* *interesting*
international in·ter·na·tsyo·*nahl* *international*
Internet ⓝ *in*·ter·net *Internet*
Interview ⓝ *in*·ter·vyoo *interview*
Intrauterinpessar ⓝ in·tra·u·te·*reen*·pe·sahr *IUD*
irgendein ir·gent·*ain* *any*
irgendetwas ir·gent·*et*·vas *anything*
irgendwo ir·gent·*vaw* *anywhere*
Irland ① *ir*·lant *Ireland*

J

ja yah *yes*
Jacke ① *ya*·ke *jacket*
Jagd ① yahkt *hunting*
Jahr ⓝ yahr *year*
Jahreszeit ① *yah*·res·tsait *season*

Japan ⓝ *yah·pahn Japan*
Jeans ⓕ pl *dzheens jeans*
jeder *yay·der everyone*
jeder ⓜ *yay·der each • every*
jemand *yay·mant someone*
Jetlag ⓜ *dzhet·leg jet lag*
jetzt *yetst now*
Jockey ⓜ *dzho·ki jockey*
Joga ⓝ *yaw·ga yoga*
Joggen ⓝ *dzho·gen jogging*
Joghurt ⓜ *yaw·gurt yogurt*
Journalist(in) ⓜ/ⓕ *zhur·na·list/ zhur·na·lis·tin journalist*
Juckreiz ⓜ *yuk·raits itch*
jüdisch *yü·dish Jewish*
Jugendherberge ⓕ *yoo·gent·her·ber·ge youth hostel*
jung *yung young*
Junge ⓜ *yung·e boy*
Jura ⓝ *yoo·ra law (subject)*

K

Kabel ⓝ *kah·bel cable*
Kaffee ⓜ *ka·fay coffee*
Kakao ⓜ *ka·kow cocoa*
Kakerlake ⓕ *kah·ker·lah·ke cockroach*
Kalbfleisch ⓝ *kalp·flaish veal*
Kalender ⓜ *ka·len·der calendar*
kalt *kalt cold*
Kamera ⓕ *ka·me·ra camera*
Kamm ⓜ *kam comb*
Kampf ⓜ *kampf fight*
Kampfsport ⓜ *kampf·shport martial arts*
Kanada ⓝ *ka·na·dah Canada*
Kanarienvogel ⓜ *ka·nah·ri·en·faw·gel canary*
Kaninchen ⓝ *ka·neen·khen rabbit*
Kantine ⓕ *kan·tee·ne canteen*
Kapelle ⓕ *ka·pe·le chapel • band (music)*
Kapitalismus ⓜ *ka·pi·ta·lis·mus capitalism*
kaputt *ka·put broken*
Karte ⓕ *kar·te map • ticket*
Karten ⓕ pl *kar·ten cards*
Kartoffel ⓕ *kar·to·fel potato*
Karton ⓜ *kar·tong box • carton*
Karwoche ⓕ *kahr·vo·khe Holy Week*

Käse ⓜ *kay·ze cheese*
Kasino ⓝ *ka·zee·no casino*
Kasse ⓕ *ka·se cash register • checkout • ticket counter*
Kassette ⓕ *ka·se·te cassette*
Kassierer(in) ⓜ/ⓕ *ka·see·rer/ ka·see·re·rin cashier*
Katholik(in) ⓜ/ⓕ *ka·to·leek/ ka·to·lee·kin Catholic*
Kätzchen ⓝ *kets·khen kitten*
Katze ⓕ *ka·tse cat*
kaufen *kow·fen buy*
Kaugummi ⓝ *kow·gu·mi chewing gum*
Kaviar ⓜ *kah·vi·ahr caviar*
Keilriemen ⓜ *kail·ree·men fanbelt*
keine *kai·ne none*
Keks ⓜ *kayks biscuit • cookie*
Keller ⓜ *ke·ler cellar*
Kellner(in) ⓜ/ⓕ *kel·ner/kel·ne·rin waiter*
kennen *ke·nen know (a person)*
Keramik ⓕ *ke·rah·mik ceramic*
Kerze ⓕ *ker·tse candle*
Kessel ⓜ *ke·sel kettle*
Ketchup ⓜ *ket·chap ketchup*
Kette ⓕ *ke·te chain*
Kichererbse ⓕ *ki·kher·erp·se chickpea*
Kiefer ⓜ *kee·fer jaw*
Kilogramm ⓝ *kee·lo·gram kilogram*
Kilometer ⓜ *ki·lo·may·ter kilometre*
Kind ⓝ *kint child*
Kinder ⓝ pl *kin·der children*
Kinderbetreuung ⓕ *kin·der·be·troy·ung childminding*
Kindergarten ⓜ *kin·der·gar·ten kindergarten*
Kinderkrippe ⓕ *kin·der·kri·pe creche*
Kindersitz ⓜ *kin·der·zits child seat*
Kino ⓝ *kee·no cinema*
Kiosk ⓜ *kee·osk convenience store*
Kirche ⓕ *kir·khe church*
Kissen ⓝ *ki·sen pillow*
Kissenbezug ⓜ *ki·sen·be·tsook pillowcase*
Kiwifrucht ⓕ *kee·vi·frukht kiwifruit*
Klasse ⓕ *kla·se class*
klassisch *kla·sish classical*
Klavier ⓝ *kla·veer piano*
Kleid ⓝ *klait dress*

Kleidung ⓕ *klai*·dung *clothing*
klein klain *little • small • short (height)*
Kleingeld ⓝ *klain*·gelt *loose change*
klettern *kle*·tern *climb*
Klettern ⓝ *kle*·tern *rock climbing*
Klima ⓝ *klee*·ma *climate*
Klimaanlage ⓕ *klee*·ma·an·lah·ge *air-conditioning*
klingeln *kling*·eln *ring (of phone)*
Klippe ⓕ *kli*·pe *cliff*
Kloster ⓝ *klaws*·ter *convent • monastery*
Knappheit ⓕ *knap*·hait *shortage*
Kneipe ⓕ *knai*·pe *pub*
Knie ⓝ *knee* knee
Knoblauch ⓜ *knawp*·lowkh *garlic*
Knöchel ⓜ *kner*·khel *ankle*
Knochen ⓜ *kno*·khen *bone*
Knopf ⓜ knopf *button*
Knoten ⓜ *knaw*·ten *lump (health)*
Koch ⓜ kokh *chef • cook*
kochen *ko*·khen *cook*
Kocher ⓜ *ko*·kher *camping stove*
Köchin ⓕ *ker*·khin *chef • cook*
Köder ⓜ *ker*·der *bait*
Koffer ⓜ *ko*·fer *suitcase*
Kofferraum ⓜ *ko*·fer·rowm *boot • trunk*
Kohl ⓜ kawl *cabbage*
Kokain ⓝ ko·ka·*een* *cocaine*
Kollege ⓜ ko·*lay*·ge *colleague*
Kollegin ⓕ ko·*lay*·gin *colleague*
kommen *ko*·men *come*
Kommunion ⓕ ko·mun·*yawn* *communion*
Komödie ⓕ ko·*mer*·di·e *comedy*
Kompass ⓜ *kom*·pas *compass*
Konditorei ⓕ kon·dee·to·*rai* *cake shop*
Kondom ⓝ ko·*dawm* *condom*
König ⓜ *ker*·nikh *king*
Königin ⓕ *ker*·ni·gin *queen*
können *ker*·nen *be able to • have permission to*
konservativ kon·zer·va·*teef* *conservative*
Konsulat ⓝ kon·zu·*laht* *consulate*
Kontaktlinsen ⓕ pl kon·*takt*·lin·zen *contact lenses*
Kontostand ⓜ *kon*·to·shtant *balance (account)*
Kontrollstelle ⓕ kon·*trol*·shte·le *checkpoint*

Konzert ⓝ kon·*tsert* *concert*
Konzerthalle ⓕ kon·*tsert*·ha·le *concert hall*
Kopf ⓜ kopf *head*
Kopfsalat ⓜ *kopf*·za·laht *lettuce*
Kopfschmerzen pl *kopf*·shmer·tsen *headache*
Kopfschmerztablette ⓕ *kopf*·shmerts·ta·ble·te *aspirin*
Korb ⓜ korp *basket*
Körper ⓜ *ker*·per *body*
korrupt ko·*rupt* *corrupt*
koscher *kaw*·sher *kosher*
kosten *kos*·ten *cost*
köstlich *kerst*·likh *delicious*
Kraft ⓕ kraft *power*
Krampf ⓜ krampf *cramp*
krank krangk *sick*
Krankenhaus ⓝ *krang*·ken·hows *hospital*
Krankenpfleger ⓜ *krang*·ken·pflay·ger *nurse*
Krankenschwester ⓕ *krang*·ken·shves·ter *nurse*
Krankenwagen ⓜ *krang*·ken·vah·gen *ambulance*
Krankheit ⓕ *krangk*·hait *disease*
Kräuter ⓝ pl *kroy*·ter *herbs*
Krebs ⓜ *krayps* *cancer*
Kreditkarte ⓕ kre·*deet*·kar·te *credit card*
Kreisverkehr ⓜ *krais*·fer·kair *roundabout*
Kreuz ⓝ kroyts *cross (religious)*
Krieg ⓜ kreek *war*
Kritik ⓕ kri·*teek* *review (arts)*
Küche ⓕ *kü*·khe *kitchen*
Kuchen ⓜ *koo*·khen *cake*
Kuckucksuhr ⓕ *ku*·kuks·oor *cuckoo clock*
Kugelschreiber ⓜ *koo*·gel·shrai·ber *pen (ballpoint)*
Kuh ⓕ koo *cow*
Kühler ⓜ *kü*·ler *radiator*
Kühlschrank ⓜ *kül*·shrangk *refrigerator*
sich kümmern um zikh *kü*·mern um *look after*
Kunde ⓜ *kun*·de *client*
kündigen *kün*·di·gen *resign*
Kundin ⓕ *kun*·din *client*

Kunst ① kunst *art*
Kunstgalerie ① *kunst·ga·le·ree*
art gallery
Kunstgewerbe ⑩ *kunst·ge·ver·be*
arts & crafts
Kunsthandwerk ⑩ *kunst·hant·verk*
handicrafts
Künstler(in) ⑩/① *künst·ler/künst·le·rin*
artist
Kunstsammlung ① *kunst·zam·lung*
art collection
Kunstwerk ⑩ *kunst·verk work of art*
Kupplung ① *kup·lung clutch (car)*
Kürbis ⑩ *kür·bis pumpkin*
kurz kurts *short*
kurzärmelig *kurts·er·me·likh*
short-sleeved
Kuss ⑩ kus *kiss*
küssen *kü·sen kiss*
Küste ① *küs·te coast*

L

lächeln *le·kheln smile*
lachen *la·khen laugh*
Lachs ⑩ laks *salmon*
Lage ① *lah·ge situation*
Lager ⑩ *lah·ger lager*
Lamm ⑩ lam *lamb*
Land ⑩ lant *country • countryside*
Landschaft ① *lant·shaft scenery*
Landwirtschaft ① *lant·virt·shaft*
agriculture
lang long *long*
langärmelig *lang·er·me·likh*
long-sleeved
langsam *lang·zahm slow • slowly*
langweilig *lang·vai·likh boring*
Laptop ⑩ *lep·top laptop*
Lastwagen ⑩ *last·vah·gen truck*
Lauch ⑩ lowkh *leek*
laufen *low·fen run*
Läuse ① pl *loy·ze lice*
laut lowt *loud • noisy*
Lautstärke ① *lowt·shter·ke volume*
(loudness)
Lawine ① *la·vee·ne avalanche*
leben *lay·ben to live*
Leben ⑩ *lay·ben life*

Lebenslauf ⑩ *lay·bens·lowf*
resume • CV
Lebensmittelhändler ⑩
lay·bens·mi·tel·hen·dler greengrocer
Lebensmittelladen ⑩
lay·bens·mi·tel·lah·den grocery store
Lebensmittelvergiftung ① *lay·bens·mi·*
tel·fer·gif·tung food poisoning
Leber ① *lay·ber liver*
Leder ⑩ *lay·der leather*
ledig *lay·dikh single (of person)*
leer lair *empty*
legen *lay·gen put (horizontal)*
Lehrer(in) ⑩/① *lair·rer/lair·re·rin*
teacher • instructor
leicht laikht *easy*
Leichtathletik ① *laikht·at·lay·tik*
athletics
leihen *lai·en borrow*
Leinen ⑩ *lai·nen linen (fabric)*
Leitungswasser ⑩ *lai·tungks·va·ser tap*
water
Lenker ⑩ *leng·ker handlebar*
lernen *ler·nen learn*
Lesbierin ① *les·bi·e·rin lesbian*
lesen *lay·zen read*
letzte *lets·te last*
Licht ⑩ likht *light*
lieben *lee·ben love*
liebevoll *lee·be·fol caring*
Liebhaber(in) ⑩/① *leep·hah·ber/*
leep·hah·be·rin lover
Lied ⑩ leet *song*
liefern *lee·fern deliver*
Lieferwagen ⑩ *lee·fer·vah·gen van*
liegen *lee·gen lie (not stand)*
Lift ⑩ lift *lift • elevator*
lila *lee·la purple*
Limonade ① *li·mo·nah·de lemonade*
Limone ① *li·maw·ne lime*
Linie ① *lee·ni·e line*
links lingks *left (direction)*
linksgerichtet *lingks·ge·rikh·tet*
left-wing
Linse ① *lin·ze lentil*
Lippen ① pl *li·pen lips*
Lippenbalsam ⑩ *li·pen·bal·zahm*
lip balm
Lippenstift ⑩ *li·pen·shtift lipstick*

Liter ⓝ *lee*-ter litre
Löffel ⓜ *ler*-fel spoon
Lohn ⓜ lawn wage
Lohnsatz ⓜ *lawn*-zats rate of pay
Lokal ⓝ lo-*kahl* bar
Luft ⓕ luft air
Luftkrankheit ⓕ *luft*-krangk-hait
  airsickness
Luftpost ⓕ *luft*-post airmail
Luftpumpe ⓕ *luft*-pum-pe pump
Luftverschmutzung ⓕ
  luft-fer-shmu-tsung air pollution
Lügner(in) ⓜ/ⓕ *lüg*-ner/*lüg*-ne-rin liar
Lungen ⓕ pl *lung*-en lungs
lustig *lus*-tikh funny
luxuriös luk-su-ri-*ers* luxury

M

machen *ma*-khen make
Mädchen ⓝ *mayt*-khen girl
Magen ⓜ *mah*-gen stomach
Magen-Darm-Katarrh ⓜ
  mah-gen-darm-ka-tar gastroenteritis
Magenschmerzen ⓜ pl
  mah-gen-shmer-tsen stomachache
Magenverstimmung ⓕ
  mah-gen-fer-shti-mung indigestion
Majonnaise ⓕ ma-yo-*nay*-ze
  mayonnaise
Makler(in) ⓜ/ⓕ *mahk*-ler/*mahk*-le-rin
  real estate agent
Maler(in) ⓜ/ⓕ *mah*-ler/*mah*-le-rin
  painter
Malerei ⓕ mah-le-*rai* painting (the art)
Mama ⓕ *ma*-ma mum • mom
Mammogramm ⓝ ma-mo-*gram*
  mammogram
manchmal *mankh*-mahl sometimes
Mandarine ⓕ man-da-*ree*-ne mandarin
Mandel ⓕ *man*-del almond
Mann ⓜ man man
Mannschaft ⓕ *man*-shaft team
Mantel ⓜ *man*-tel overcoat • cloak
Margarine ⓕ mar-ga-*ree*-ne margarine
Marihuana ⓝ ma-ri-hu-*ah*-na marijuana
Markt ⓜ markt market
Marktplatz ⓜ *markt*-plats
  market square
Marmelade ⓕ mar-me-*lah*-de jam

Maschine ⓕ ma-*shee*-ne machine
Masern pl *mah*-zern measles
Massage ⓕ ma-*sah*-zhe massage
Masseur(in) ⓜ/ⓕ ma-*ser*(-in) masseur/
  masseuse
Material ⓝ ma-te-ri-*ahl* material
Matratze ⓕ ma-*tra*-tse mattress
Matte ⓕ *ma*-te mat
Mauer ⓕ *mow*-er wall (outer)
Maurer(in) ⓜ/ⓕ *mow*-rer/*mow*-re-rin
  bricklayer
Maus ⓕ mows mouse
Mechaniker(in) ⓜ/ⓕ me-*khah*-ni-ker/
  me-*khah*-ni-ke-rin mechanic
Medien pl *may*-di-en media
Meditation ⓕ me-di-ta-*tsyawn*
  meditation
Medizin ⓕ me-di-*tseen* medicine
Meer ⓝ mair sea
Meeresküste ⓕ *mair*-res-küs-te seaside
Meerrettich ⓜ *mair*-re-tikh horseradish
Mehl ⓝ mayl flour
mehr mair more
nicht mehr nikht mair not any more
mein mine • my
Meinung ⓕ *mai*-nung opinion
Meisterschaften ⓕ pl *mais*-ter-shaf-ten
  championships
Melodie ⓕ me-lo-*dee* tune
Melone ⓕ me-*law*-ne melon
Mensch ⓜ mensh person
Menschen ⓜ pl *men*-shen people
Menschenrechte ⓝ pl *men*-shen-rekh-te
  human rights
menschlich *mensh*-likh human
Menstruation ⓕ mens-tru-a-*tsyawn*
  menstruation
Menstruationsbeschwerden ⓕ pl mens-
  tru-a-*tsyawns*-be-shver-den period pain
Messe ⓕ *me*-se mass (Catholic) • trade
  fair
Messer ⓝ *me*-ser knife
Metall ⓝ me-*tal* metal
Meter ⓜ *may*-ter metre
Metzgerei ⓕ mets-ge-*rai*
  butcher's shop
mieten *mee*-ten rent • hire
Mietvertrag ⓜ *meet*-fer-trahk lease
Migräne ⓕ mi-*gray*-ne migraine

Mikrowelle ① *mee*·kro·ve·le *microwave*
Milch ① milkh *milk*
Milchprodukte ⑩ pl milkh·pro·duk·te
  dairy products
Militär ⑩ mi·li·tair *military*
Millimeter ⑩ mi·li·may·ter *millimetre*
Million ① mi·lyawn *million*
Mineralwasser ⑩ mi·ne·rahl·va·ser
  mineral water
Minute ① mi·noo·te *minute*
mischen mi·shen *mix*
mit mit *with*
Mitglied ⑩ mit·gleet *member*
Mittag ⑩ mi·tahk *noon*
Mittagessen ⑩ mi·tahk·e·sen *lunch*
Mitteilung ① mi·tai·lung *message*
Mitternacht ① mi·ter·nakht *midnight*
Mittwoch ⑩ mit·vokh *Wednesday*
Möbel ⑩ pl mer·bel *furniture*
Modem ⑩ maw·dem *modem*
mögen mer·gen *to like*
möglich merk·likh *possible*
Mohrrübe ① mawr·rü·he *carrot*
Monat ⑩ maw·nat *month*
Montag ⑩ mawn·tahk *Monday*
Morgen ⑩ mor·gen
  morning (6am – 10am)
morgen mor·gen *tomorrow*
morgen früh mor·gen frü
  tomorrow morning
Moschee ① mo·shay *mosque*
Moskitospirale ① mos·kee·to·shpi·rah·le
  mosquito coil
Moslem ⑩ mos·lem *Muslim*
Moslime ① mos·lee·me *Muslim*
Motor ⑩ maw·tor/mo·tawr *engine*
Motorboot ⑩ maw·tor·bawt *motorboat*
Motorrad ⑩ maw·tor·raht *motorcycle*
Möwe ① mer·ve *seagull*
müde mü·de *tired*
Müll ⑩ mül *rubbish*
Mülleimer ⑩ mül·ai·mer *rubbish bin*
Mund ⑩ munt *mouth*
Mundfäule ① munt·foy·le
  thrush (medical condition)
Münzen ① pl mün·tsen *coins*
Muschel ① mu·shel *mussel*
Museum ⑩ mu·zay·um *museum*
Musik ① mu·zeek *music*

Musiker(in) ⑩/① moo·zi·ker/
  moo·zi·ke·rin *musician*
Muskel ⑩ mus·kel *muscle*
Muskelzerrung ① mus·kel·tser·rung
  sprain
Müsli ⑩ müs·li *muesli*
mutig moo·tikh *brave*
Mutter ① mu·ter *mother*

N

nach nahkh *after • towards*
Nachkomme ⑩ nahkh·ko·me
  descendant
Nachmittag ⑩ nahkh·mi·tahk *afternoon*
Nachname ⑩ nahkh·nah·me *surname*
Nachrichten pl nahkh·rikh·ten *news*
nächste naykhs·te *next • nearest*
Nacht ① nakht *night*
Nadel ① nah·del *sewing needle •
  syringe*
Nagelknipser ⑩ pl nah·gel·knip·ser
  nail clippers
nahe nah·e *close (nearby)*
in der Nähe in dair nay·e *nearby*
nähen nay·en *sew*
Name ⑩ nah·me *name*
Nase ① nah·ze *nose*
nass nas *wet*
Natur ① na·toor *nature*
Naturheilkunde ① na·toor·hail·kun·de
  naturopathy
Naturreservat ⑩ na·toor·re·zer·vaht
  nature reserve
neben nay·ben *next to*
neblig nay·blikh *foggy*
Neffe ⑩ ne·fe *nephew*
nehmen nay·men *take*
nein nain *no*
nett net *nice • kind*
Netz ⑩ nets *net*
neu noy *new*
Neujahrstag ⑩ noy·yahrs·tahk
  New Year's Day
Neuseeland ⑩ noy·zay·lant
  New Zealand
nicht nikht *not*
Nichte ① nikh·te *niece*
Nichtraucher- nikht·row·kher·
  non smoking

nichts nikhts *nothing*
nie nee *never*
Niederlande pl nee·der·lan·de *Netherlands*
niedrig nee·drikh *low*
noch nicht nokh nikht *not yet*
Nonne ① no·ne *nun*
Norden ⑩ nor·den *north*
normal nor·mahl *ordinary*
normale Post ① nor·mah·le post *surface mail*
Notfall ⑩ nawt·fal *emergency*
Notizbuch ⑪ no·teets·bookh *notebook*
notwendig nawt·ven·dikh *necessary*
Nudeln pl noo·deln *noodles • pasta*
null nul *zero*
Nummer ① nu·mer *number*
nur noor *only*
Nuss ① nus *nut*
nützlich nüts·likh *useful*

O

obdachlos op·dakh·laws *homeless*
oben aw·ben *upstairs*
Objektiv ⑩ op·yek·teef *lens (camera)*
Obsternte ① awpst·ern·te *fruit picking*
oder aw·der *or*
Ofen ⑩ aw·fen *oven*
offen o·fen *open*
offensichtlich o·fen·zikht·likh *obvious*
öffentlich er·fent·likh *public*
öffnen erf·nen *open*
Öffnungszeiten ① pl erf·nungks·tsai·ten *opening hours*
oft oft *often*
ohne aw·ne *without*
Ohr ⑪ awr *ear*
Ohrenstöpsel ⑩ aw·ren·shterp·sel *earplugs*
Ohrringe ⑩ pl awr·ring·e *earrings*
Öl ⑪ erl *oil*
Olive ① o·lee·ve *olive*
Olivenöl ⑪ o·lee·ven·erl *olive oil*
Olympische Spiele ⑪ pl o·lüm·pi·she shpee·le *Olympic Games*
Oma ① aw·ma *grandmother*
Onkel ⑩ ong·kel *uncle*
Opa ⑩ aw·pa *grandfather*

Oper ① aw·per *opera*
Operation ① o·pe·ra·tsyawn *operation*
Opernhaus ⑪ aw·pern·hows *opera house*
Optiker(in) ⑩/① op·ti·ker/op·ti·ke·rin *optician*
orange o·rahngzh *orange (colour)*
Orange ① o·rahng·zhe *orange*
Orangenmarmelade ① o·rahng·zhen·m ar·me·lah·de *marmalade*
Orangensaft ⑩ o·rahng·zhen·zaft *orange juice*
Orchester ⑪ or·kes·ter *orchestra*
organisieren or·ga·ni·zee·ren *organise*
Orgasmus ⑩ or·gas·mus *orgasm*
Orgel ① or·gel *organ (church)*
Original- o·ri·gi·nahl· *original (not copied)*
örtlich ert·likh *local*
Osten ⑩ os·ten *east*
der Nahe Osten ⑩ dair nah·e os·ten *Middle East*
Ostern ⑪ aws·tern *Easter*
Österreich ⑪ ers·ter·raikh *Austria*
Ozean ⑩ aw·tse·ahn *ocean*
Ozonschicht ① o·tsawn·shikht *ozone layer*

P

Paar ⑪ pahr *pair (couple)*
ein paar ain pahr *a few*
Packung ① pa·kung *packet (general)*
Paket ⑪ pa·kayt *package • parcel*
Pampelmuse ① pam·pel·moo·ze *grapefruit*
eine Panne haben ai·ne pa·ne hah·ben *break down*
Papa ⑩ pa·pa *dad*
Papagei ⑩ pa·pa·gai *parrot*
Papier ⑪ pa·peer *paper*
Papiertaschentücher ⑪ pl pa·peer·ta·shen·tü·kher *tissues*
Paprika ① pap·ri·kah *paprika • capsicum • bell pepper*
Parfüm ⑪ par·füm *perfume*
Park ⑩ park *park*
Parkplatz ⑩ park·plats *carpark*
Parlament ⑪ par·la·ment *parliament*

Partei ① par·*tai* party (politics)
Pass ⓜ pas *pass* • *passport*
Passnummer ① *pas*·nu·mer *passport number*
Pause ① *pow*·ze *intermission*
eine Pause machen ai·ne *pow*·ze *ma*·khen *rest*
Pedal ⓝ pe·*dahl* pedal
Penis ⓜ *pay*·nis penis
Pension ① pahng·*zyawn* boarding house • bed & breakfast
pensioniert pahng·zyo·*neert* retired
Person ① per·*zawn* person
Personalausweis ⓜ per·zo·*nahl*·ows·vais *identification card*
persönlich per·*zern*·likh personal
Petersilie ① pay·ler·zee·li·e parsley
Petition ① pe·ti·*tsyawn* petition
Pfad ⓜ pfaht path • trail
Pfanne ① *pfa*·ne pan
Pfeffer ⓜ *pfe*·fer pepper
Pfefferminzbonbons ⓜ pl pfe·fer·*mints*·bong·bongs mints
Pfeife ① *pfai*·fe pipe
Pferd ⓝ pfert horse
Pfirsich ⓜ *pfir*·zikh peach
Pflanze ① *pflan*·tse plant
Pflaster ⓝ *pflas*·ter Band-aids
Pflaume ① *pflow*·me plum
pflücken *pflü*·ken pick (flowers)
Pfund ⓝ pfunt pound (weight)
Phantasie ① fan·ta·*zee* imagination
Physik ① fü·*zeek* physics
Picknick ⓝ *pik*·nik picnic
Pilgerfahrt ① *pil*·ger·fahrt pilgrimage
Pille ① *pi*·le pill
die Pille dee *pi*·le the Pill
Pilz ⓜ pilts mushroom
Pinzette ① pin·*tse*·te tweezers
PKW-Zulassung ①
 pay·kah·vay·*tsoo*·la·sung *car registration*
Plakat ⓝ pla·*kaht* poster
Planet ⓜ pla·*nayt* planet
Plastik ⓝ *plas*·tik plastic
Platz ⓜ plats place • seat (train, cinema) • square (town) • court (tennis)

Platz am Gang plats am gang *aisle seat*
Poker ⓝ *paw*·ker poker (game)
Politik ① po·li·*teek* politics • policy
Politiker(in) ⓜ/① po·*lee*·ti·ker/ po·*lee*·ti·ke·rin politician
Polizei ① po·li·*tsai* police
Polizeirevier ⓝ po·li·*tsai*·re·veer *police station*
Pollen ⓜ *po*·len pollen
Pony ① *po*·ni pony
Porto ⓝ *por*·to postage
Post ① post mail
Postamt ⓝ *post*·amt post office
Postkarte ① *post*·kar·te postcard
postlagernd *post*·lah·gernt *poste restante*
Postleitzahl ① *post*·lait·tsahl postcode
praktisch *prak*·tish practical
prämenstruelle Störung ① *pray*·mens·tru·e·le *shter*·rung *premenstrual tension*
Präsident(in) ⓜ/① pre·zi·*dent*/ pre·zi·*den*·tin president
Preis ⓜ prais price
Premierminister(in) ⓜ/① prem·*yay*·mi·nis·ter/ prem·*yay*·mi·nis·te·rin prime minister
Priester ⓜ *prees*·ter priest
privat pri·*vaht* private
Privatklinik ① pri·*vaht*·klee·nik *private hospital*
pro praw per
produzieren pro·du·*tsee*·ren produce
Programm ⓝ pro·*gram* program
Projektor ⓜ pro·*yek*·tor projector
Prosa ① *praw*·za fiction
Prostituierte ① pros·ti·tu·*eer*·te prostitute
Protest ⓜ pro·*test* protest
protestieren pro·tes·*tee*·ren protest
Prozent ⓝ pro·*tsent* percent
prüfen *prü*·fen check
Psychologie ① psü·kho·lo·*gee* psychology
Pullover ⓜ pu·*law*·ver Jumper • sweater
Pumpe ① *pum*·pe pump
Punkt ⓜ pungkt point
Puppe ① *pu*·pe doll

Q

Qualifikationen ⓕ pl
kva·li·fi·ka·tsyaw·nen *qualifications*
Qualität ⓕ kva·li·tayt *quality*
Quarantäne ⓕ ka·ran·tay·ne *quarantine*
Querschnittsgelähmte ⓜ&ⓕ
kvair·shnits·ge·laym·te *paraplegic*
Quittung ⓕ kvi·tung *receipt*

R

Rabatt ⓜ ra·bat *discount*
Rad ⓝ raht *wheel*
radfahren raht·fah·ren *cycle*
Radfahrer(in) ⓜ/ⓕ raht·fah·rer/
raht·fah·re·rin *cyclist*
Radio ⓝ rah·di·o *radio*
Radsport ⓜ raht·shport *cycling*
Radweg ⓜ raht·vayk *bike path*
Rahmen ⓜ rah·men *frame*
Rallye ⓕ re·li *rally*
Rasiercreme ⓕ ra·zeer·kraym
shaving cream
rasieren ra·zee·ren *shave*
Rasierer ⓜ ra·zee·rer *razor*
Rasierklingen ⓕ pl ra·zeer·kling·en
razor blades
Rassismus ⓜ ra·sis·mus *racism*
Rat ⓜ raht *advice*
raten rah·ten *advise • guess*
Ratte ⓕ ra·te *rat*
Raub ⓜ rowp *robbery*
rauchen row·khen *smoke*
Raum ⓜ rowm *space*
realistisch re·a·lis·tish *realistic*
Rebe ⓕ ray·be *vine*
Rechnung ⓕ rekh·nung *bill • check*
rechts rekhts *right (direction)*
rechtsgerichtet rekhts·ge·rikh·tet *right-
wing*
Rechtsanwalt ⓜ rekhts·an·valt *lawyer*
Rechtsanwältin ⓕ rekhts·an·vel·tin
lawyer
recyceln ri·sai·keln *recycle*
Regal ⓝ re·gahl *shelf*
Regeln ⓕ pl ray·geln *rules*
Regen ⓜ ray·gen *rain*

Regenmantel ⓜ ray·gen·man·tel
raincoat
Regenschirm ⓜ ray·gen·shirm *umbrella*
Regierung ⓕ re·gee·rung *government*
Region ⓕ re·gyawn *region*
Regisseur(in) ⓜ/ⓕ re·zhi·ser/
re·zhi·ser·rin *director*
reich raikh *wealthy*
Reifen ⓜ rai·fen *tyre*
Reifenpanne ⓕ rai·fen·pa·ne *puncture*
rein rain *pure*
Reinigung ⓕ rai·ni·gung *cleaning*
Reis ⓜ rais *rice*
Reise ⓕ rai·ze *journey • trip*
Reisebüro ⓝ rai·ze·bü·raw
travel agency
Reiseführer ⓜ rai·ze·fü·rer *guidebook*
Reisekrankheit ⓕ rai·ze·krangk·hait
travel sickness
reisen rai·zen *travel*
Reisende ⓜ/ⓕ rai·zen·de
passenger (train)
Reisepass ⓜ rai·ze·pas *passport*
Reiseroute ⓕ rai·ze·roo·te *itinerary*
Reisescheck ⓜ rai·ze·shek
travellers cheque
Reiseziel ⓝ rai·ze·tseel *destination*
Reißverschluss ⓜ rais·fer·shlus *zipper*
Reiten ⓝ rai·ten *horse riding*
reiten rai·ten *ride (horse)*
Reitweg ⓜ rait·vayk *bridle path*
Religion ⓕ re·li·gyawn *religion*
religiös re·li·gyers *religious*
Reliquie ⓕ re·lee·kvi·e *relic (religious)*
Rennbahn ⓕ ren·bahn *racetrack*
rennen re·nen *run*
Rennen ⓝ re·nen *race (sport)*
Rennrad ⓝ ren·raht *racing bike*
Rentner(in) ⓜ/ⓕ rent·ner/rent·ne·rin
pensioner
reparieren re·pa·ree·ren *repair*
Republik ⓕ re·pu·bleek *republic*
Reservereifen ⓜ re·zer·ve·rai·fen
spare tyre
reservieren re·zer·vee·ren *reserve*
Reservierung ⓕ re·zer·vee·rung
reservation
Restaurant ⓝ res·to·rahng *restaurant*
retten re·ten *save (someone)*

Rettich ⓜ re·tikh *radish*
R-Gespräch ⓝ air·ge·shpraykh *collect call • reverse-charge call*
Rhythmus ⓜ rüt·mus *rhythm*
Richter(in) ⓜ/ⓕ rikh·ter/rikh·te·rin *judge*
richtig rikh·tikh *right (correct)*
riesig ree·zikh *huge*
Rindfleisch ⓝ rint·flaish *beef*
Ring ⓜ ring *ring (on finger)*
Risiko ⓝ ree·zi·ko *risk*
Ritt ⓜ rit *ride*
Rock ⓜ rok *skirt*
Rockgruppe ⓕ rok·gru·pe *rock group*
Rockmusik ⓕ rok·mu·zeek *rock (music)*
Rodeln ⓝ raw·deln *tobogganing*
Roggenbrot ⓝ ro·gen·brawt *rye bread*
roh raw *raw*
Rollschuhfahren ⓝ rol·shoo·fah·ren *in-line skating*
Rollstuhl ⓜ rol·shtool *wheelchair*
Rolltreppe ⓕ rol·tre·pe *escalator*
romantisch ro·man·tish *romantic*
rosa raw·za *pink*
Rosenkohl ⓜ raw·zen·kawl *Brussels sprouts*
Rosine ⓕ ro·zee·ne *raisin*
rot rawt *red*
Rotwein ⓜ rawt·vain *red wine*
Route ⓕ roo·te *route*
Rucken ⓜ rü·ken *back (body)*
Rückfahrkarte ⓕ rük·fahr·kar·te *return (ticket)*
Rucksack ⓜ ruk·zak *backpack • knapsack*
Rückzahlung ⓕ rük·tsah·lung *refund*
Rudern ⓝ roo·dern *rowing*
Rugby ⓝ rag·bi *rugby*
ruhig roo·ikh *quiet*
Ruinen ⓕ pl ru·ee·nen *ruins*
Rum ⓜ rum *rum*
rund runt *round*

S

Sabbat ⓜ za·bat *Sabbath*
Safe ⓜ sayf *safe*
Safe Sex ⓜ sayf seks *safe sex*

Saft ⓜ zaft *juice*
sagen zah·gen *say*
Sahne ⓕ zah·ne *cream*
Salami ⓕ za·lah·mi *salami*
Salat ⓜ za·laht *salad*
Salz ⓝ zalts *salt*
Samstag ⓜ zams·tahk *Saturday*
Sand ⓜ zant *sand*
Sandalen ⓕ pl zan·dah·len *sandals*
Sänger(in) ⓜ/ⓕ zeng·er/zeng·e·rin *singer*
Sardine ⓕ zar·dee·ne *sardine*
Sattel ⓜ za·tel *saddle*
sauber zow·ber *clean*
Sauce ⓕ zaw·se *sauce*
Sauerstoff ⓜ zow·er·shtof *oxygen*
Sauerteigbrot ⓝ zow·er·taik·brawt *sourdough bread*
Sauna ⓕ zow·na *sauna*
Schach ⓝ shakh *chess*
Schaf ⓝ shahf *sheep*
Schaffner(in) ⓜ/ⓕ shaf·ner/shaf·ne·rin *conductor*
Schal ⓜ shahl *scarf*
Schatten ⓜ sha·ten *shade • shadow*
einen Schaufensterbummel machen ai·nen show·fens·ter·bu·mel ma·khen *go window-shopping*
Schaumwein ⓜ showm·vain *sparkling wine*
Schauspiel ⓝ show·shpeel *play (theatre) • drama*
Schauspieler(in) ⓜ/ⓕ show·shpee·ler/show·shpee·le·rin *actor*
Scheck ⓜ shek *cheque (bank)*
einen Scheck einlösen ai·nen shek ain·ler·zen *cash a cheque*
Scheckkarte ⓕ shek·kar·te *cheque card*
Scheinwerfer ⓜ pl shain·ver·fer *headlights*
Schere ⓕ shair·te *scissors*
schieben shee·ben *push*
Schiedsrichter(in) ⓜ/ⓕ sheets·rikh·ter/shoots·rikh·te·rin *referee*
schießen shee·sen *shoot (gun)*
Schiff ⓝ shif *ship*
Schild ⓝ shilt *sign*
Schinken ⓜ shing·ken *ham*
schlafen shlah·fen *sleep*

schläfrig *shlayf*·rikh *sleepy*
Schlafsack ⓜ *shlahf*·zak *sleeping bag*
Schlaftabletten ① pl *shlahf*·ta·ble·ten
   sleeping pills
Schlafwagen ⓜ *shlahf*·vah·gen *sleeping
   car*
Schlafzimmer ⓝ *shlahf*·tsi·mer *bedroom*
Schläger ⓜ *shlay*·ger *racquet*
Schlamm ⓜ *shlam mud*
Schlange ① *shlang*·e *queue • snake*
Schlauch ⓜ *shlowkh tube (tyre)*
schlecht *shlekht bad • off (of food)*
schlechter *shlekh*·ter *worse*
schließen *shlee*·sen *close (shut)*
Schließfächer ⓝ pl *shlees*·fe·kher
   luggage lockers
Schloss ⓝ *shlos lock • palace*
Schlucht ① *shlukht gorge*
Schlüssel ⓜ *shlü*·sel *key*
schmackhaft *shmak*·haft *tasty*
Schmalz ⓝ *shmalts lard*
Schmand ⓜ *shmant sour cream*
Schmerz ⓜ *shmerts pain*
schmerzhaft *shmerts*·haft *sore • painful*
Schmerzmittel ⓝ *shmerts*·mi·tel
   painkillers
Schmetterling ⓜ *shme*·ter·ling *butterfly*
Schmiermittel ⓝ *shmeer*·mi·tel *lubricant*
Schminke ① *shming*·ke *make-up*
Schmuck ⓜ *shmuk jewellery*
schmutzig *shmu*·tsikh *dirty*
Schnecke ① *shne*·ke *snail*
Schnee ⓜ *shnay snow*
Schneefeld ⓝ *shnay*·felt *snowfield*
schneiden *shnai*·den *cut*
Schneider/in ⓜ/① *shnai*·der/
   shnai·de·rin *tailor*
schnell *shnel quick*
Schnorcheln ⓝ *shnor*·kheln *snorkelling*
Schnuller ⓜ *shnu*·ler *dummy • pacifier*
Schnur ① *shnoor string*
Schokolade ① *sho·ko·lah*·de *chocolate*
schon *shawn yet • already*
schön *shern beautiful*
Schönheitssalon ⓜ *shern*·haits·za·long
   beauty salon
Schottland ⓝ *shot*·lant *Scotland*
Schramme ① *shra*·me *bruise*
Schrank ⓜ *shrangk cupboard*

Schraubenzieher ⓜ *shrow*·ben·tsee·er
   screwdriver
schrecklich *shrek*·likh *terrible*
Schreibarbeit ① *shraip*·ar·bait
   paperwork
schreiben *shrai*·ben *write*
Schreibwarenhandlung ①
   shraip·vah·ren·han·dlung *stationer*
schreien *shrai*·en *shout*
Schrein ⓜ *shrain shrine*
Schreiner(in) ⓜ/① *shrai*·ner/*shrai*·ne·rin
   carpenter
Schriftsteller(in) ⓜ/① *shrift*·shte·ler/
   shrift·shte·le·rin *writer*
schüchtern *shükh*·tern *shy*
Schuhe ⓜ pl *shoo*·e *shoes*
Schuld ① *shult (someone's) fault*
schulden *shul*·den *owe*
schuldig *shul*·dikh *guilty*
Schule ① *shoo*·le *school*
Schulter ① *shul*·ter *shoulder*
Schüssel ① *shü*·sel *bowl*
Schutzimpfung ① *shuts*·im·pfung
   vaccination
schwach *shvakh weak*
schwanger *shvang*·er *pregnant*
Schwangerschaftserbrechen ⓝ
   shvang·er·shafts·er·bre·khen
   morning sickness
Schwangerschaftstest ⓜ
   shvang·er·shafts·test
   pregnancy test kit
Schwanz ⓜ *shvants tail*
schwarz *shvarts black*
schwarzer Pfeffer ⓜ *shvar*·tser *pfe*·fer
   black pepper
schwarzweiß *shvarts*·vais *B&W (film)*
Schwein ⓝ *shvain pig*
Schweinefleisch ⓝ *shvai*·ne·flaish *pork*
Schweiz ① *shvaits Switzerland*
schwer *shvair difficult (task) • heavy*
Schwester ① *shves*·ter *sister*
Schwiegermutter ① *shvee*·ger·mu·ter
   mother-in-law
Schwiegersohn ⓜ *shvee*·ger·zawn
   son-in-law
Schwiegertochter ① *shvee*·ger·tokh·ter
   daughter-in-law
Schwiegervater ⓜ *shvee*·ger·fah·ter
   father-in-law

schwierig *shvee·rikh* difficult
Schwimmbad ⓝ *shvim·baht* swimming pool
schwimmen *shvi·men* swim
Schwimmweste ⓕ *shvim·ves·te* lifejacket
schwindelig *shvin·de·likh* dizzy
schwul *shvool* gay
schwül *shvül* muggy
Secondhandgeschäft ⓝ *se·kend·hend·ge·sheft* second-hand shop
See ⓜ *zay* lake
seekrank *zay·krangk* seasick
Segeln ⓝ *zay·geln* sailing
segnen *zayg·nen* bless
sehen *zay·en* see • look
sehr *zair* very
Seide ⓕ *zai·de* silk
Seife ⓕ *zai·fe* soap
Seifenoper ⓕ *zai·fen·aw·per* soap opera
Seil ⓝ *zail* rope
Seilbahn ⓕ *zail·bahn* cable car
sein *zain* his
sein *zain* be
seit (Mai) *zait (mai)* since (May)
Seite ⓕ *zai·te* side • page
Sekretär(in) ⓜ/ⓕ *ze·kre·tair/ze·kre·tair·rin* secretary
Sekundarschule ⓕ *ze·kun·dahr·shoo·le* high school
Sekunde ⓕ *ze·kun·de* second
Selbstbedienung ⓕ *zelpst·be·dee·nung* self-service
selbstständig *zelpst·shten·dikh* self-employed
selten *zel·ten* rare
senden *zen·den* send
Senf ⓜ *zenf* mustard
Serie ⓕ *zair·ri·e* series
Serviette ⓕ *zer·vye·te* napkin
Sessellift ⓜ *ze·se·lift* chairlift (skiing)
Sex ⓜ *seks* sex
Sexismus ⓜ *sek·sis·mus* sexism
sexy *sek·si* sexy
Shampoo ⓝ *sham·poo* shampoo
Shorts pl *shorts* shorts • boxer shorts
Show ⓕ *shoh* show
sicher *zi·kher* safe
Sicherheit ⓕ *zi·kher·hait* safety

Sicherheitsgurt ⓜ *zi·kher·haits·gurt* seatbelt
Sicherung ⓕ *zi·khe·rung* fuse
sie *zee* she • they
Sie *zee* you sg&pl pol
Sieger(in) ⓜ/ⓕ *zee·ger/zee·ge·rin* winner
silbern *zil·bern* silver
Silvester ⓝ *zil·ves·ter* New Year's Eve
Singapur ⓝ *zing·a·poor* Singapore
singen *zing·en* sing
Single ⓜ *singl* single (of person)
sinnlich *zin·likh* sensual
Sitz ⓜ *zits* seat (car)
sitzen *zi·tsen* sit
Skateboarden ⓝ *skayt·bor·den* skateboarding
Skibrille ⓕ *shee·bri·le* goggles (skiing)
skifahren *shee·fah·ren* ski
Skulptur ⓕ *skulp·toor* sculpture
Slipeinlage ⓕ *slip·ain·lah·ge* panty liner
Snack ⓜ *snek* snack
Snowboarden ⓝ *snoh·bor·den* snowboarding
Socken ⓟ pl *zo·ken* socks
sofort *zo·fort* immediately
Sohn ⓜ *zawn* son
Sojamilch ⓕ *zaw·ya·milkh* soy milk
Sojasauce ⓕ *zaw·ya·zaw·se* soy sauce
Sommer ⓜ *zo·mer* summer
Sonne ⓕ *zo·ne* sun
Sonnenaufgang ⓜ *zo·nen·owf·gang* sunrise
Sonnenbrand ⓜ *zo·nen·brant* sunburn
Sonnenbrille ⓕ *zo·nen·bri·le* sunglasses
Sonnencreme ⓕ *zo·nen·kraym* sunblock
Sonnenuntergang ⓜ *zo·nen·un·ter·gang* sunset
sonnig *zo·nikh* sunny
Sonntag ⓜ *zon·tahk* Sunday
Soße ⓕ *zaw·se* sauce
Souvenir ⓝ *zu·ve·neer* souvenir
Souvenirladen ⓜ *zu·ve·neer·lah·den* souvenir shop
Sozialhilfe ⓕ *zo·tsyahl·hil·fe* welfare
sozialistisch *zo·tsya·lis·tish* socialist

Sozialstaat ⓜ zo·tsyahl·shtaht
welfare state
Spanien ⓝ shpah·ni·en Spain
sparen shpah·ren save (money)
Spargel ⓜ shpar·gel asparagus
Spaß ⓜ shpahs fun
Spaß haben shpahs hah·ben have fun
spät shpayt late
Spaten ⓜ shpah·ten spade
Speichen ⓕ pl shpai·khen spokes
Speisekarte ⓕ shpai·ze·kar·te menu
Speisewagen ⓜ shpai·ze·vah·gen
dining car
Spezialist(in) ⓜ/ⓕ shpe·tsya·list/
shpe·tsya·lis·tin specialist
speziell shpe·tsyel special
Spiegel ⓜ shpee·gel mirror
Spiel ⓝ shpeel match (sport)
spielen shpee·len play (game) •
play (instrument)
Spielzeug ⓝ shpeel·tsoyk toy
Spinat ⓜ shpi·naht spinach
Spinne ⓕ shpi·ne spider
Spitze ⓕ shpi·tse lace
Spitzhacke ⓕ shpits·ha·ke pickaxe
Spitzname ⓜ shpits·nah·me nickname
Sport ⓜ shport sport
Sportler(in) ⓜ/ⓕ shport·ler/shport·le·rin
sportsperson
Sprache ⓕ shprah·khe language
Sprachführer ⓜ shprahkh·fü·rer
phrasebook
sprechen shpre·khen speak
springen shpring·en jump
Spritze ⓕ shpri·tse syringe
Spülung ⓕ shpü·lung conditioner
Staat ⓜ shtaht state
Staatsangehörigkeit ⓕ shtahts·an·ge·
her·rikh·kait nationality
Staatsbürgerschaft ⓕ
shtahts·bür·ger·shaft citizenship
Stadion ⓝ shtah·di·on stadium
Stadium ⓝ shtah·di·um stage
Stadt ⓕ shtat city • town
Standby-Ticket ⓝ stend·bai·ti·ket
stand-by ticket
stark shtark strong
Start ⓜ shtart start (sport)

statt shtat instead of
Statue ⓕ shtah·tu·e statue
Steak ⓝ stayk steak (beef)
Stechmücke ⓕ shtekh·mü·ke mosquito
Stecker ⓜ shte·ker plug (electricity)
stehlen shtay·len steal
Stehplatz ⓜ shtay·plats standing room
steil shtail steep
Stein ⓜ shtain stone
stellen shte·len put (vertical)
sterben shter·ben die
Stereoanlage ⓕ shtair·re·o·an·lah·ge
stereo
Sterne ⓜ pl shter·ne stars
Sternzeichen ⓝ shtern·tsai·khen star
sign • zodiac
Steuer ⓕ shtoy·er tax
Stich ⓜ shtikh bite (insect)
Stickerei ⓕ shti·ke·rai embroidery
Stiefel ⓜ shtee·fel boot (footwear)
Stil ⓜ shteel style
stilles Wasser ⓝ shti·les va·ser
still water
Stimme ⓕ shti·me voice
Stock ⓜ shtok floor (storey)
stoned stohnd stoned (drugged)
stoppen shto·pen stop
Stöpsel ⓜ shterp·sel plug (bath)
stornieren shtor·nee·ren cancel
Strand ⓜ shtrant beach
Straße ⓕ shtrah·se street • road
Straßenbahn ⓕ shtrah·sen·bahn tram
Straßenkarte ⓕ shtrah·sen·kar·te
road map
Straßenkinder ⓝ pl shtrah·sen·kin·der
street kids
Straßenmusiker(in) ⓜ/ⓕ
shtrah·sen·moo·zi·ker/
shtrah·sen·moo·zi·ke·rin busker
Streichhölzer ⓝ pl shtraikh·herl·tser
matches
streiken shtrai·ken (to be) on strike
Streit ⓜ shtrait quarrel
streiten shtrai·ten argue
Strom ⓜ shtrawm current (electricity)
Stromschnellen ⓕ pl shtrawm·shne·len
rapids
Strümpfe ⓜ pl shtrüm·fe stockings

Strumpfhose ① *shtrumpf·haw·ze* pantyhose

Stück ⓝ *shtük* piece

Student(in) ⓜ/① *shtu·dent/shtu·den·tin* student

Studentenausweis ⓜ *shtu·den·ten·ows·vais* student card

studieren *shtu·dee·ren* study

Studio ⓝ *shtoo·di·o* studio

Stufe ① *shtoo·fe* step (stairs)

Stuhl ⓜ *shtool* chair

stumm *shtum* mute

stur *shtoor* stubborn

Sturm ⓜ *shturm* storm

suchen nach *zoo·khen nahkh* look for

Süchtige ⓜ/① *zükh·ti·ge* addict

Süden ⓜ *zü·den* south

Supermarkt ⓜ *zoo·per·markt* supermarket

Suppe ① *zu·pe* soup

Surfbrett ⓝ *serf·bret* surfboard

surfen *ser·fen* surf

süß *züs* sweet/candy

Süßigkeiten ① pl *zü·sikh·kai·ten* lollies

Synagoge ① *zü·na·gaw·ge* synagogue

synthetisch *zün·tay·tish* synthetic

T

Tabak ⓜ *ta·bak* tobacco

Tabakladen ⓜ *ta·bak·lah·den* tobacconist

Tag ⓜ *tahk* day

Tagebuch ⓝ *lah·ge·bookh* diary (journal)

täglich *tayk·likh* daily

Tal ⓝ *tahl* valley

Tampons ⓜ pl *tam·pons* tampons

Tankstelle ① *tangk·shte·le* service station

Tante ① *tan·te* aunt

tanzen *tan·tsen* dance

Tasche ① *ta·she* bag • pocket

Taschenbuch ⓝ *ta·shen·bookh* paperback

Taschenlampe ① *ta·shen·lam·pe* torch • flashlight

Taschenmesser ⓝ *ta·shen·me·ser* penknife

Taschenrechner ⓜ *ta·shen·rekh·ner* calculator

Tasse ① *ta·se* cup

Tastatur ① *tas·ta·toor* keyboard

taub *towp* deaf

Tauchen ⓝ *tow·khen* diving

Taufe ① *tow·fe* baptism • christening

tausend *tow·zent* thousand

Taxi ⓝ *tak·si* taxi

Taxistand ⓜ *tak·si·shtant* taxi stand

Technik ① *tekh·nik* technique

Tee ⓜ *tay* tea

Teelöffel ⓜ *tay·ler·fel* teaspoon

Teil ⓝ *tail* part

teilen *tai·len* share

Teilzeit ① *tail·tsait* part-time

Telefon ⓝ *te·le·fawn* telephone

Telefonauskunft ① *te·le·fawn·ows·kunft* directory enquiries

Telefonbuch ⓝ *le·le·fawn·bookh* phone book

telefonieren *te·le·fo·nee·ren* phone

Telefonkarte ① *te·le·fawn·kar·te* phone card

Telefonzelle ① *te·le·fawn·tsel·le* phone box

Telefonzentrale ① *te·le·fawn·tsen·trah·le* telephone centre

Telegramm ⓝ *te·le·gram* telegram

Teleskop ⓝ *te·les·kawp* telescope

Teller ⓜ *te·ler* plate

Tempel ⓜ *tem·pel* temple

Temperatur ① *tem·pe·ra·toor* temperature (weather)

Tennis ⓝ *te·nis* tennis

Tennisplatz ⓜ *te·nis·plats* tennis court

Teppich ⓜ *te·pikh* rug

Termin ⓜ *ter·meen* appointment

Terminkalender ⓜ *ter·meen·ka·len·der* diary (for appointments)

Terrasse ① *te·ra·se* patio

Test ⓜ *test* test

teuer *toy·er* expensive

Theater ⓝ *te·ah·ter* theatre

Theaterkasse ① *te·ah·ter·ka·se* ticket office (theatre)

Theke ① *tay·ke* counter (at bar)

Thermosflasche ① *ter·mos·fla·she* thermos

Thunfisch ⓜ *toon*-fish *tuna*
tief *teef* *deep*
Tier ⓝ *teer* *animal*
Tisch ⓜ *tish* *table*
Tischdecke ⓕ *tish*-de-ke *tablecloth*
Tischtennis ⓝ *tish*-te-nis *table tennis*
Toast ⓜ *tawst* *toast*
Toaster ⓜ *taws*-ter *toaster*
Tochter ⓕ *tokh*-ter *daughter*
Tofu ⓜ *taw*-fu *tofu*
Toilette ⓕ to-a-*le*-te *toilet*
Toilettenpapier ⓝ to-a-*le*-ten-pa-peer *toilet paper*
toll *tol* *terrific*
Tomate ⓕ to-*mah*-te *tomato*
Tomatensauce ⓕ to-*mah*-ten-zaw-se *tomato sauce*
Topf ⓜ *topf* *pot (ceramics)*
Töpferwaren ⓕ pl *terp*-fer-vah-ren *pottery*
Tor ⓝ *tawr* *gate • goal*
Torhüterin ⓕ *tawr*-hü-te-rin *goalkeeper*
Torwart ⓜ *tawr*-vart *goalkeeper*
ein Tor schießen *ain tawr shee*-sen *score a goal*
tot *tawt* *dead*
töten *ter*-ten *kill*
Tour ⓕ *toor* *tour*
Tourist(in) ⓜ/ⓕ tu-*rist*/tu-*ris*-tin *tourist*
Touristenklasse ⓕ tu-*ris*-ten-kla-se *economy class*
tragen *trah*-gen *carry • wear*
Training ⓝ *tray*-ning *workout*
trampen *trem*-pen *hitchhike*
Transitraum ⓜ tran-*zeet*-rowm *transit lounge*
Transport ⓜ trans-*port* *transport*
trauen *trow*-en *trust*
träumen *troy*-men *dream*
traurig *trow*-rikh *sad*
treffen *tre*-fen *meet*
Treppe ⓕ *tre*-pe *stairway*
treten *tray*-ten *kick*
trinken *tring*-ken *drink*
Trinkgeld ⓝ *tringk*-gelt *tip (gratuity)*
trocken *tro*-ken *dry*
Trockenobst ⓝ *tro*-ken-awpst *dried fruit*
trocknen *trok*-nen *dry (clothes)*
Truthahn ⓜ *troot*-hahn *turkey*

T-Shirt ⓝ *tee*-shert *T-shirt*
tun *toon* *do*
Tür ⓕ *tür* *door*
Turm ⓜ *turm* *tower*
Türsteher ⓜ *tür*-shtay-er *bouncer (club heavy)*
Tüte ⓕ *tü*-te *carton (milk)*
Typ ⓜ *tüp* *type*
typisch *tü*-pish *typical*

U

U-Bahn ⓕ *oo*-bahn *subway (underground)*
U-Bahnhof ⓜ *oo*-bahn-hawf *metro station*
Übelkeit ⓕ *ü*-bel-kait *nausea*
über *ü*-ber *about • above • over*
Überbrückungskabel ⓝ *ü*-ber-*brü*-kungks-kah-bel *jumper leads*
Überdosis ⓕ *ü*-ber-daw-zis *overdose*
überfüllt *ü*-ber-*fült* *crowded*
Übergepäck ⓝ *ü*-ber-ge-pek *excess baggage*
übermorgen *ü*-ber-mor-gen *day after tomorrow*
übernachten *ü*-ber-*nakh*-ten *stay (at a hotel)*
Überraschung ⓕ *ü*-ber-*ra*-shung *surprise*
Überschwemmung ⓕ *ü*-ber-*shve*-mung *flooding*
übersetzen *ü*-ber-*ze*-tsen *translate*
Uhr ⓕ *oor* *clock • watch*
Ultraschall ⓜ *ul*-tra-shal *ultrasound*
umarmen um-*ar*-men *hug*
Umfrage ⓕ *um*-frah-ge *polls*
Umkleideraum ⓜ *um*-klai-de-rowm *changing room*
Umsatzsteuer ⓕ *um*-zats-shtoy-er *sales tax*
umsteigen *um*-shtai-gen *change (trains)*
Umtausch ⓜ *um*-towsh *exchange*
Umwelt ⓕ *um*-velt *environment*
Umweltverschmutzung ⓕ *um*-velt-fer-shmu-tsung *pollution*
unbequem *un*-be-kvaym *uncomfortable*
und *unt* *and*

unfair un·fair *unfair*
Unfall ⓜ un·fal *accident*
ungefähr un·ge·fair *approximately*
ungewöhnlich un·ge·vern·likh *unusual*
Ungleichheit ⓕ un·glaikh·hait
inequality
Uniform ⓕ u·ni·form *uniform*
Universität ⓕ u·ni·ver·zi·tayt *university*
Universum ⓝ u·ni·vair·zum *universe*
unmöglich un·merk·likh *impossible*
unschuldig un·shul·dikh *innocent*
unser un·zer *our*
unten un·ten *down • at the bottom*
unter un·ter *among • below • under*
Unterhemd ⓝ un·ter·hemt *singlet*
Unterkunft ⓕ un·ter·kunft
accommodation
Unterschrift ⓕ un·ter·shrift *signature*
Untertitel pl un·ter·tee·tel *subtitles*
Unterwäsche ⓕ un·ter·ve·she
underwear
Urlaub ⓜ oor·lowp *holiday*

V

Vagina ⓕ va·gee·na *vagina*
Vater ⓜ fah·ter *father*
Vegetarier(in) ⓜ/ⓕ ve·ge·tah·ri·er/
ve·ge·tah·ri·e·rin *vegetarian*
Vene ⓕ vay·ne *vein*
Ventilator ⓜ ven·ti·lah·tor *fan (machine)*
Verabredung ⓕ fer·ap·ray·dung
date (appointment)
Veranstaltungskalender ⓜ
fer·an·shtal·tungks·ka·len·der
entertainment guide
Veranstaltungsort ⓜ
fer·an·shtal·tungks·ort *venue*
Verband ⓜ fer·bant *bandage*
Verbandskasten ⓜ fer·bants·kas·ten
first-aid kit
Verbindung ⓕ fer·bin·dung *connection*
verbrennen fer·bre·nen *burn*
verdienen fer·dee·nen *earn*
Vergangenheit ⓕ fer·gang·en·hait *past*
Vergaser ⓜ fer·gah·zer *carburettor*
vergessen fer·ge·sen *forget*
vergewaltigen fer·ge·val·ti·gen *rape*

Verhaftung ⓕ fer·haf·tung *arrest*
verhindern fer·hin·dern *prevent*
Verhütungsmittel ⓝ
fer·hü·tungks·mi·tel *contraceptives*
verkaufen fer·kow·fen *sell*
Verkehr ⓜ fer·kair *traffic*
Verlängerung ⓕ fer·leng·e·rung
extension (visa)
verlegen fer·lay·gen *embarrassed*
verletzen fer·le·tsen *hurt*
Verletzung ⓕ fer·le·tsung *injury*
verlieren fer·lee·ren *lose*
Verlobte ⓜ&ⓕ fer·lawp·te
fiance • fiancee
Verlobung ⓕ fer·law·bung
engagement (marriage)
verloren fer·law·ren *lost*
Vermieter(in) ⓜ/ⓕ fer·mee·ter/
fer·mee·te·rin *landlord/landlady*
vermissen fer·mi·sen
miss (feel absence of)
Vermittlung ⓕ fer·mit·lung *operator*
vernünftig fer·nünf·tikh *sensible*
verpassen fer·pa·sen *miss (the bus)*
Verpflegung ⓕ fer·pflay·gung
provisions
verrückt fer·rükt *crazy*
Versicherung ⓕ fer·zi·khe·rung
insurance
Verspätung ⓕ fer·shpay·tung *delay*
versprechen fer·shpre·khen *promise*
verstehen fer·shtay·en *understand*
Verstopfung ⓕ fer·shtop·fung
constipation
versuchen fer·zoo·khen *try (attempt)*
Vertrag ⓜ fer·trahk *contract*
Verwaltung ⓕ fer·val·tung
administration
Verwandte ⓜ&ⓕ fer·van·te
relation (family)
verzeihen fer·tsai·en *forgive*
Videokassette ⓕ vee·de·o·ka·se·te
video tape
viel feel *a lot (of) • plenty*
viele fee·le *many*
vielleicht fi·laikht *maybe*
Viertel ⓝ feer·tel *quarter*
vierzehn Tage ⓜ pl feer·tsayn tah·ge
fortnight

Virus ⓜ *vee*·rus *virus (health) • virus (computer)*

Visum ⓝ *vee*·zum *visa*

Vitamine ⓕ pl vi·ta·*mee*·ne *vitamins*

Vogel ⓜ *faw*·gel *bird*

Volksentscheid ⓜ *folks*·ent·shait *referendum*

voll fol *full*

Vollkornbrot ⓝ *fol*·korn·brawt *wholemeal bread*

Vollkornreis ⓜ *fol*·korn·rais *brown rice*

Vollzeit ⓕ *fol*·tsait *full-time*

Volumen ⓝ vo·*loo*·men *volume*

von fon *from*

vor fawr *in front of • before*

vor kurzem fawr *kur*·tsem *recently*

vor uns fawr uns *ahead*

vorbereiten fawr·be·*rai*·ten *prepare*

vorgestern fawr·*ges*·tern *day before yesterday*

Vorhängeschloss ⓝ *fawr*·heng·e·shlos *padlock*

Vormittag ⓜ *fawr*·mi·tahk *morning (10am – 12pm)*

Vorname ⓜ *fawr*·nah·me *Christian/given name*

Vorort ⓜ *fawr*·ort *suburb*

Vorrat ⓜ *fawr*·raht *stock*

vorsichtig fawr·zikh·tikh *careful*

Vorwahl ⓕ *fawr*·vahl *area code*

vorziehen fawr·*tsee*·en *prefer*

W

wachsen vak·sen *grow*

sich waschen zikh va·shen *wash (oneself)*

Waffe ⓕ va·fe *weapon*

Wagen ⓜ *vah*·gen *carriage (train)*

wählen *vay*·len *choose • vote*

Wahlen ⓕ pl *vah*·len *elections*

Wählton ⓜ *vayl*·tawn *dial tone*

wahr vahr *true*

während vair·rent *during*

Währung ⓕ *vair*·rung *currency*

Wald ⓜ valt *forest*

wandern van·dern *hike*

Wanderstiefel ⓜ pl *van*·der·shtee·fel *hiking boots*

Wanderweg ⓜ van·der·vayk *hiking route*

wann van *when*

wann immer van *i*·mer *whenever*

Warenhaus ⓝ *vah*·ren·hows *department store*

warm varm *warm*

warnen var·nen *warn*

warten var·ten *wait*

Wartesaal ⓜ var·te·zahl *waiting room (train station)*

Wartezimmer ⓝ var·te·tsi·mer *waiting room (doctor's)*

warum va·rum *why*

was vas *what*

Wäscheleine ⓕ ve·she·lai·ne *clothesline*

waschen va·shen *wash (something)*

Wäscherei ⓕ ve·she·rai *laundrette*

Waschküche ⓕ vash·kü·khe *laundry (room)*

Waschlappen ⓜ vash·la·pen *wash cloth (flannel)*

Waschmaschine ⓕ vash·ma·shee·ne *washing machine*

Waschpulver ⓝ vash·pul·ver *washing powder*

Wasser ⓝ va·ser *water*

wasserdicht va·ser·dikht *waterproof*

Wasserfall ⓜ va·ser·fal *waterfall*

Wasserflasche ⓕ va·ser·fla·she *water bottle*

Wasserhahn ⓜ va·ser·hahn *faucet • tap*

Wassermelone ⓕ va·ser·me·law·ne *watermelon*

Wasserskifahren ⓝ va·ser·shee·fah·ren *waterskiing*

Watte-Pads pl va·te·pedz *cotton balls*

Wechselgeld ⓝ vek·sel·gelt *change (coins)*

Wechselkurs ⓜ vek·sel·kurs *exchange rate*

wechseln vek·seln *exchange (money)*

Wecker ⓜ ve·ker *alarm clock*

Weg ⓜ vayk *track (path) • way*

wegen vay·gen *because of*

Wegweiser ⓜ vayk·vai·zer *signpost*

sich weh tun zikh vay toon *hurt (yourself)*

Wehrdienst ⓜ vair·deenst
military service

Weihnachten ⓝ vai·nakh·ten Christmas

Weihnachtsbaum ⓜ vai·nakhts·bowm
Christmas tree

Weihnachtsfeiertag ⓜ
vai·nakhts·fai·er·tahk Christmas Day

weil vail because

Wein ⓜ vain wine

Weinberg ⓜ vain·berk vineyard

Weinbrand ⓜ vain·brant brandy

Weintrauben ⓕ pl vain·trow·ben grapes

weiß vais white

Weißbrot ⓝ vais·brawt white bread

weißer Pfeffer ⓜ vai·ser pfe·fer
white pepper

weißer Reis ⓜ vai·ser rais white rice

Weißwein ⓜ vais·vain white wine

weit vait far

Welle ⓕ ve·le wave

Welt ⓕ velt world

Weltmeisterschaft ⓕ velt·mais·ter·shaft
World Cup

wenig vay·nikh (a) little

wenige vay·ni·ge few

weniger vay·ni·ger less

wenn ven when • if

wer vair who

Werkstatt ⓕ verk·shtat
garage (car repair)

Werkzeug ⓝ verk·tsoyk tools

Wert ⓜ vert value (price)

wertvoll vert·fol valuable

Wespe ⓕ ves·pe wasp

Westen ⓜ ves·ten west

Wette ⓕ ve·te bet

Wetter ⓝ ve·ter weather

Whisky ⓜ vis·ki whisky

wichtig vikh·tikh important

wie vee how

wie viel vee feel how much

wieder vee·der again

wiederverwertbar vee·der·fer·vert·bahr
recyclable

wiegen vee·gen weigh

wild vilt wild

willkommen vil·ko·men welcome

Wind ⓜ vint wind

Windel ⓕ vin·del nappy (diaper)

Windeldermatitis ⓕ
vin·del·der·ma·tee·tis nappy rash

windig vin·dikh windy

Windschutzscheibe ⓕ vint·shuts·shai·be
windscreen

Windsurfen ⓝ vint·ser·fen windsurfing

Winter ⓜ vin·ter winter

winzig vin·tsikh tiny

wir veer we

wissen vi·sen know (something)

Wissenschaft ⓕ vi·sen·shaft science

Wissenschaftler(in) ⓜ/ⓕ vi·sen·shaft·ler/
vi·sen·shaft·le·rin scientist

Witz ⓜ vits joke

wo vaw where

Wochenende ⓝ vo·khen·en·de
weekend

Wodka ⓜ vot·ka vodka

Wohlfahrt ⓕ vawl·fahrt social welfare

wohnen vaw·nen reside

Wohnung ⓕ vaw·nung
apartment (flat)

Wohnwagen ⓜ vawn·vah·gen caravan

Wolke ⓕ vol·ke cloud

wolkig vol·kikh cloudy

Wolle ⓕ vo·le wool

wollen vo·len want

Wort ⓝ vort word

Wörterbuch ⓝ ver·ter·bookh dictionary

wunderbar vun·der·bahr wonderful

wünschen vün·shen wish

Würfel ⓜ vür·fel dice

Würmer ⓜ pl vür·mer worms

Wurst ⓕ vurst sausage

würzig vür·tsikh spicy

Wüste ⓕ vüs·te desert

wütend vü·tent angry

Z

Zahl ⓕ tsahl number

zählen tsay·len count

Zahlung ⓕ tsah·lung payment

Zahn ⓜ tsahn tooth

Zahnarzt ⓜ tsahn·artst dentist

Zahnärztin ⓕ tsahn·erts·tin dentist

Zahnbürste ⓕ tsahn·bürs·te toothbrush

Zähne ⓜ pl tsay·ne teeth

Zahnfleisch ⓝ tsahn·flaish gum (mouth)

Zahnpasta ⓕ tsahn·pas·ta toothpaste

Zahnschmerzen pl *tsahn*·shmer·tsen
  toothache
Zahnseide ① *tsahn*·zai·de *dental floss*
Zahnstocher ⓜ *tsahn*·shto·kher
  toothpick
Zauberer(in) ⓜ/① *tsow*·be·rer/
  tsow·be·re·rin *magician*
Zaun ⓜ tsown *fence*
Zehe ① *tsay*·e *toe* • *clove (of garlic)*
zehn tsayn *ten*
zeigen *tsai*·gen *show* • *point*
Zeit ① tsait *time*
Zeitschrift ① *tsait*·shrift *magazine*
Zeitung ① *tsai*·tung *newspaper*
Zeitungshändler ⓜ *tsai*·tungks·hen·dler
  newsagency
Zeitungskiosk ⓜ *tsai*·tungks·kee·osk
  newsstand
Zeitunterschied ⓜ *tsait*·un·ter·sheet
  time difference
Zelt ⓝ tselt *tent*
zelten *tsel*·ten *camp*
Zeltplatz ⓜ *tselt*·plats *campsite*
Zentimeter ⓜ tsen·ti·*may*·ter *centimetre*
Zentralheizung ① tsen·*trahl*·hai·tsung
  central heating
Zentrum ⓝ *tsen*·trum *centre*
zerbrechen tser·*bre*·khen *break*
zerbrechlich tser·*brekh*·likh *fragile*
Zertifikat ⓝ tser·ti·fi·*kaht* *certificate*
Zeugnis ⓝ *tsoyk*·nis *reference (work)*
Ziege ① *tsee*·ge *goat*
ziehen *tsee*·en *pull*
Ziel ⓝ tseel *target* • *finish (sport)*
Zigarette ① tsi·ga·*re*·te *cigarette*
Zigarre ① tsi·*gar*·re *cigar*

Zimmer ⓝ *tsi*·mer *room*
Zimmernummer ① *tsi*·mer·nu·mer
  room number
Zirkus ⓜ *tsir*·kus *circus*
Zitrone ① tsi·*traw*·ne *lemon*
Zoll ⓜ tsol *customs*
Zoo ⓜ tsaw *zoo*
zu tsoo *too* • *at*
zu Hause tsoo *how*·ze *(at) home*
Zucchini ① tsu·*kee*·ni
  zucchini • *courgette*
Zucker ⓜ *tsu*·ker *sugar*
Zuckererbse ① *tsu*·ker·erp·se *snow pea*
Zufall ⓜ *tsoo*·fal *chance*
Zug ⓜ tsook *train*
zugeben *tsoo*·gay·ben
  admit (accept as true)
Zukunft ① *tsoo*·kunft *future*
Zulassung ① *tsoo*·la·sung
  car registration
zum Beispiel tsum *bai*·shpeel
  for example
Zündung ① *tsün*·dung *ignition*
zurück tsu·*rük* *back (return)*
zurückkommen tsu·*rük*·ko·men *return*
zusammen tsu·*za*·men *together*
Zusammenstoß ⓜ tsu·*za*·men·staws
  crash
zustimmen *tsoo*·shti·men *agree*
Zutat ① *tsoo*·taht *ingredient*
zweimal *tsvai*·mahl *twice*
zweite *tsvai*·te *second*
Zwerchfell ⓝ *tsverkh*·fel *diaphragm*
Zwiebel ① *tsvee*·bel *onion*
Zwillinge ⓜ pl *tsvi*·ling·e *twins*
zwischen *tsvi*·shen *between*

E

F

D